SEVENTY-ONE GUNS

David Tossell has 20 years' experience in sports journalism and public relations. Formerly Executive Sports Editor of *Today*, he is currently head of European public relations for the National Football League (NFL) and is the author of one previous book, on American football.

MAINSTREAM / SPORT

SEVENTY-ONE GUNS

THE YEAR OF THE FIRST ARSENAL DOUBLE

DAVID TOSSELL

MAINSTREAM
PUBLISHING

EDINBURGH AND LONDON

First published in Great Britain in 2002 by
MAINSTREAM PUBLISHING COMPANY (EDINBURGH) LTD
7 Albany Street
Edinburgh EH1 3UG

ISBN 1 84018 776 X

This edition, 2003

A catalogue record for this book is available from the British Library

Typeset in Berkeley and Capitals
Printed and bound in Great Britain by
Cox & Wyman Ltd

CONTENTS

Acknowledgements

Books of this nature rely on the cooperation of many people. Most importantly, *Seventy-One Guns* would never have seen the light of day without the members of the 1970–71 Arsenal playing and coaching staff who happily and freely gave their time to talk about the old days. In thanking all of those Gunners, and their opponents, who shared memories of a remarkable time in their careers, there are some whose contribution deserves to be highlighted. Bob McNab was a constant source of information, encouragement, helpful suggestions and contacts, while thanks are also due to Sammy Nelson for opening up his address book.

In particular, I would like to express my gratitude to Bob Wilson, who has given great support to this project from day one, including his contribution of a foreword. I am delighted that a percentage of the royalties from sales of the book will be assisting the work of the Willow Foundation, established by Bob and his wife, Megs, in 1999. More information about the charity can be found at the back of the book.

Thanks are due to everyone at Mainstream Publishing for their professionalism and their faith in the book, while Mal Butler at the *News of the World*, Tim Parks of *The Mirror* and Paul Mace at Leicester City FC all made valuable contributions. I am indebted to the numerous writers, publishers and television companies whose printed material and video footage have provided priceless research material; and to Lucy Parks, whose sub-editor's eye helped to produce the final manuscript.

Finally, this book is dedicated to Amy, Sarah and Laura, who continue to tolerate their father's obsessions, and to my own father, who I hope would have been as proud of the finished product as I remain of him.

Foreword by Bob Wilson

There are still times when the events surrounding Arsenal Football Club in the 1970–71 season seem unbelievable. I was talking to Frank McLintock, our captain, about it recently and we ended up saying, 'Can you really believe we did it? Was it really us?'

At the time there were few people who gave us a chance of achieving what only Tottenham Hotspur had previously managed in the 20th century – to win the coveted Double of League Championship and FA Cup. We were totally written off more than once, especially with a couple of months to go in the season when Leeds United, the most successful team of the era, were storming away with the title – or so it seemed. They were seven points ahead of us, and that was in the days when there were only two points for a win. It drives me mad now when people say you can't get back a 10-point difference. Win 5 games on the bounce and you have got 15 points. In effect, that is what we had to do and it's why I think our achievement was such a great one. And don't forget that we had the FA Cup running alongside our League programme and we were drawn away in every round!

In my mind, there was a very important moment towards the end of the season when we had a meeting at Highbury in the dressing-room. Our manager, Bertie Mee, and first team coach, Don Howe, sat everybody down and I could see that Bertie was getting quite shaky about the whole thing. I remember seeing his hands trembling and thinking how nervous he was. He said to us, 'Look, you have a chance here to put your names into the history book for always. But to do so, you have got to make football the priority of your life, at the expense of your family, your wife and everything else. You have got to try to explain to them that this is your chance for

9

glory.' It was put very plainly and simply that our names could be in that book for ever, which they will be. You might not pick up a football book for years at a time but when you look at the *Rothmans Football Yearbook* or whatever, there are our names – from Armstrong to Wilson. The timing of that meeting was fantastic. The gap was down to four or five points and we knew Leeds had to slip up and we had to keep winning. And that is exactly what happened.

The fact it was at Tottenham that we played our final League game and clinched the title – well, you just couldn't have written it like that. There was no way they wanted us to win the Double and there we were with the chance to do the first half of it on their patch. It was incredibly dramatic.

By then we had got to the point where we simply refused to believe we could be beaten, even when we were two goals down in the FA Cup semi-final against Stoke, even when we went behind again in the final against Liverpool. The strength of the team was its togetherness. Everyone was part of the jigsaw and everyone would have given everything for the guy next to him on the pitch. And we did – so much so that on the day after the final, when we had our victory parade around Islington on a bus, Frank fell asleep on the steps of the Town Hall. He was just exhausted with the effort of the previous nine months.

Almost 30 years later, we were all standing round the graveside at Geordie Armstrong's funeral. Everyone was there. Bob McNab had even flown in from California. Tony Adams, the Arsenal captain, said to me, 'I think it's amazing that you are all here. I wonder if the same would happen with our team in 25 years' time.' But it wouldn't. The geography of today's game makes it impossible for one thing. But we were like family, and still are. Every time we get together, even if we haven't seen each other for a few years, it is just like we are back together as a team.

It was that spirit that saw us through some difficult times, that spirit that bonds us together even now, and that spirit I hope you will experience through the pages of this book.

March 2002

INTRODUCTION

THE MIDDLE SATURDAY OF AUGUST 1970. THE RENEWED RITUAL OF brotherhood at the start of a football season. Arsenal's team coach pulled to a halt outside the main entrance of Everton Football Club, the champions of the Football League. On board, the Gunners players, themselves the newly-crowned holders of the European Fairs Cup, were unaware that the brief trip from Liverpool's Adelphi Hotel had been the beginning of a journey that would secure a place in the history of their sport. The Londoners' arrival was greeted by the usual mass of curious faces, some straining at the effort of spying a familiar figure making his way down the aisle in his club blazer, others snarling insults at the enemy. Those not preoccupied with catching an early glimpse of the opposition pushed on toward their chosen turnstile, the numbers swelling as more bodies emerged from the terraced streets that ran regimentally into Goodison Road.

Appropriately, the Arsenal players who were to dominate the first full season of the 1970s, found themselves kicking off in the city that characterised so much of the changing face of English football, and society, during the 1960s. The previous decade had seen Liverpool become England's new centre of popular culture, with groups like The Beatles and Gerry and The Pacemakers – along with entertainers such as Cilla Black and Jimmy Tarbuck – bringing an added sense of identity and pride to its inhabitants. Success on the football field had more or less kept pace with the number one singles as Liverpool and Everton totalled three League Championships and a couple of FA Cups between them in the years since 'Love Me Do' first hit the charts.

Throughout the 1960s, the boundaries separating the world of Cilla, Tarby and Paul McCartney from the environment inhabited by Kop legend Ian St John and Goodison Park hero Alan Ball had become increasingly difficult to distinguish. The abolition of the maximum wage of £20 per week early in the decade meant celebrity status for players who could suddenly afford to be seen alongside television and movie stars at trendy nightclubs. Footballers no longer earned the same wages and drank at the same local as your dad. And they didn't look like him either. They were fashion conscious, from their burgeoning sideburns to their widening trouser bottoms. The advent of youth-orientated weekly football magazines like *Goal* and *Shoot* glamorised them even more, along with the frenzy in school playgrounds over the annual collection of soccer stickers.

Football had gone from being a stadium sport to a multimedia property, with television viewers the major shareholders. More than 30 million watched the replay of the 1970 FA Cup final. Highlights of the opening day of the new season would be seen by close to 20 million on *Match of the Day* – preparing to premiere its new and soon-to-be-famous theme tune – and ITV's regional Sunday afternoon counterpart. But while the weekly diet of thrills and spills helped to raise the players' profiles, it also served to disguise the game's faults, especially from a younger generation who were not yet travelling regularly to games. By the beginning of the 1970–71 season, the game had never been more to the fore of the public's consciousness, yet there were worrying signs that crowds at some clubs had begun to show a decline. Perhaps it was because those at the grounds could see the advent of a new defensive age. The game might have more glamour and glitz than ever before, but the product itself was becoming more factory production line than London Palladium.

The 1960s had brought, of course, England's 1966 World Cup triumph plus significant achievements by English teams in club competitions, highlighted by Manchester United's lifting of the European Cup in 1968. The victory by Sir Alf Ramsey's England team had been good for the game's attendance for a while. But it also proved that you could win through pragmatism instead of inventiveness, by placing the emphasis on defence rather than attack. As the rewards for winning grew, so did the cost of defeat and consequently strength, fitness and organisation were often emphasised over quick-thinking and creativity, heavy-handedness over lightness of touch. That also meant the man devising the tactics was stepping out of the shadows of his players, and with the likes of Bill Shankly, Brian Clough, Don Revie and Tommy Docherty as its flag-bearers, the cult of the celebrity manager was born.

INTRODUCTION

In August 1970, British music was preparing to don its platform shoes and totter into the age of 'Glam and Glitter'. And while the safe, boring pop charts of Gilbert O'Sullivan and Dawn were getting ready to find a home for Marc Bolan and David Bowie, so an increasingly defensive-minded Football League still had room for the likes of Rodney Marsh, Charlie Cooke and a precocious young Londoner by the name of Charlie George. It was the very lack of imagination in so much that surrounded them that made their contributions so stimulating to the senses.

The 1970 FA Cup final between Chelsea and Leeds symbolised the battle of philosophies at the turn of the decade. Chelsea were a spontaneous and flashy throwback to the Manchester United of a few years earlier. They were blessed with the ideal front man in Peter Osgood, whose hairdressing style, incidentally, was evolving towards that of Ray Dorset, the hirsute singer of Mungo Jerry, whose 'In The Summertime' monopolised the number one position for several weeks. Leeds, to their critics, were the cynical icons for the new age of win-at-all-costs. Uplifting moments like Eddie Gray's trickery with the ball or a sublime pass by Johnny Giles were hidden, or conveniently forgotten, in the face of joyless professionalism. Even the most avid of Leeds-bashers, however, had to grudgingly sympathise with the team that ended the 1969–70 season without a single trophy. League champions the previous season with a record points total, Don Revie's side fell between three stools, missing out on the League, FA Cup and European Cup in the chaotic closing weeks of an over-crowded season, shortened by the forthcoming Mexico World Cup.

Chelsea's FA Cup victory, coming on the heels of a League Championship triumph by Harry Catterick's stylish Everton side, did more than simply set the stage for a Blue summer that was completed by the general election victory of Edward Heath's Conservative Party. For a while at least, it restored faith that skill was still football's most valuable commodity – a belief wonderfully reinforced by the 'beautiful game' of Pelé's Brazilian World Cup winners. Disappointment in England at the failure to hold a 2–0 lead in the quarter-final against West Germany was erased somewhat by the thrall in which football fans were held as Jairzinho, Gerson, Rivelino and the world's greatest player danced their samba around the opposition.

It all contributed to a renewed feeling of optimism as the 1970–71 season kicked off and crowds on the first day of the season would show a 40,000 increase on the previous year. Nowhere was the mood more upbeat than at Goodison Park, where the first trophy of the new season was already residing. A week before Arsenal's arrival, Everton had beaten Chelsea 2–1 at Stamford Bridge to win the FA Charity Shield, a game less notable for goals by Alan Whittle and Howard Kendall than the appearance of Alan Ball in a pair of white boots. It marked the beginning of a fashion movement followed by style-conscious schoolboys everywhere and continued by high-profile players like Terry Cooper, Alan Hinton, Colin Todd and Asa Hartford. Even Arsenal skipper Frank McLintock joined in at the start of the following season, but with his white footwear horribly obvious at the bottom of red socks, he looked like the kid who had forgotten his football boots and was made to do PE in his plimsoles.

On the day of the Charity Shield there had been a more pertinent pointer to the shape of football to come, when Derby County defeated Manchester United 4–1 in the final of the Watney Cup. Introduced as an event for the two top-scoring teams in each division who had failed to qualify for Europe or gain promotion, the tournament would help to pave the way for the sponsorship of the major competitions in English football. The 1970–71 season would also see the debut of the Texaco Cup, a trophy contested by the also-rans of the English, Scottish and Irish leagues. Remembered at a distance as a trophy for which the phrase 'tin-pot' might have been invented, the competition would, in fact, regularly produce crowds in excess of 20,000, with a respectable 51,000 attending the two legs of the inaugural final between Wolves and Hearts.

The Texaco Cup put an additional £100,000 into the game's coffers but Football League secretary Alan Hardaker admitted there had been resistance to such a concept in the past. Even a tournament as innocuous as the Watney Cup – a week-long pre-season knockabout that diverted £25,000 of the sponsor's money to the County Football Associations – had been close to three years in the planning stage. Hardaker pointed out, 'A company entering the field of sponsorship in football cannot hope to achieve its objective simply by using the game to advertise its product. There has to be a genuine interest in the welfare of the game, and a tremendous amount of work by the sponsors, not only to publicise their own activities, but to publicise the competition and the game.

'I believe that sponsorship in football has now arrived. Its financial influence could well revolutionise football during the next decade, but it must be remembered by administrators at every level that the game's birthright must never be sold cheaply to a sponsor just for the sake of financial gain.'

Hardaker, exhibiting slightly less foresight, predicted, 'I do not think anyone in the game wants to see in this country the kind of advertising prevalent on the continent where one team's shirts endorse a certain brand of alcohol, while another team carries plugs urging male supporters to use a particular brand of eau-de-cologne. This is not sponsorship, it is merely advertising which does nothing whatsoever for the game.' Imagine telling that to Manchester United 20 years later.

Other stories capturing attention as the season kicked off included some worrying security issues. Bobby Moore, still waiting to hear if he faced charges after being accused of stealing a necklace from a Colombian jewellers before the World Cup, was kept out of one of West Ham's pre-season friendlies following a kidnap threat to his wife, Tina. Meanwhile, Peter Osgood reported that he had received a threat that he would be shot during Chelsea's game against Manchester United.

At Manchester City, as well as disappointment at the sending off of winger Mike Summerbee for striking an opponent in the opening game against Southampton, manager Joe Mercer was shaking his head in disbelief at Sir Alf Ramsey's blinkered view of the footballing world. Not only had the England manager chosen not to remain in Mexico to watch the latter stages of the World Cup after England's premature exit, he also claimed that English football had nothing to learn from the new champions of the world. Mercer, who would follow Ramsey into the England manager's chair four years later, countered, 'While he must make and stand by his own decisions he should not carry them to the point of arrogance. He should appreciate that you can't stand still in this game. But even after we had lost in Mexico he refused to learn by staying on to watch Brazilian technique.'

Meanwhile, Wolves centre-forward Derek Dougan, one of the game's most outspoken figures and a hit on ITV's revolutionary World Cup panel during the summer, was elected as chairman of the Professional Footballers' Association, succeeding former Arsenal defender Terry Neill.

At Goodison Park, the manner of Everton's nine-point Championship victory had fans feeling buoyant about their prospects of challenging for the title once again. Many experts forecast another two-horse race between the Merseyside team and Leeds. Bobby Charlton, writing his weekly column in *Goal*, described the champions as being, 'full of fight, skill and confidence'. He added, 'They must be the best starters of all-time. They just seem to click into gear straight away, while some of us are still struggling to find our feet.'

True to Charlton's words, Everton opened the game against Arsenal like champions and dominated the opening stages. The visitors' defence had the Welshman John Roberts playing in place of Peter Simpson, hospitalised for a cartilage operation, and they could not prevent Joe Royle diving to head in a cross from the England right-back Tommy Wright with almost 30 minutes played. By the time the game entered its final 20 minutes, Arsenal could consider themselves somewhat fortunate to be still only one goal behind. Bob McNab had cleared off the line from Whittle, the little blond firebrand whose goals had been so vital to Everton's title challenge in the closing months of the previous season, and their goal had been threatened on numerous other occasions. But as Everton pushed forward in search of a decisive second goal, Arsenal broke with pace and purpose and Charlie George beat goalkeeper Gordon West to John Radford's pass to equalise. The goal was to prove costly, however, as George was stretchered from the field, two ankle bones broken in the collision with West.

Parity lasted until six minutes from time. Wright crossed, goalkeeper Bob Wilson turned the ball against the inside of the post and Alan Ball, with either head or hand depending on your allegiance, set up winger Johnny Morrissey to score a close-range goal. But this Arsenal team had already demonstrated its resilience, coming from three goals down to win the Fairs Cup final four months earlier, and would do so time and again in the coming months. It was no more than a taste of things to come when they grabbed another equaliser. Roberts was the unlikely provider, his square pass being met by a subtle chip by George Graham that left West beaten.

A valuable point had been won by Arsenal but, despite a dogged performance, there was little to indicate a passing of the baton from one champion to another. There was certainly no hint of the incredible months to come. The Gunners were clearly efficient, professional and combative, with their share of skill. Championship contenders perhaps, but not a team on the brink of greatness.

In a few months' time, and for many years to come, discussions would rage about just how good this Arsenal team was. To some, the Gunners seemed horribly grey in the fall-out from the explosion of colour that was Brazil's World Cup triumph. Few, not even the players themselves, would argue that they were as extraordinarily blessed with talent as Leeds, their greatest rivals. And while Manchester United had George Best, Bobby Charlton and Denis Law, Arsenal had Charlie George, Peter Storey and John Radford. But in sport, like life, achievements are sometimes all the more extraordinary for being performed by ordinary men.

Five hours after arriving at Goodison Park, the Arsenal team bus pulled away from the remaining autograph seekers still enjoying the early evening sun. Settling back in their seats were a group of ordinary men, who just happened to be engaged in a profession that was becoming increasingly extraordinary in the summer of 1970. Their remarkable journey had begun.

1

CAPTAIN FANTASTIC

FOR MOST OF THE 1960S, HIGHBURY WAS NOT THE HAPPIEST OF PLACES TO watch and play football. Older Arsenal fans, fed a diet of regular success until midway through the previous decade, wondered why their team could suddenly no longer sit at football's top table with the elite of Manchester, Merseyside and, worst of all, the other side of north London. Younger fans simply wondered if they would ever know the kind of feast their fathers and older brothers spoke about. In the meantime, they made sure to steer clear of Tottenham fans in the playground.

Players lured to Arsenal by the international stature and winning tradition of the club were left frustrated when the medals and glory for which they had signed failed to materialise. As the expectations and frustrations grew, both on the terraces and within the dressing-room, it was Frank McLintock who felt it more than most. Passionate about his chosen career and driven by inner demons, McLintock had left Leicester City to experience the joy of winning trophies instead of the pain of losing finals, which he had endured twice with the Filbert Street club. But by the end of the decade, the square-jawed, clench-fisted captain of the Arsenal team had merely lost twice more at Wembley. His own misfortunes had become the personalised story line in the wider drama of Highbury's search for lost glory.

Had the fates, and Leicester's management, operated differently, McLintock could already have been a medal-winning member of the Leeds team whose domination of English football Arsenal were trying to undermine, or even playing for the Liverpool side who were to cross Arsenal's path of destiny in the 1970–71 season.

Born in Glasgow in the last week of 1939, McLintock moved south to sign for Leicester City as an energetic, enthusiastic 17 year old early in 1957. Within three years he was establishing himself as one of the best attacking right-halves in the country and helped Leicester reach the 1961 FA Cup final, where they lost to Tottenham's Double winners. Two seasons later, it was Leicester themselves who were at one point pushing for both domestic honours, but, having seen their championship challenge peter out, they went down tamely at Wembley to a Manchester United side in the throes of reconstruction. By then, however, McLintock had grudgingly admitted to himself that his ambitions could best be fulfilled away from the comforting family atmosphere of the Midlands club.

'I loved Leicester,' he recalls. 'I met my wife, Barbara, there and two of my children were born there. But I wanted to get international caps and play in Europe. I had played in Europe once at Leicester and we were unlucky to go out in the second round to Atletico Madrid. I enjoyed that and I wanted more. So I kept asking for a transfer. I needed to go another step.'

McLintock, who in recent years has re-established his public profile as a hard-working part of Sky Sports' televised football team, explains, 'There has always been a drive in me. Even now, I am probably working as hard as I did when I was 25. If I have a lapse I am looking for something to do.'

It was that quality that prompted Bill Shankly to approach him about a move to Liverpool. 'Shanks tapped me up in 1961, just after we played in the Cup final. He and Ian St John met me on the dance floor at the dinner after the game and he came up, as bold as brass, and said, "Hello, son. How would you like to play for a good team?" We were in the top flight and he was in the Second Division at that time. He tried to get me there, but in those days it was so difficult to get away.'

Leeds United's Don Revie was the next to try. 'He offered me £8,000 in cash and £60 a week basic wage when I was on £20 a week. Phenomenal money, but I still couldn't get away. Eventually our chairman, Sid Needham, said, "Look, I'll buy you a newsagent and a sweet shop if you'll stay." I told him it was not just about money and when they realised there were other reasons for wanting to get away, they wished me all the best and let me go.

'Mr Needham was a lovely man, so was the manager, Matt Gillies. Looking back I didn't give them enough credit at the time. They were fatherly people, they had principles. I had a drive to get to a bigger club and Arsenal came in at the right time. Billy Wright talked to me on the phone and told me he was going to get Gordon Banks and Ray Wilson at the club and I thought, bloody hell, that will be terrific. That's how it all came about.'

In the autumn of 1964, Arsenal and Leicester agreed a fee of £80,000, a

British record for a wing-half, and McLintock headed south into a Highbury set-up that turned out to be far from what he had expected – and been promised. 'The team wasn't properly balanced. There were some excellent players like George Eastham, but there were some players who maybe weren't up to the Arsenal standard. It was a mishmash. Players like myself and Don Howe had arrived and hadn't settled in yet. I put extra pressure on myself. I wanted to justify that fee. So instead of being a free-wheeling attacking midfield player with bundles of energy, who shot at goal every five minutes, I was so uptight I was tackling everyone within 50 yards. I should just have thought, "To hell with it, it's not my fault if the team's not great." But that's not the type of person I am. I take the responsibility on my shoulders, even though I shouldn't do. I tried too hard and when you do that you don't play as well. You have got to have an element of relaxation within yourself to make yourself perform to your best. The other way just tires you.'

Added to the pressure of an under-achieving team in the present was the weight of past glories – seven League titles and three FA Cup victories. 'You felt the pressure, and you felt it big time because they'd had so much success. All the old names, like Cliff Bastin, Joe Mercer, Ted Drake, would come up and we felt, "Fuck it, we've achieved nothing."'

Billy Wright was the man who had been charged with bringing success back to the club. Appointed in the summer of 1962, nine years after the Gunners' last League championship victory, he arrived with a track record as a leader of men, 90 of his record 105 England caps having been won as captain. But the former Wolves legend proved to be no genius as a manager. With England striker Joe Baker leading the attack, Arsenal could score three goals on any day, only to concede four at the other end. Disorganisation was the name of the game.

McLintock decided that a change in tradition was needed. 'I had the cheek to ask Billy to get the club to change the strip, because we felt as though we were living in the past all the time. They did it for a year.' So it was that Arsenal played the 1965–66 season in Manchester United-style red shirts without the white sleeves that had become recognisable around the world. Embarrassed to this day, McLintock adds, 'When I look back on it, what a bloody cheek I had to put in a suggestion like that. Dopey. I felt we needed something to break the cycle; what was really needed was better players.'

Peter Storey, a young first-teamer who had seen Wright follow George Swindin into the manager's office, cringes at the memory of his last season in charge. 'That must have been the lowest point for the club. We were in danger of being relegated. They'd taken us for pre-season training to the West Indies, but we never did a day's training. We had a riot in Jamaica. Joe Baker head-butted one of the Jamaican players and the game got abandoned and we all came off. In another game Joe slung his boots at Billy and said, "You do better."

'There was terrible friction, a terrible rift. On one side of the changing-room were Joe Baker, George Eastham and the big signings, and the other half was the young guys like me who cost nothing. I never felt like Billy took much interest in the younger players and we tended to get the blame for everything. There were arguments during training and games. Frank was always arguing with him and it was a terrible atmosphere. Billy was a nice bloke but the pressure was too much. It all went wrong and he started hitting the bottle a bit. He was drunk some of the time. I think they did him a big favour giving him the sack.'

Arsenal finished the season in 14th place, winning only 12 games and plunging to new depths when only 4,544 turned up at Highbury to see a hastily arranged end of season game against Leeds. Wright's subsequent dismissal came as no surprise.

As fans and players wondered which big name would be next into the managerial office, the Arsenal board announced the appointment of the club's physiotherapist, Bertie Mee, as the new manager. Even the players who knew Mee, whose only playing experience had been brief and unspectacular spells with Derby County and Mansfield, were shocked. Bob Wilson, still waiting to establish himself as the club's number one goalkeeper, recalls, 'It was certainly no surprise when Billy was fired. What was a surprise was when we heard that Bertie had got the job. He was a great organiser and we thought he had just been put in charge for a short while to get affairs in order before someone else took over. But Bertie's greatest strength was that he surrounded himself with very good people.'

To fill the position of first team coach, Mee brought in Dave Sexton, a former forward with West Ham and several other London clubs, who had been coaching at Fulham. The growing maturity of young players introduced by Wright – defenders Simpson and Storey, midfielder Jon Sammels and striker John Radford – plus the tactical awareness of Sexton, produced immediate signs of improvement. A couple of signings, Huddersfield left-back Bob McNab and Chelsea forward George Graham, provided additional experience and proven ability.

'Dave Sexton was a revelation,' says Sammels, who still has a framed picture of himself and Sexton during a Highbury training session hanging on his wall. 'We would play a game on Saturday and he'd go over to Italy on Sunday to watch training sessions and games, and he'd bring back ideas. Doggies, a series of sprints, was one. We used to do those as part of our fitness training. We were down in Sussex before a cup game, training at Lancing College and staying in Hove. Dave would get us up early in the morning – we used to say it was because he couldn't sleep – and at seven o'clock he'd have us doing these doggies along the sea-front. You certainly didn't want a fried breakfast by the time you got back to the hotel.'

Centre-forward John Radford adds, 'Dave was a brilliant coach for me because he loved working with the forwards and midfield players. I would work with Dave morning, afternoon and night on different things. I had not been given much attention before then.'

Sexton would go on to earn a reputation as a great attack-minded manager with Chelsea, Queens Park Rangers and Manchester United, but he did work on making Arsenal a tighter unit all over the field. McLintock explains, 'What Dave started working on was closing down as a team, like a chain reaction. The right-back would push forward, the right-sided centre-half would push over. We always used to try to keep the line, although we never talked about it much. As soon as the ball was cleared and the forwards pushed upfield, we would all push up as well. The idea was always to keep your team up and down the pitch, no more than about 45 yards apart. If you can do that, and Liverpool did it for years, your midfield players are always in support of your forwards and always in support of your back four. You only need to run 20 or 30 yards because the team is not all spread out. So Dave started on that, the closing down.'

After improving to seventh in the table in Mee's first season, McLintock clearly remembers the feeling when, early in 1967–68, Sexton left to succeed Tommy Docherty as manager of Chelsea. 'We were furious when Bertie let Dave go. Maybe he couldn't have stopped him, or maybe he should have done more to keep him there. But it was the first time we had found somebody we felt could do what was a very difficult job. It was a mission impossible with the expectations the club had, the players that were there and having a new manager in charge.'

But Mee made another good choice, promoting Don Howe from the position of reserve team coach. The former England right-back had begun his coaching career after breaking a leg in the spring of 1966, two years after signing for Arsenal from West Bromwich. Sexton, however, was a tough act to follow. 'It was difficult for Don because we were all moaning and groaning about Dave going,' says McLintock.

Radford recalls, 'It went on for a few weeks after Don took over. One day we were working in the top gym at Highbury and the players weren't really putting it in properly. I remember Don just blowing his top. He stopped everything, sat everyone down and gave us the biggest bollocking we'd ever had.'

McLintock continues, 'Don said, "Right, I have fucking had enough of you lot. I am Don Howe. Dave Sexton has gone. I am the coach and from now on you will do what I say. Right, come on! We are going to do double laps. Go! Go!" And from then on you could tell he was in charge. We had been so pissed off. Don grabbed us by the scruff of the neck, and gave himself a good kick up the bollocks as well, knowing that he had got to start acting properly. He just got better and better as a coach.'

Graham adds, 'We knew Don because he had been a player and then reserve team coach, so we had seen him on the training ground. So there was continuity. That is one of the reasons why it worked. It was the same kind of continuity that Liverpool had for so many years.'

The 1967–68 season brought Arsenal's first Wembley appearance in 16 years, a 1–0 defeat to Leeds in a disappointing League Cup final. The following season, McLintock was at last playing in an Arsenal team that, for a while at least, appeared capable of a sustained challenge for the League Championship. An unbeaten run of 11 games at the start of the season represented the club's best opening for 20 years and silenced unrest among fans over the absence of a big-name summer signing. Having led the title race early in the season, the challenge stumbled, but there remained the prospect of another League Cup final against Swindon and the continued development of a side that might even become consistent challengers to the best teams from the north of England.

In goal, Wilson, the former schoolteacher, was growing increasingly comfortable in his first full season as a First Division player. In front of him, the uncompromising Storey and McNab flanked a defence that had adapted well to Howe's zonal marking system and in which the underrated but skilful Simpson had become indispensable. Further forward, Graham displayed the vision and mind of a top-quality midfield player, more than making up for the lack of speed that had ultimately exposed him as an out-and-out striker. Leading the attack was the big Yorkshireman, Radford, awarded his first England cap earlier in the season.

Professionalism was the key word, although critics were already describing the Gunners as a negative side. Howe countered during the season, 'This defensive tag people hang on us just isn't true. They are fooled into thinking it because we have had so few goals scored against us. This is because we have a good defence, not because we are defensive-minded.'

Mee added, 'It is no use playing entertaining football and losing every match. The proof is in the pudding. We are beginning to be successful in terms of results and the crowds are coming back to Highbury.'

By the time the Gunners prepared to face Third Division Swindon, they had conceded only 18 goals in 30 League games. In the League Cup itself, the Gunners had progressed with the minimum of fuss in the fewest possible number of games. Their six ties included a 2–1 win against one-time League leaders Liverpool and a bad-tempered two-legged semi-final triumph against neighbours Tottenham.

McLintock had already played in, and lost, three Wembley finals. On a disgrace of a pitch – which had needed hundreds of gallons of water pumped off before an England international a few weeks earlier – he was destined to lose for a fourth time. 'We really felt we had a great chance of winning it, even though six of us had the flu that week. Up to 90 minutes I was still bombing forward on a pitch that was about a foot thick in mud. But as soon as 90 minutes were up, someone blew out my candle. I couldn't lift my legs after that.'

Swindon were inspired to a 3–1 extra-time victory by their winger Don Rogers and goalkeeper Peter Downsborough, having been helped on their way by an appalling first-half mix-up between Wilson and the blond Scottish centre-half Ian Ure. McLintock still wears a look of disbelief as he remembers, 'Bob was shouting for the ball and Ian kept on dribbling it back to him instead of releasing it. He was probably a bit worried about the surface. All of a sudden he gave it to Bob from about five yards away and it bounced off him and they put it in the net. We actually played pretty well and bombarded Swindon but their goalkeeper was unbelievable.'

Although Bobby Gould grabbed a fortuitous equaliser four minutes from time, Arsenal had nothing left to give during an extra 30 minutes on Wembley's unforgiving mix of mud and sand. Howe made a hugely optimistic, and inevitably unsuccessful, plea to referee Bill Handley to abandon the game, and Rogers, who had skirted around the fringes of the action for 90 minutes, wrote his name into football folklore with a pair of goals.

McLintock, overwhelmed by fatigue and disappointment, wandered in a daze among the uniformed men of the Royal Engineers' band as, yet again, he made his way back to the losers' dressing-room. 'To lose once at Wembley is heartbreaking, but four times is like a nightmare come true. I was knackered and shell-shocked. It was a terrible experience. I said to myself, am I ever going to win anything? You keep getting close and you see other people picking up cups and you feel it. Luckily enough I have an attitude of mind that eventually gets over it and puts it behind me. Maybe it was the start of us getting closer as a team and getting better players in a few positions.'

To improve the defence, Howe suggested switching the 5 ft 10 in. McLintock to the centre of the back four, a move that prompted resistance from the player himself and scepticism from teammates. Sammels, for several years McLintock's central midfield partner, explains, 'As midfield players, we had a good understanding and both of us would be all over the field. Some teams used to play three in the middle there, but we always felt we could cover the same ground with just me and Frank. I thought he wouldn't have the discipline to play at the back and I don't think I was alone.'

McNab adds, 'I thought Frank was finished before he switched. We were in Malta in 1969 and Frank had mentioned that they were toying with this idea and our eyebrows went up. Frank was so undisciplined, he ran out of gas after 70 minutes. His legs ran his brain. Don had said to me, "I think you should be captain." I said I didn't feel ready or have the respect of the lads and I wasn't bothered about being captain. So Don said, "Who are we going to have?" I mentioned Frank, and Don said, "Frank's not going to be here."

'Frank couldn't have kept going on the way he was, but he came to me and said, "Can you help me to be a defender?" I didn't have a lot of enthusiasm for it. But to be fair to Frank, he took to it like a duck to water. He is so enthusiastic and it is infectious and he picked it up 100 times quicker than I would have thought. We worked with him and he liked it. He loved playing people offside and the little tricks we used to do and he loved it when they worked. He became so comfortable.'

Even McLintock concedes, 'It was a dangerous thing to do, but Don and Gordon Clark, the chief scout, said they thought I would extend my career and do better for the club if I didn't play as someone who was driving forward the whole time, trying to do everything. I was too conscientious. I needed to try to switch back a couple of gears. I was a good passer and tackler and they knew I was good in the air for my height. But I thought it was like getting the elbow.

'I remember playing in my first match and Ian Ure came in after the game and said he was knackered. I said, "You're knackered? I could go out and play another match." But after a year or so of doing that I would get just as tired as him. Your body adjusts to whatever you are doing, but at first I felt as fresh as a daisy and felt I could go out dancing after the game or whatever. I was impetuous and strong-willed. If I didn't agree with somebody I would just say, "Fuck off." But I slipped into it very quickly. I would say that within three or four weeks I wasn't making many mistakes.'

McLintock's partnership with Simpson quickly became the bedrock of Arsenal's success in the seasons to come and he found himself back in his country's national squad after an absence of three years. He had also inherited the job of club captain from Irish centre-half Terry Neill, a move that McNab recalls was welcomed by many of the players. 'I thought Terry couldn't play,' he says. 'That's why some people didn't like him.'

Sammels, who befriended McLintock on his arrival from Leicester and even helped decorate his new house, almost glows when talking about his captain. 'I think a lot of him as a man and a player. He was a great leader, an inspiration. Simple as that. I compare him to Dave Mackay at Tottenham and I know Frank thought a lot of Dave. The great players in the Tottenham team used to idolise Dave Mackay and our lads had the same respect for Frank. Even if he wasn't playing well, which wasn't very often, you always wanted him in the side. He could pick everybody up or give them a rollicking when they needed it.'

McLintock was an important influence on the young players who were finding their way into the team. As Eddie Kelly explains, 'I spoke to Frank a lot, a lot of the young lads did. And he would pass it on to Don Howe. When you are young it is hard to communicate with managers so it was great having Frank there to talk to; it really worked for me.'

Taking charge on the field was a side of McLintock's game that had always come naturally to him. 'I was very good at sorting people out, pushing them around, exaggerating praise for people. Even at 19 I was talking and shouting instructions and I had just walked into the team as a part-time professional. I'd go, "Hey, push in there or do this or do that." It never even entered my head that I shouldn't tell someone what they should be doing.'

Even as he sits in the conservatory of his north London house, it is easy to imagine McLintock cajoling and organising his defence for a corner kick. He is constantly on the edge of his seat while he speaks, punctuating his recollections with arm movements, pounding his fist into his hand, straining his neck to win imaginary headers. It is tiring just to watch and listen – and easy to believe Peter Simpson when he says, 'Playing between Frank and Bob McNab, who was also very verbal, could give you a headache.' The only time McLintock eases up is when a young boy toddles happily into the room and the fiery captain temporarily, and proudly, turns into Grandad.

McLintock picks up his thread. 'It was all part of having so much energy. I was training and I was working from half past seven to five at night in the early days, so I could do a forty-hour week and get Saturdays off. It was ridiculous really. Cycling to my job and back again, training and getting home at ten o'clock at night and still getting in the first team. People said I had a million to one chance of making it. But I had such determination and drive and it was making me strong and fit. It helped keep my feet on the ground and realise that playing football is a joy.'

There was plenty of joy around Highbury one year and one month after the disappointment of Swindon as McLintock became the first Arsenal captain since Joe Mercer 17 years earlier to hold aloft a piece of silverware. When the final whistle blew to complete Arsenal's victory over Anderlecht in the final of the Fairs Cup, the pitch disappeared under a tidal wave of human celebration, players and fans joining together to cast free the shackles of the club's monumental past.

This particular chapter in Arsenal history had begun rather more sedately with an unremarkable victory against Glentoran, a tie most notable for the sending off in Ireland of 18-year-old Charlie George for insulting a linesman. Then an assured defensive performance in Portugal and a penalty save by reserve goalkeeper Geoff Barnett helped dispose of Sporting Lisbon. While Arsenal fans might have been resigned to another season without a title challenge, their form in Europe maintained the growing feeling of optimism around the club and a quarter-final place was gained through two uninspiring games against Rouen of France, settled late in the second leg by Sammels.

It was a somewhat refurbished Arsenal side that took up the challenge of Romania's Dynamo Bacau. The players used in the tie were basically those who would dominate on the Gunners' behalf the following season, with Neill, midfielder David Court, striker Bobby Gould and winger Jimmy Robertson having played their last games in the competition. Before long all four would be gone from the club. After a comfortable away victory, Arsenal scored seven at home – Radford, George and Sammels happily helping themselves to two goals each.

The brushing aside of the powerful Dutch side Ajax was as unexpected as the Highbury demolition of Dynamo had been predictable. Ajax, on their way to a three-year domination of the European Cup, boasted the exciting talent of Johan Cruyff, yet Gunners manager Bertie Mee welcomed the semi-final draw, believing Arsenal's style was better suited to the team from Amsterdam than tackling Inter Milan or Belgium's Anderlecht. Mee's optimism proved well-founded as Ajax were overwhelmed at Highbury. Frustrated by Ajax's negative tactics after George's early goal, Arsenal sparked into life when Peter Marinello, the much-trumpeted £100,000 signing from Hibernian, was replaced by the dependable George Armstrong. Two goals followed, including another by George, for whom the night represented something of a coming of age. It was not only his flowing locks that had developed since his shorn-headed debut on the opening day of the season. Used in selective games early on, his unconventional, instinctive skills were adding an extra dimension to the methodical efficiency of Arsenal under Mee and Howe, and earning a legion of worshippers on Highbury's North Bank.

After the unflappable Simpson and the maturing Kelly helped ensure that Ajax's early goal in Amsterdam was their only success, Anderlecht were waiting for the Gunners in the final. The Parc Astrid Stadium in Brussels, with 30,000 packed onto its cramped terraces, provided a hostile backdrop and, to a deafening soundtrack of firecrackers, horns and sirens, Arsenal fell behind by three goals.

'Playing in Europe was such a different tempo to playing at somewhere like Newcastle,' says McLintock. 'They just knocked the ball about and were very patient. You were not getting elbows across the face, they were not knocking in balls behind you. But all of a sudden it's, *boom!*, a goal. You're thinking, "Lucky bastards". They go back to the same tempo again, probing, probing, probing. It lulls you into a false sense of security. Suddenly another goal, two–nothing down, and you feel as though you have been doing well and they haven't dominated you. Suddenly, it's three–nothing.'

No team had ever reversed a three-goal deficit in a European final, but with his first touch of the ball substitute Ray Kennedy headed home a goal that promised to change the complexion of the tie. Then came, according to many, McLintock's finest hour. 'Frank was the most impulsive person you could ever meet,' Bob Wilson explains. 'He'd see you and say, "I love that tie, where can I get one?" or, "Where can I get that shirt?" But if he couldn't get it there and then, five minutes later he would have forgotten about it and moved on to something else.

'After we lost to Anderlecht in the first leg of the final, I remember him going into the shower feeling as down as anyone. He came out five minutes later and he was like Mel Gibson in *Braveheart*. "We can do it, we can win this Cup, they can't stop us," he was shouting. By the time we left the dressing-room to go back to the hotel, we were all convinced we could win.'

McLintock adds, 'I was just saying, "Come on, get your heads up. We can beat this lot. If we really concentrate at the back and don't give them a chance and if we bomb them and get stacks of balls into their centre-halves, we can pulverise them."'

One week later, floodlights bouncing off the spring evening's rainfall, Anderlecht were duly pulverised. The visitors were confidently into their stride, but Arsenal weathered an early storm and the game was changed by a flash of brilliance by the young Scot, Kelly. Receiving the ball from McLintock following Armstrong's corner, the 19 year old took two paces and slammed an unstoppable shot into the roof of the net from 20 yards. 'I thought Highbury was going to burst,' said the scorer. 'I was just hovering around waiting for something to happen and it did. I just decided to have a go.' Arsenal swarmed all over their opponents, with Armstrong 5 ft 6 in. of perpetual motion on either flank. The second goal arrived with 20 minutes remaining, Radford propelling himself through the air to meet McNab's cross. Two minutes later Sammels, authoritative in the centre of midfield, converted an intelligent pass from the quick-thinking George and 17 years of futility was washed away.

Europe having been conquered, Arsenal were ready to take on the best teams in the English game. 'That win gave the players the confidence that what Bertie and Don were doing must be right,' Graham explains. 'When you are teaching people to absorb what you are putting across, once they take it on board and have success with it they think, "I like this teacher, I am going to work even more." Those two games in the Fairs Cup were a crucial time.'

McLintock concludes, 'We played magnificently. On the night, as a team, individually and collectively, we couldn't have played any better. Everyone was on fire and the crowd was really behind us. Winning that cup was so important to me and to the club. The first trophy in 17 years. We were becoming a good team and now we had the confidence to go with it.'

2

BACK TO THE FUTURE

TWO DAYS AFTER OPENING THE 1970-71 SEASON BY RESCUING A POINT at Everton, Arsenal faced another away game at West Ham. The team at Upton Park saw Ray Kennedy joining John Radford in attack in place of the injured Charlie George, a move that would have long-lasting implications. Peter Storey reverted to his former right-back position, occupied at Everton by the now-injured Pat Rice, while Peter Marinello came into a midfield missing Jon Sammels, who had cracked a bone in his right ankle during a pre-season game in Denmark.

With Peter Simpson another long-term casualty, manager Bertie Mee lamented, 'To get three key men hurt, one from each section of the team, is an awful way to begin. In effect, we have lost a quarter of the team for perhaps a quarter of the season. But I would like to think the strength of the squad is enough to carry us through such a period.'

Arsenal's depleted team gained their second point of the season with a 0–0 draw, although it was a rearguard action for much of the evening. Frank McLintock gave a captain's performance, including a vital goal-line clearance from West Ham's Bermudan centre-forward Clyde Best. Jimmy Greaves shot just over from six yards and came close from distance, while Arsenal's only near miss of the first half came via the head of Hammers defender Alan Stephenson. Efforts from Radford and George Armstrong were evidence of Arsenal's increased authority in the second half, but their first win of the season would have to wait for another five days.

Arsenal opened their home programme against Manchester United in front of 54,117 fans, the biggest crowd in the country on the second Saturday of the season. A sunny day in London found the Gunners in irresistible form against a United team who looked a lot more than two years removed from their conquest of Europe. Storey was back in midfield, putting himself about among the blue shirts of the visitors and saving special attention, as usual, for George Best.

Those with memories of Swindon in 1969 had little sympathy for former Arsenal centre-back Ian Ure when he gave away a 14th minute free-kick. Bob McNab's cross went via the head of Eddie Kelly to an unmarked Radford, who wrong-footed sometime England goalkeeper Alex Stepney for the first of the day's four goals. Ure, it must be said, had played decently at times for a struggling United side during the 1969–70 season, but this was not to be his day. Radford and Kennedy caused repeated confusion in the centre of the United defence and Armstrong, with his direct style, was clearly revelling in the presence of two such dangerous targets for his crosses. Best did force Wilson into the kind of save that had become the keeper's calling card, hurling himself head first to steal the ball from the attacker's feet. It was such a perfect example of Wilson's trademark style that he still has the moment framed for posterity at his home in Hertfordshire.

The second Arsenal goal arrived without much further delay. Exchanging positions with Armstrong, Kennedy found himself on the right flank with Ure in pursuit. The forward delivered a cross that proved too high for Armstrong in the centre but fell for Radford to control at the far post and score with a low drive. Two more goals followed the half-time interval. Kennedy headed down a cross for Radford to volley in his hat-trick goal after George Graham linked skilfully with Rice and Storey. That was the signal for Stepney to leave with an injured shoulder and hand his jersey to central defender David Sadler. The makeshift keeper was powerless to stop Graham's header looping under the crossbar after United's defence was once again beaten in the air from an Armstrong cross. The visitors were left with one point and no goals in three games and, writing in the *Daily Mail*, Brian James claimed, 'I don't remember seeing a worse United side.'

Any euphoria Arsenal fans might have felt over their unbeaten start to the season was tempered somewhat two days later by the revelation that one of their stalwarts, left-back McNab, might not be around to share in any future success. After an ongoing 15-month battle for more money, McNab stated, 'I am having to think of asking for a transfer because I am losing money every week.'

McNab's comments turned the spotlight on the Highbury salary structure, in which each first-team player earned a basic wage of between £70 and £90 per week, considered low by First Division standards. Players were free to negotiate their own deals within those narrow limits and, on top of the basic pay, they received the standard win bonuses. If the team were successful that would at least bring them into line with their First Division peers. Then there was the controversial 'loyalty bonus', through which players received an additional 12.5 per cent of their bonus money for every completed year at Highbury. That meant £1,000 worth of win bonuses produced an additional £250 for a player with two years' service. For McNab, who signed in 1966, bonus payments totalled considerably less than someone like Armstrong, an Arsenal professional since 1961. Newspapers pointed out that, despite playing 53 first team games the previous season, McNab had earned £2,000 less than Terry Neill and David Court, who played only 25 and 30 games respectively.

McNab remembers his frustration clearly, explaining, 'It was a very irritating situation. It was a good idea, but it just didn't work. It is a good idea to reward loyalty but when two players who are basically reserves are getting more than someone who is in England squads and is playing every game week in, week out, there must be something wrong. I thought it was fundamentally unfair. There had already been talk of us trying to sign players like Alan Ball and common sense told you he wouldn't be coming to Arsenal to earn £2,000 less than me. My feeling was that they would do something for that type of new player but not for me.'

Arsenal's public response was to explain that players bought by the club normally received five or ten per cent of the transfer fee. McNab had received £5,000 after his £50,000 move from Huddersfield. 'The money worked out at £1,250 a year over four years – about £800 a year after tax. I had just bought a home in Huddersfield for £2,250 and after joining Arsenal I didn't have enough money to buy a house. In the end, I was able to buy the townhouse in New Southgate that Arsenal had found for me to rent.

'I didn't want to leave Arsenal. We had won the Fairs Cup, I had a leadership role in the team and I had been in the England squad that went to South America before the World Cup. But I had been approached by a very big club who were winning championships and was told that someone connected with that club would give me enough money to buy a house. I knew damn well I would be out of pocket at Arsenal. At that time, you had done well if you'd paid for your house by the time you finished your career. I loved London, I loved the team and I could see we had got something special coming up, but there was a lot of money being talked about.'

Publicly, Arsenal chairman Denis Hill-Wood displayed the club's reluctance to change its policy and seemed resigned to losing McNab, saying, 'I hope we don't lose him, but I am sure we will.'

According to McNab, however, Hill-Wood was adamant that his unsettled left-back was going nowhere. 'I adored the chairman. He was a lovely fellow, an absolute gentleman and he always used to tell me and Peter Storey that we were his favourite players. I requested a meeting with him and I got summoned to his office at the Ambro Bank, next to the Bank of England, in Threadneedle Street. It was in this huge office and it reminded me of the Arsenal boardroom. It was beautiful, walnut everywhere, pictures of tea clippers on the walls.

'He said to me, "You know you are one of my favourite players, Bob, and I don't want to let you go. If I have to I will sit you in the stand next to me for two years." I said to him, "But you could get £200,000 for me," which was a fortune in those days. He just said, "I don't know if you noticed where you are as you came in. That's not really a lot of money – not when you are sat next to the Bank of England."

'Basically he smacked me on the bum and sent me on my way and I didn't ask for a transfer. If I had not liked the chairman it might have been different. But he was always nice to me and I loved him. In the end they scrapped the loyalty system when Alan Ball signed the following season.' McNab continued to insist in the press that it was a 'matter of principle' rather than hard cash, but assured Arsenal fans he would not ask for a transfer.

McNab, aged 27 and at the height of his powers, had proved his heart belonged to Arsenal four years earlier when he had been forced to make a choice between Highbury and Anfield. It was the kind of opportunity he had feared would never present itself after chronic injury problems early in his career.

'I had been playing for Huddersfield's first team since the age of 21 but I had been out for about a year and a half. I'd had two cartilage operations on my knee. There had been nothing wrong with the second one, it was caused by the rehabilitation. To say it was a joke would be an understatement. The bloke would come in from cleaning the boots and my leg would be about six foot wide and he'd say, "Right" and put it under the heat lamp all day. The worst thing for fluid is a heat lamp and I sat under one for three hours a day. As soon as the fluid went away they would have me out running three miles and the next day the fluid was back again.

'Ian Greaves arrived from Manchester United as manager and said, "I hear you are a good player." I said to him, "Well, you must have a good memory." He said that if I came in at nine in the mornings he would come in with me and give me some exercises. Within three weeks I was back and I had a year and a half in the first team. We had a good team and a good system and just missed promotion, but my transfer was a financial thing. I was their most valuable asset. They created a scenario where the first team wage was £35 a week and mine was still £25 plus £10 appearance money. I was the most valuable player in the club but they offered me the same again. What could I do? I wrote a transfer request, and before I could hand it in, it was in the papers. They said, "We can't keep an unhappy player, his demands are too much."

'About two days later the manager called me in and said, "I've sold you. You are seeing Bill Shankly at Liverpool this morning and in the afternoon you are going to see Bertie Mee. They have both agreed a fee and it is up to you."'

McNab recalls his appointment at Liverpool with an icy chill. 'Shanks gave me high blood pressure. When they tested it at Arsenal later on, it was low. I found Shanks a totally overbearing man. We were in a room the size of a table and I was stark naked. He stood next to me and he was so close he was almost touching me. He started prodding me. I had been a joiner and builder for almost five years before I signed for Huddersfield as a nineteen year old so I had a powerful upper body and big arms for someone my size. He said, "I never realised you were such a strong wee man. You're the best left-back in Britain." I said, "I don't know about that, what about Ray Wilson at Everton?" So he says, "Aye, but you're better in the air. Did you see that goal against the Germans?" He was talking about the first goal in the World Cup final, where Ray headed it down and they scored. I was all shook up after that meeting. Shanks never spoke to me for four years after that. He just used to glare at me whenever he saw me and eff and blind at me during games.'

After meeting the ultra-polite Mee, it was Arsenal for whom McNab signed, partly because of his desire to live in London. Arriving within weeks of George Graham from Chelsea and inside-forward Colin Addison from Nottingham Forest, Britain's most expensive full-back found a club in the throes of overhaul on and off the field. In all, Mee used 22 players in his first season as manager and such a state of flux was the last thing McNab needed, especially as his first few months at Highbury were unsettling on a personal level.

'When I signed I was injured with what turned out to be a thigh strain that had calcified through playing with injuries at Huddersfield. A soft tissue x-ray showed the calcification, which I was informed could be extremely serious if not attended to. Arsenal made the decision to treat it rather than operate and it worked. Then Bertie himself worked me twice a day for ten days after the injured leg was healed. I knew he had been a physio with the army, but at the time I thought he was from the Gestapo torture section. But I had six months of repeated injuries and illness, including pleurisy and a serious ankle strain which required an operation to manipulate the ankle and regain complete movement.

'The only reason I was in the team was because they had paid £50,000 for me. I had lost my confidence and I felt intimidated. Coming from Huddersfield in 1966 was like coming from Costa Rica nowadays. Everybody was laughing at my clothes because we were two years behind up there and they were taking the piss out of me. Where I had come from, if someone had taken the piss out of me in the dressing-room I would have chinned them. It got to the point where I'd had enough. I ate it for a while and I am not proud of the way I turned it around. I sorted a few of them out on the training ground. I had done five years on a building site so I was strong. I even got sent home two or three times. I started to get a reputation for being a bit crazy, and I deliberately picked on those who were supposed to be the tough ones. Everyone is always scared of someone they think is a bit doolally. All of a sudden I got a bit of respect.'

McNab's role in the team grew after Don Howe's appointment as first team coach and, a few months later, his decision to scrap the man-for-man marking system introduced by Dave Sexton in an attempt to shore up Arsenal's woeful defence. For a thoughtful player like McNab, Howe's methods were a breath of fresh air.

'Dave was the first coach I had ever seen. I was 23 and had never seen a coach. I loved him, but I didn't like playing for his defence. I could understand why he did it as a coach because they had been such a mess in defence. If you give someone an assignment and say, "Right, mark him" and that fellow scores, you know whose fault it is. Personally, I thought it was a mindless way of playing football. The centre-halves at Huddersfield were better than the centre-halves we had. I would just switch my brains off in the dressing-room before the game.

'I love to overlap and on one occasion Bertie and Dave called me in and said, "Bob, you are not overlapping." We had been playing Fulham and I had been marking a very poor player who had ended up playing in behind the front two. So I was stuck in the middle just in front of our centre-halves, man-to-man marking someone who didn't even merit being marked. Well, I'd like to have seen somebody bloody overlap from that position. I liked the training Dave did, except when he did defending work. Then I just cringed. He was giving erroneous information, not what I would have done at all.

'I knew we could do better; my problem was convincing players like

Peter Simpson and Peter Storey, who had never won anything. I think I drove Don mad. Pat Rice always says he remembers Don and I debating it in a bar for hours and hours. Don eventually changed it at the end of his first season. It was a brave decision to change a system that had got us to the League Cup final against Leeds, which was the first hint of success they'd had for years. I was flattered to see that Don said he was happy to play the zonal system because he had me on the field to manage it. I think I did that. I was a thinker, while Frank was very emotional, someone who would beat the drum. And the lads listened, even though I used to slaughter them sometimes.'

Playing alongside McNab was Peter Simpson, who admits, 'It was difficult to make the switch at first because you had to start using your head. Not being the brainiest of people I found that difficult! We got it off pat in the end, but we had the players for it.'

Skipper McLintock, the new boy at the back, explains, 'Don and Bob McNab helped me a lot. Especially with holding the line and not running into the corner flags, although I would get dragged in sometimes. You go with someone and you know they are taking you into a false position, so I learned to just back off two or three yards because you don't want your centre-halves getting in positions where there are holes up the side of you. If I drifted a bit too far one way, he'd shout, "Oi, you cunt. Get fucking back here and stop dragging me across." It wasn't just, "Frank, don't go as much as that." He would let you have it and it made me pick it up more quickly.

'We used to pass men over. If my centre-forward was running out to the right wing I could have ended up running into corner flags and the back four would be pulled all over the place. So when the centre-forward started his run into the channel I would start to run with him for five or ten yards so he couldn't get between the two of us. Then the right-back just used to come and get him. Peter Simpson would do the same with Bob on the left. It was carefully mapped out and Don was a great help, as was Bob, who was a great tactician. He could hardly run, but no one ever got by him because his positional play was superb.'

Like his coach, McNab knew that playing football was not a popularity contest and admits, 'I would say the cruellest things on the field. I could be criminal, but the lads knew it wasn't personal. But a few years after the Double season, when I was captain, I was called into the office and was told not to say anything to the players on the field because they were so upset with the things I was saying to them. They were going through a rebuilding phase with a lot of young players and I think the youngsters were making excuses. So I agreed not to say a word. We played and I kept my mouth shut, even though all sorts was going on. Bertie called me in maybe two or three games later and said, "You can say what the hell you like to them." I asked him to go and tell the players that in front of me. So Bertie called them over and said, "I have just unleashed Bob on you again."'

Graham recalls McNab as having a 'great tactical defensive brain'. He continues, 'He was a tremendous defender, quick in the tackle, and could read situations very well. His only weakness was crossing over the halfway line. We used to have a laugh about Bob, saying he used to find the guys in the six rows behind the goal with his crosses more than anyone else.'

Victory against McNab's former Huddersfield team sent Arsenal to the top of the First Division, albeit for only 24 hours. But there was little in a scrappy victory over the newly-promoted Yorkshire team to compare with their play of three days earlier against United. The Highbury crowd watched in a dissatisfied hush for much of the game and it needed good goalkeeping from Wilson to keep Huddersfield at bay. There were only 15 minutes left when Kennedy – carrying the attack on his own after Radford left the game with a calf injury – headed the winner.

It was a victory with little to recommend it other than the capture of two points, but McNab argues, 'If you only win games when you play well, you win nothing. We probably had 12 games that season where we were an absolute nightmare. But because we had strength, discipline, organisation and fighters, we maybe won four of them and drew four of them.'

At Stamford Bridge the following Saturday, however, Arsenal suffered their first defeat of the season, their hopes undermined by a John Hollins effort that was to earn ITV's Golden Goal award for the season. Shortly before half-time, the tireless Hollins took a pass from Ron Harris and surged from midfield before lobbing the ball over the advancing Wilson. Having seen his effort rebound off the bar, Hollins kept running and hit the ball home sweetly on the rebound. As the ball lay in the back of the goal, the two dominant personalities in the Arsenal back four, McLintock and McNab, came face to face in red-faced fury. 'I had been on the line in case the ball dropped in,' McNab remembers. 'When it hit the bar, I knew I had to explode off the line and get out to Hollins before he hit it. The field was bone hard in the middle and I had long studs on because it was soft out on the wings. I had to get out 12 yards to Hollins, bending my run, faking him a little, anything to try to make him look at me instead of at the ball. But I couldn't get out there because my back foot slipped out. Frank exploded at me, "Why didn't you fucking get out there?" I was in his face screaming, "Because I fucking slipped!" On Monday, Frank said to me, "Sorry. I saw on telly that you slipped." What irritated me was that Frank should have known better. Common sense says I couldn't do anything in a 12-yard goal without my hands, so I would have tried to get out.'

It was not until ten years later that McNab realised it was the Stamford Bridge slip that caused a deep-rooted pelvic injury that reduced his mobility for the rest of the season and caused him to sit out much of the following year.

Kelly's second-half header put Arsenal back on level terms, but when Peter Osgood set up Irish right-back Paddy Mulligan for his first League goal, the Gunners were condemned to defeat. It had been a typically hard-fought London derby, featuring one scuffle between McLintock and Osgood, and it was clearly not to the liking of the watching Brazil manager, Mario Zagallo. He commented, 'How can players enjoy games such as this? Pelé and our other great players would not survive in games like this week after week.' Now, if Zagallo had really wanted a taste of English football he should have stayed around London for another three days.

3

HARD BASTARDS

THE CHELSEA RESULT WAS A DISAPPOINTING WAY FOR ARSENAL TO PREPARE
for the visit by Leeds United, the outstanding team of the era. The Yorkshire
side, stung by the disappointment of the previous season, had begun the
new campaign with obvious intent. While Arsenal were losing in west
London, Leeds were beating West Ham to maintain their 100 per cent
record.

It was the kind of success rate to which they had become accustomed
under their manager, Don Revie, a man widely misunderstood and unloved
beyond the boundaries of Yorkshire. Ridiculed by most people in 1961 when
he declared his intention of turning a poor Second Division side into the best
in Europe, Revie was then condemned for the way in which he approached
the fulfilment of that dream. In taking his club from the brink of the Third
Division to European conquests, Revie saw his accomplishments denigrated
because of Leeds' often cold-hearted approach. In addition, the fact that they
finished as runners-up in so many competitions was seen as proof that his
men lacked the character to rise to the ranks of the truly great. Less was said
about Revie's qualities as one of the game's most astute tacticians, a man who
could spot and nurture unproven talent, and as a leader able to mould men
of diverse skills into a formidable, coherent unit.

Frank McLintock, despite his admiration for Arsenal's great adversaries,
shares the belief that Leeds went beyond acceptable boundaries. 'I thought
they were a great side, but they just got too dirty, too cynical. They didn't
need to do it because they were good enough not to. They were never liked
because of that. It's a great shame because they had possibly the best team
of the late '60s and early '70s.'

Don Revie, born in Middlesbrough in 1927, signed for Leicester in 1944 before moving to Hull City six years later. But it was at Manchester City, where his elegant skills resided from 1952 to 1956, that he reached his peak as a player and earned all six of his England caps. In 1954–55 he was named Footballer of the Year and helped City to the FA Cup final, where they were beaten by Newcastle. The following season Revie led City back to Wembley, where he successfully employed 'The Revie Plan' to beat Birmingham. Wearing his usual number 9 shirt, Revie operated from a deep position, where his exact passing was more effective. The tactic flummoxed the Birmingham defence and resulted in a 3–1 win for City. A two-year spell at Sunderland proved to be his last stop-off before his fateful arrival at Leeds for a transfer fee of £18,000.

By March 1961, Revie, a player past his best, could sense the atmosphere of defeat and self-pity that was seeping through the club. Billy Bremner, who was to become Revie's on-field general, admitted, 'The situation was depressing. No one cared. Players couldn't be bothered to train any more. They were so sick of losing that I'm sure they would have left the club at the drop of a hat. The entire conversation in the dressing-room concerned how many goals we would be defeated by in our next game.'

Less than a season after being in the First Division, Leeds were staring at relegation to Division Three. The city was more interested in the local rugby league team and crowds had slumped to 7,000. It was then that chairman Harry Reynolds, with the foresight that had made him a millionaire in the business world, decided Revie was the man to take over the running of the team from Raich Carter, who had led Leeds to eighth in Division One in 1956–57. 'I immediately took to Don,' said Reynolds. 'I could tell he was the man for the job. He had no experience of management and some felt this was not a good thing, but the decision to appoint him was unanimous.'

Revie's first task was to restore the club's self-esteem. From now on, nothing but the best would be good enough for his team – which meant a new kit, new equipment, first-class travel and five-star accommodation. Revie explained, 'I wanted to instill the right attitude into everyone with the club. A successful club must think big, act in a big way, and I hoped that by adopting this approach the players would respond to it. Players who didn't like it were told that Leeds had nothing to offer them. Either they thought and acted like me or they left.

'I was going to make sure that every player on the staff was a man of terrific character. Men with backbone who I knew wouldn't quit if the going got tough, men who would almost give their lives for the club. So when we signed youngsters as apprentices, we tried to ensure they were lads of strong character. They had to have ability – that went without question – but they also had to show guts and determination.'

Revie eventually patched up his relationship with defender Jack Charlton. Shortly before his appointment as manager, he had snapped at his teammate, 'If I was the manager I wouldn't even pick you.' The comment festered for a while and Charlton came close to joining Manchester United before the two settled their differences and Revie assured Charlton, 'What I said is in the past. With the right attitude you can still become the best centre-half in Europe.'

Leeds managed to maintain their Division Two status, but suddenly the new manager's plans came under threat from the boardroom. With the club in dire need of funds, Revie discovered the directors had agreed to sell Bremner for £25,000. He marched straight into the chairman's office. 'I said that if Billy went, I went too. I told the chairman there were two men on the staff I needed to build the team around and Bremner was one. "He is going to be one of the finest players the world has ever seen," I said. And with that, I marched out again. It was a dreadful decision to make, but by now I was convinced that Leeds United were going to be great.'

The board relented, Bremner stayed and Revie was free to set about building a team which, if it did not always reflect the grace of Revie as a player, epitomised the uncompromising, ruthless way in which he tackled the job of manager. Leeds became embroiled in a disproportionate number of controversial, ugly games as they rose to the upper reaches of the Football League. Their football was based on the philosophy of not losing and Revie's first priority was a solid, technically correct defence. In this regard he was not so much guilty of heresy against the gospel of attacking football as he was one of the first managers to recognise the harsh new wave of reality that was soon to wash over the English game.

Revie's approach brought Leeds the Division Two title in 1963–64. In their first year back in the First Division they almost pulled off the League and Cup Double, losing the Championship to Manchester United on goal average and being beaten in extra time by Liverpool in the final of the FA Cup.

It was to be a familiar story until 1968, when Revie's side won the League Cup by beating Arsenal 1–0 and overcame Hungarian side Ferencvaros over two legs in a Fairs Cup final that was delayed until the start of the 1968–69 season. The victories ended Leeds' sequence of finishing second in four major competitions in the previous four years, as well as being beaten semi-finalists on three more occasions.

Inevitably, Revie's first success was shrouded in bitterness. For some time, controversy had been building over Leeds' tactics at corner kicks. Pursuing a plan hatched during a kick-around with brother Bobby and Jimmy Greaves at an England training session, Charlton had taken to stationing his 6 ft 1 in. frame right on the goal-line, directly in front of the opposing goalkeeper. The England defender was accused of standing on keepers' feet, obstructing them, pushing them, backing into them – just about everything short of stealing their wallets. 'When he stands on the goal-line he is there to try and score,' said Revie. 'There is nothing in the rules against it.'

At Wembley, Arsenal were adamant that Charlton had impeded goalkeeper Jim Furnell at a corner, leaving him stranded when Cooper volleyed in from ten yards. Arsenal midfielder Jon Sammels recalls, 'It wasn't a very good game and we cancelled one another out. Charlton fouled Furnell, but we knew that would happen because that was what they were about in those days – up to all tricks.'

A few weeks later more silverware arrived at Elland Road, courtesy of a Mick Jones goal in the home leg against Ferencvaros and an impressive display of teamwork in a staunch rearguard action in Budapest. The same close-knit group would provide the cast of leading characters in Leeds' triumphs under Revie. Of the thirteen men who performed over the two legs against Ferencvaros, eleven were to be key components of the club's achievements over the next six years.

In goal was the error-prone Welshman Gary Sprake, the man who once literally threw the ball into his own net at Anfield. Blond and somewhat fragile-looking, his prolonged presence in the Leeds team bears testament to his manager's loyalty as much as to his own ability.

At right-back was Paul Reaney, master of the goal-line clearance and a man who saved his best performances for games against Manchester United, where he appeared to spend the entire 90 minutes inside George Best's shirt. Occupying the other side of the defence was Terry Cooper, the finest attacking left-back of his time. In the centre stood the imposing monument of Charlton, nicknamed 'The Giraffe'. Shorts pulled high over endless legs, Charlton, despite his 35 years at the beginning of the 1970–71 season, was still playing with the energy of a teenager. Partnering him was Norman Hunter, denied more than his 28 England caps by the birth of a certain Bobby Moore and denied greater recognition for his ability as a ball player by his reputation as a man who would happily tackle a freight lorry head on.

In midfield, Billy Bremner and Johnny Giles were the heart of the team. Bremner was the stereotypical short, red-headed Scot; a cocktail of passion, rage and love of a scrap. But the image concealed a sophisticated footballing brain, considerable skill and the happy knack of scoring some spectacular goals in the most important of games. Giles personified the paradox of this immensely gifted, yet often cynical, Leeds team. A creative genius around the halfway line – all subtlety, perception and acute angles – he could display a ruthless streak of self-preservation in the heat of a midfield battle. Having played in Manchester United's FA Cup-winning side of 1963, Giles was bought by Revie that summer to add guile and know-how to what was then an inexperienced Leeds team. Despite fielding Giles in the outside right position at Wembley, United never believed he would develop into a truly outstanding player and happily let the little Irishman join Leeds for £32,000. It would prove to be the best purchase of Revie's career.

Bremner felt that his new colleague, having come from the free-and-easy atmosphere of Old Trafford, needed to allow some of the Leeds style to rub off on him. 'When he joined us he lacked the fire and devil to go with his undoubted footballing talents,' said Bremner. 'It wasn't long before he acquired that devil because every Leeds player must possess that determination and drive.'

An astute thinker about the game, evident in his subsequent careers as manager and football pundit, Giles revelled in the more disciplined and tactical approach he discovered at Elland Road, although he bristled at suggestions he had become a physical player. 'The club has never put pressure on me to tackle strongly, I've always had this streak of toughness in me since I was a kid,' he argued. 'Being a creative player, people will go out to kick you and I can protect myself. If people want to play football then I want to play football. If someone wants to mix it I can take care of myself.'

As devilish as they could be for opponents, Giles and Bremner were heaven-sent as far as Revie was concerned. Discussing the partnership, Giles said, 'Obviously it has grown stronger over the years we've played together but it's still instinctive. You can plan and devise all sorts of ploys in practice but in the end it's your instinctive reaction to a situation that counts. I like to try to find a bit of extra space to give myself extra time to react and that's where Billy and I read each other perfectly.'

Spearheading the Leeds attack was Mick Jones, bought from Sheffield United for £100,000 in 1967. A tireless runner and selfless worker for the team, Jones was often consigned to the shadows because his teammates stood so tall in the spotlight. Men like Scot Peter Lorimer, whose right-foot specials from the edge of the penalty area were the stuff of legend. Wide on the left were the dancing feet of Eddie Gray, capable of outrageous trickery.

Gray often appeared to have paid for the prodigious talent in his lower limbs with their low resistance to injury, preventing him from fulfilling seemingly unlimited potential at the peak of his career, although he did eventually play on for Leeds until the age of 36. Gray's finest hour came in the drawn 1970 FA Cup final against Chelsea, when he skipped and danced through Wembley's clinging mud, toying with poor David Webb like a young Cassius Clay tormenting a befuddled opponent. Paul Madeley, elegant and unassuming, was the man who never had a position of his own at Elland Road but had an important task to perform in just about every big game Leeds every played under Revie.

Leeds' European success in the autumn of 1968 proved to be the launch pad for their first League Championship, which they won with a record 67 points. Playing up front alongside Jones and Lorimer during the triumphant campaign was Mike O'Grady, but when he moved on to Wolves and Allan Clarke arrived from relegated Leicester in the summer of 1969, the Revie jigsaw was complete.

'Sniffer' Clarke, a slightly built forward for whom Leicester paid a British record £150,000 to Fulham in the summer of 1968, had hardly set the League alight during his year at Filbert Street. He scored only 12 League goals and was linked on several occasions with a move to Manchester United. He was also rumoured not to be seeing eye-to-eye with Leicester manager Frank O'Farrell, but it was his goal that beat holders West Brom in the semi-final of the FA Cup. In the final, despite playing on the losing side against Manchester City, Clarke was magnificent, spraying passes around like a wing-half and winning the Man of the Match award.

Clarke stepped into a Leeds team that for a time threatened an achievement that would have marked them down as one of football's greatest-ever teams. But their pursuit of the European Cup, League Championship and FA Cup in the 1969–70 season ended in heartbreak on all three fronts. Faced with an irresistible run of form by Everton after Christmas, Revie was forced to concede defeat and save his men for the cup games. Two days before the European Cup semi-final first leg against Celtic, Revie sent out a reserve side for a ridiculously scheduled game against Derby, Leeds' eighth in fourteen days. Unapologetic for flying in the face of League regulations that demanded a full-strength team be fielded, Revie said, 'We must consider the players' health and the club doctor has advised against them playing.'

A Sprake blunder and a late equaliser from Chelsea's Ian Hutchinson were to blame for Leeds' failure to finish off Chelsea in the FA Cup final. Sprake's error was a classic, the kind that made his dubious reputation. A hopeful shot from the edge of the box by Peter Houseman was completely lacking in menace, yet suddenly the ball squirmed through the keeper's arms as he dived to his left.

Four days after 120 punishing minutes at Wembley, Leeds' European Cup bid ended in front of 136,000 fans at Glasgow's Hampden Park. Trailing 1–0 from the first leg of their semi-final against Scottish champions Celtic, Leeds levelled the tie through the indomitable Bremner, only for Celtic to score twice in the second half.

Revie, who had said earlier in the season, 'To win all three trophies would be the eighth wonder of the world,' sent out his team at Old Trafford two weeks later in search of the one pot still on offer. But in the FA Cup's first final replay since 1912, a magnificent first-half goal – carved out by Clarke and executed by Jones – was again cancelled out by a late equaliser. In the extra half-hour of a bad-tempered game, Webb scored Chelsea's winner. It was scant consolation that Leeds' efforts were recognised in the awarding of the Footballer of the Year trophy to Bremner, while Revie was named Manager of the Year.

As well as being dedicated, honest and cooperative to outsiders, Revie's greatest asset as a club manager may have been in his relationship with his players. Manchester United's Matt Busby once told a young Revie that treating players well was the most important part of being a manager. And Revie was rewarded for following that dictum by the fierce loyalty shown him by the Leeds players. Bremner, a former teammate of Revie's who became something of a surrogate son, said at the height of Leeds' powers, 'The boss is first and foremost a players' man. He looks after you, provided you give everything you've got on the field. He cares about everyone in the club. He looks after the ground staff boys the same way he looks after the first team players.'

The players' loyalty to Revie was never more apparent than in their anger at the lack of credit given to the team for their footballing ability, particularly after the Championship season of 1968–69 when Leeds did attempt to open up their style of play. 'If people think we can't score goals then we'll just have to go out and start proving them wrong, won't we?' Revie had said during that championship campaign. 'If people want proof we can attack they can have it.'

George Graham is unabashed in his admiration for Revie's team. 'Leeds at the time were fantastic. Some of their play, their passing, was unbelievable and it stemmed from Bremner and Giles. They should have won more trophies because they were phenomenal. We knew that if we could get anywhere near Leeds we were going to have a good season.'

While Arsenal might not have matched Leeds for their streak of nastiness, their solid, organised approach was not so far removed from the Elland Road methods. It meant that any game between the two clubs was guaranteed to be tight, tense and not very pretty.

'It was a war of attrition,' Bob McNab recalls. 'In certain games you could have taken the ball off and nobody would have noticed. I'll never forget an incident in one game involving Billy Bremner and Peter Storey. When you are going to do somebody, you let them get the ball first. The ball was in between them and they were both standing and waiting for the other to get it. It was just a few seconds I suppose but it seemed like ages and somebody else eventually came in between them and got it. Neither of them dared put their foot in because the other would have ripped it off.'

Gunners coach Don Howe says, 'They were shocking games. Everybody in those games was too professional. We all knew how to stop the game and hold the momentum if one team got on top. The games against Leeds were not for the supporters. They were for the coaches and the players.'

John Radford adds, 'Leeds at that time were dominating things and bullying people. Losing to them in the League Cup in 1968 was a good game for us in some ways because from then on we started to get a little bit like that ourselves and we were probably the first side to stand up to them. You had to look after yourselves, especially in midfield. Early on it was a question of who could get one over on anyone else. It was accepted. Whoever got the first one in, good luck to them. If the laws were the way they are today there would have been nobody left on the pitch.'

Says Sammels, 'When we played Leeds up there we used to stay in Wakefield and before we got on the coach we had our pre-match meeting. I remember Don Howe saying once, "You know we are playing Leeds today. You know what it's going to be like. Is there anyone who doesn't want to play?" They had very skilful players but they were very intimidating. From one to eleven, including the keeper, they could all be physical.

'Johnny Giles was probably the best midfield player in the country, a terrific passer with both feet. But he was a hard little devil. As for Norman Hunter, well I can remember one of my earliest games at Leeds when I was maybe 19. I'd scored a little earlier and I got this ball on the far side and I knocked it past Hunter. I can't remember anything else except finding myself on the gravel track with all the ligaments in my left ankle damaged. When you played Leeds you knew you were going to get whacked in the first minutes of the game, whoever was marking you.'

Gunners full-back Sammy Nelson points out, 'They sorted you out in the first few minutes. It was all about trying to intimidate you, stopping you from concentrating on the ball, getting you looking over your shoulder instead.'

Defenders who lined up against Leeds knew their day's work would be just as punishing as that faced by the forwards who had to take on Charlton and Hunter. Peter Simpson explains, 'Their forwards gave our defenders more stick than we gave them. Allan Clarke was all elbows and it was always very physical. They went over the top and all that sort of thing, but it was done well, very professional.'

The battle could be a verbal one as well. Bob Wilson recalls, 'I always remember Paul Madeley saying things about my wife or family. They would try anything. Leeds had a defining part in my growth as a goalie because they had those corner kick tactics at the time I started in the first team. Charlton scored a goal at Elland Road with Peter Storey supposedly marking him. From then I had no one on the goal-line, it would just be me against him. Not only did I want it one-to-one, I would try to intimidate as badly as they would. It wouldn't just be, "Leave him to me," it would be, "Leave that bastard to me," right in his ear. You have to learn to live with it – you compete or you die.'

So when Leeds arrived at Highbury on the night of Tuesday, 1 September 1970, no one was under any illusions about what lay in store. 'It was like a game of chess when we played,' McLintock remembers. 'You had to work at every header, you had to do something brilliant just to get some space to get in a shot. Overall, you had to work so hard for everyone. Nobody gave up anything cheaply and nobody made any mistakes. We were both so efficient you always knew there would be only one goal in it.

'And it was dirty. They would try to win games by fair means or foul. They would go down injured, one player after another, trying to break up your attacks. I remember the referee cottoning on one time at Highbury after Hunter had gone down. The referee waved play on and Hunter jumped up and headed the ball out for a corner. The crowd were booing and swearing. I knew a lot of their players and they were smashing lads. But I would say it to their faces that they spoiled themselves because they were too good to do things like that, and should have won more than they did. They were a magnificent side with magnificent balance in their team – a team made in heaven.'

In later years an even darker side to the Leeds' success story would emerge. Hushed whispers of attempts by Revie to bribe opponents eventually developed into fully fledged accusations in print by Bob Stokoe – dating to when he had been manager of Bury in Division Two – and Wolves defender Francis Munro. One of the Arsenal players, wishing to remain anonymous on this subject, claims, 'Don tried to get to me to throw a game in the Marble Hall.'

Former *Sunday People* writer Mike Langley said recently that 'most of the knowledgeable football writers thought Revie was bent'. But Trevor Cherry, the England defender who would play for Leeds after transferring from Huddersfield, responds to accusations that Revie attempted to fix games by saying, 'If he did, I've always been in the wrong dressing-room. That's pub talk.'

Following Leeds' impressive start to the 1970–71 season, several managers, including Manchester City's Joe Mercer and Liverpool's Bill Shankly, picked out Arsenal as one of the few teams able to threaten them. Wilson says, 'I think Leeds thought we were the only side who could stop them, and we thought they were the only team who could live with us. We were the best two sides in the country and we knew it. It sounds arrogant but you have to have a certain arrogance and belief otherwise you will never win anything.'

The rivals' first meeting of the young season fell quickly into the expected pattern, making no allowances for the faint-hearted in the 48,000 crowd. The Gunners welcomed back Radford in place of Nelson, who had played at Chelsea three days earlier, but they lost Eddie Kelly after only 28 minutes of the game. Kelly was sent off by Welsh referee Iowerth Jones for lashing out at Bremner shortly after the Leeds captain had clattered into him from behind. While Bremner stayed down apparently injured, the furious Arsenal players surrounded the referee to protest at Kelly's dismissal. Mr Jones would eventually need an eight-man police escort at the end of the game.

Kelly recalls, 'Bremner went over the top on me and got my knee and my thigh. A couple of minutes later I retaliated. Billy knew what he was doing, he knew I was a young lad and he knew I had been playing well for Arsenal. You couldn't be a coward in those games. Your own players would know and the opposition would know – they would soon figure out if you were a bit of a bottler. So at the next throw-in I tried to scissor-kick him. It was stupid. My wife, Sylvie, came to the game and got there late and she was sitting beside Charlie George's girlfriend, Susan. She said to her, "How come Eddie is not playing?" So Susan said, "He was – he's been sent off!"'

With the crowd baying at Bremner's every move, Cooper incensed the North Bank further with a late challenge on Rice that earned him a booking. The Arsenal players' response was as impassioned as the crowd's. Rarely were Leeds able to take advantage of their extra man, with Cooper's effort against a post and Clarke's miss from three yards being the closest they came to scoring. As the second half wore on, there were even chances for Arsenal to snatch both points.

Such was the Gunners' brave response that manager Bertie Mee said, 'This was the best performance I have ever seen by an Arsenal team against a side the calibre of Leeds. If my youngsters can live through a game like that they can live through anything.'

Writing in the *Evening Standard*, Jim Manning was less complimentary, calling it 'one of the foulest matches between two Football League teams I have seen since the war'.

The following night, the game between Crystal Palace and Blackpool featured a series of ugly tackles that degenerated into an all-out brawl late in the match. Two police officers even ventured onto the field of play in an attempt to break up the mayhem, which continued as the players disappeared into the tunnel.

The events at Highbury and Selhurst Park were typical of the kind of games the Football Association had set out to eradicate. On the eve of the season they had announced plans to make clubs more accountable for the actions of their players. Vernon Stokes, the head of the FA's disciplinary committee, said, 'If certain clubs have a bad record they will have to answer to me as chairman or the committee. The clubs will be warned first time. A manager could be suspended *sine die* or for a period of, say, two months. Directors could also be suspended. For years now the FA have called clubs with bad records to task, but never have the rules been fully applied. This time it will be different.'

A change in policy had also been announced whereby bookings gained in the previous season would now be carried over, meaning three cautions in any twelve-month period would be punishable by suspension.

Forwards like Kennedy and Radford, however, knew not to wait for the referees to come to their rescue. 'If you try to hold the ball you get clobbered,' Kennedy explained. 'I can take it but it seems a bit one-sided. There's hardly a week goes by when I don't end up with bumps and bruises. It seems to be an accepted part of football. I've got to take it – especially in the box, where defenders get more desperate and referees are frightened to give you a penalty if you are fouled.'

West Ham's England striker Geoff Hurst became an obvious target for over-zealous defenders following his World Cup heroics. 'There's less protection for front runners now,' he said during the 1970–71 season. 'It's an accepted thing for teammates to ask me on a Thursday or Friday if I have got rid of my bruises after seeing me on the treatment table. There's not much you can do about it. Strikers come in for a lot of punishment and we accept this, but the tackle from behind is another thing. It's up to referees to give proper protection. There is a danger of strikers being kicked out of the game.'

Radford recalls the precautions he took to prevent such a fate befalling him. 'I used to wear these little felt chiropody pads, a quarter of an inch thick. The felt wasn't as tough as plastic but it used to fit nicely up the back of your leg. I never used to wear shin pads because you never used to get tackled from the front, everything was from behind. You knew that when the first ball came in, you were going to get done. Most teams had players who could put it about a bit.'

The player who fitted that bill for Arsenal was Peter Storey, who claims that Leeds were responsible for starting a trend that other teams could not ignore. 'They started all the rough stuff when they got promoted and other teams thought: if we can't beat them, join them. So we all started going that way and it was a conscious effort to take them on at their own game.

'At the start of a game, you think, "Right, I am going to do him first." You know that early on you are not going to get your name taken, so if you are going to commit a bad foul you do it early. The ref will just blow for a foul and you get away with it. Looking back, it was not right, but all the teams were doing it.'

It was, therefore, somewhat in keeping with the pervading mood of the time when Kelly's claim that he had simply retaliated against Bremner was accepted by the FA. The disciplinary hearing agreed he had been 'provoked' on the field, fining him £50 and suspending the usual ban for four weeks. Less than two weeks after Kelly's dismissal, another player, Southampton's Jimmy Gabriel, had claimed to be victim of what he called, 'The same old pattern – sent off against Leeds.' Gabriel added, 'Time and again it happens. They exaggerate incidents. Check the records and see how many men have been sent off against them. I was smacked on the jaw and kicked in the back while lying on the floor waiting for treatment. They make me sick with their methods.' Gabriel, too, would be spared further punishment.

By the week of Kelly's hearing, more controversy was blowing up around Leeds. In a television interview, Jack Charlton revealed that he kept a 'little black book' in which were the names of two players he intended to 'do'. He was reported to have said in the interview, 'I would kick them four yards over the touch-line if I got the chance.' Charlton was banned from England and representative games pending an FA hearing and was charged with bringing the game into disrepute. However, a newspaper survey of First Division centre-forwards claimed that all 21 of those polled thought

Charlton should not be banned. In the end, the FA agreed with Charlton that his remarks in the interview had been reported out of context and no ban was enforced.

Still, it all served to intensify the mystique surrounding the team Arsenal knew they would have to overcome to win their first title in 18 years. At least they had already taken one point from them, and who knew how important that might turn out to be?

4

WINGING IT

THE OPENING LINE OF A CHAPTER IN THE 1970 *ARSENAL FOOTBALL BOOK* announces, 'Wingers are like bosoms. Sometimes they are in. Sometimes they are out. Fashions fluctuate.' Putting aside the interesting choice of metaphor, it is a testament to George Armstrong's long Arsenal career that he was never out of fashion for long.

Since signing as a Highbury professional in 1961 and forcing his way into the team early the following year, Armstrong had fought off changing trends and rival wingers to play more than 300 first team games by the start of the 1970–71 season. A succession of Arsenal strikers, from Joe Baker to John Radford and Ray Kennedy, had cause to thank his energy and crossing ability for many of their tally of goals. The fans loved 'Geordie' for his willingness to give everything for the cause, and by quarter to five on the first Saturday of September, there was not a more popular man in Highbury. Never the most prolific of scorers, Armstrong had struck twice to see off the great rivals from Tottenham.

'This is the best start I have made to a season,' Armstrong told reporters. 'For the past couple of years I have gotten an early injury and then been unable to come back into the team because the lads have been doing so well. The way Arsenal have looked after me – the loyalty bonus is right up my street – has been a consolation when I have been fighting to get my place back. I just want to be part of what is going to be a great season for Arsenal.'

England's World Cup victory of 1966, the triumph of Alf Ramsey's 'Wingless Wonders' did the likes of George Armstrong no favours. He, along with players like Wolverhampton's Dave Wagstaffe, Derby's Alan

Hinton and previous Ramsey selections like Liverpool's Peter Thompson and Ian Callaghan, saw the door to the England team closed in their faces. By the time he was proving to be Arsenal's matchwinner in the first north London derby of the season, Armstrong had long since been lumbered with the label of one of England's best uncapped players. Even at club level, the evolution of the game forced a re-evaluation of Armstrong's talents. Arriving at Highbury as an inside-forward but soon becoming established as an orthodox winger, his role developed into the kind of bustling wide midfield position that required as much willingness to throw himself into covering tackles as to get outside opposing full-backs.

'It used to be murder going up and coming back again,' Armstrong admitted. 'Now I'm not finding it nearly so hard. When you are winning, everything is easier. The game has changed a lot in the last five years – especially for wingers. Wingers were out. But at Arsenal now I am playing a more orthodox wing role again, I'm using the flanks more and crossing for the strikers, although away from home I have got to drop a bit deeper to make more space for the front runners and tighten up the middle.'

Armstrong's place as a regular in the side had not been earned without the threat of competition. Early in his career he competed for a place against Scottish international Johnny MacLeod, a high profile signing from Hibernian, and Alan Skirton, the 'Highbury Express'. In later years, Arsenal's switch to a 4–3–3 style meant there was only room for one wide man, someone who could operate on either flank as well as drop back into midfield. So when Jimmy Robertson, the Scottish winger, arrived at Highbury from Tottenham in a swap deal for forward David Jenkins early in the 1968–69 season, Armstrong was forced to look over his shoulder once more.

His consistency won out and Robertson was soon preparing to pack his bags for Ipswich. But in the meantime there emerged an even greater threat in the shape of Peter Marinello, a frail-looking but fleet-footed 19 year old from Hibernian. His £100,000 transfer at the beginning of 1970 captured the imagination of the younger Highbury fans, earned column inches in teenagers' pop magazines and prompted talk of the arrival of the new George Best. With what turned out to be unfortunate irony, Marinello's debut was at Old Trafford, where he sent the headline writers into raptures with a stunning individual goal in the first half. For Armstrong, it signalled the beginning of another battle for first-team survival, while for the long-haired Marinello it meant advertising deals, modelling assignments and distractions that made it impossible for him to live up to his grand entrance into English football.

John Radford, one of the men Marinello was bought to supply, believes Arsenal were taken by surprise at the reaction to the transfer. 'I remember during the first half at United, he picked up the ball in his own half, went on a run and beat half their team and put the ball in the net. When I got home that night my wife asked how the new lad had played and I said, "He is going to be a great player." But he never played that well again.

'He had so much going on, with all the modelling and the magazines and all the other stuff. In later years a team would protect their young players from all of that – like Alex Ferguson did at Manchester United with Ryan Giggs and then David Beckham. Arsenal were probably at fault for not protecting Peter better, saying, "No, you can't do this or that, you need to concentrate on your football and your training," but that kind of thing had never really happened before so I suppose it was understandable that they weren't ready for it.'

Marinello's natural ability was never in doubt. Jon Sammels recalls, 'Peter was very skilful and could beat people easily. He had a long stride for a small chap and was very quick, no one could beat him in a sprint. It all happened too soon for him. If he had come down two or three years later it would have been fairer on him. After the goal at Manchester United everyone expected him to do it every game. In the squad system now it would be great to have him on the bench and when the game is getting stretched and defenders are getting tired, bring him on. With his speed, he would cause havoc. Perhaps at a different time he would have been a regular player. But who was he going to replace? George Armstrong? You couldn't leave Geordie out of the team for any length of time.'

So it proved, the turning point being Marinello's substitution in the Fairs Cup semi-final against Ajax. Armstrong, who had started only three League games in three months following Marinello's arrival, came on to produce a scintillating cameo performance.

Eddie Kelly was one of the players closest to Marinello after his arrival from Edinburgh and felt for his fellow countryman. 'Wee Geordie was that consistent that Peter never really got a chance,' he says. 'Peter was a very good player, very different to George. Even if George was having a bad game his work rate was superb, and that was the biggest thing he had over Peter. If Peter wasn't having a good game, you wouldn't get a lot of work rate from him, he wasn't that type of player. Peter really admired George for that part of his game.

'I thought Peter was a great signing. He could beat men better than George and was more flamboyant and I suppose Bertie thought at the time that we needed that. Peter gave you an extra dimension and George was certainly put under pressure by Peter. But George was so consistent and would get every cross in whereas Peter could get the ball and go past two or three players, but his crossing wasn't always great. What knocked Peter for six was when he missed a chance in the first few minutes against Ajax. After George came back there was no way you could have left him out.'

Reserve team coach Steve Burtenshaw was given the job of building up Marinello physically to meet the demands of the First Division. 'Peter didn't really work out straight away, so they gave him to me to strengthen and toughen up. We had him working three days a week on the weights, even on a Friday before a reserve game. We were never going to turn him into a Storey or McNab but it never did him any harm and he played stronger. Peter worked hard at it and we never had any trouble with him. We aimed to treat him as an individual, toughen him up mentally. Weights was one way we did it. He worked hard at it and any failings he had at Arsenal were not through lack of effort. He was a hell of a talent.'

Despite Burtenshaw's endorsement of the weight programme, Marinello did claim at the time that Arsenal's tough regime had taken its toll. 'In some early games my legs were feeling like lumps of lead right from the start. The worst part was when they decided my upper body wasn't as well developed as it should be and I was on weight training for months to build it up. It was murder.'

Bob McNab laughs when he recalls, 'I will never forget Peter and Sammy Nelson trying to bench-press 60 lb. Their little left arms were bent down here and the bar was diagonal. Peter wasn't a threat to Geordie. He had no strength in his upper body.'

By the time Armstrong was scoring twice against Tottenham, Marinello had already made the last of his three League appearances of the 1970–71 season and would have only one game as substitute in the Fairs Cup to look forward to for the rest of the campaign. He was left lamenting his fortunes in the press. 'I'm the forgotten man of football all right,' he said. 'The way things have worked out since joining Arsenal has made me pretty bitter towards a lot of people. I'm not talking about anybody at Highbury – I mean some of the guys who were going to help me business-wise when I came down here. You've no idea of the trouble some of these characters went to in order to try to make me sign contracts for just about everything you could think of. They thought I was going to be the biggest story of the century.'

No such fanfare had accompanied the young Armstrong's arrival in London a decade earlier. One of nine children born in Hepburn to a Tyneside shipyard worker, Armstrong spent a few weeks on Newcastle's books as an amateur, but grew tired of having to ask permission to leave his job as an apprentice electrician to attend training. So when Arsenal asked him down to London for a week's trial, he happily accepted, although he soon realised that he would have to switch from inside-forward. 'That was the position I was playing when an Arsenal scout spotted me at 16,' Armstrong said, 'but George Swindin, then manager at Highbury, said they had plenty of inside-forwards and asked me if I would mind operating on the flank.'

His performance at the trial stuck in the memory of future teammate Sammels. 'I remember Geordie coming down from the shipyards. We were watching him and it was unbelievable the way he was buzzing around. It was the same when he got older.'

Armstrong impressed enough to be offered a contract and to be handed a first-team debut at the age of 17, setting up the winning goal in a victory at Blackpool. He blossomed under Billy Wright, and earned five England Under-23 caps. He even scored both goals in his final appearance against Turkey three months before the 1966 World Cup, although only West Ham's Martin Peters made it from that team into the full squad. Sammels reveals, 'Alf Ramsey picked him to play for England Under-23s and Geordie scored and had a good game. Alf came back to him and said something like, "In case I don't see you again, it was nice to have met you!"'

The writing was on the wall as far as England was concerned, but Armstrong's value to Arsenal continued to soar. 'Geordie was a bit of everything, winger and midfielder,' says Sammels. 'He could play left and right, cross with either foot, or he could tuck in and work back. Bob McNab used to love it when Geordie was playing in front of him. If he went forward he knew Geordie would be back covering for him. It was lovely for a full-back to have Geordie playing in front of him. He was ideal for any system. And Geordie was the best crosser of the ball with both feet I have seen. Alan Hinton was the only one I can compare with him.'

Frank McLintock agrees, 'If three people were running into the box, he wouldn't just hit it into the general area, he would ping it right at the fella.'

Sammy Nelson adds, 'He was a great guy to have around, great for the team. I can remember him popping up on our line to head the ball away and next minute he'd be up there crossing the ball for John Radford.'

McNab developed a great understanding with Armstrong on Arsenal's left flank, although he reveals, 'Now and again I could strangle him. You'd practise things all week and as soon as the whistle went and the ball started rolling, he'd forget everything. Sometimes you'd do a throw-in where you bounced it and you'd throw it to the right place and he'd go to the wrong place. But he countered that with all the wonderful things he did for the club. Geordie could deliver a perfect ball with either foot and he'd ask you how you wanted him to deliver it – drive it, bend it, ping it? "Where do you want it, just tell me," he'd say. If you haven't got someone who can deliver the ball where it should be delivered six times out of ten, you can practise corners all day long and you'll be wasting your time.

'He could float lovely little balls in to the front players at the edge of the box, and it's tough for defenders in that situation, even if the attacker has his back to goal. You have only got to mistime your tackle and it's a foul.'

Completing an effective triangle on Arsenal's left was George Graham, who says, 'Geordie, Bob and I had a great understanding. I would just tell Geordie, "You give me the ball and get on your bike. Just go."'

Against Tottenham, Armstrong for once grabbed the glory himself instead of serving it up for someone else to feed upon. Early in the game his tireless running put him in position to open the scoring, rounding off a move that could not have been more straightforward. McLintock fired the ball forward to Radford, who had sprung the offside trap, and the centre-forward poked the ball first-time under the body of Tottenham goalkeeper Ken Hancock, playing only his second game in two years. The effort was almost certainly goalbound when Armstrong followed in energetically to knock home his first goal of the season.

He did not have to wait long for his second. George Graham freed Kelly on the right, Kennedy failed to make clean contact at the near post and Armstrong was first to the ball in the six-yard box to fire into the roof of the net. Arsenal's 2–0 half-time lead was never threatened and the Spurs fans, whose team had now won only two of their first seven games, went home so unhappy that Martin Peters needed police protection from his own supporters to board the team bus. The former West Ham midfielder, a stalwart of two World Cups, was still struggling to win over the Tottenham crowd since a transfer that had sent White Hart Lane legend Jimmy Greaves to Upton Park in a deal valued at a British record £200,000.

Armstrong's place in Highbury history would already be firmly established by the end of the 1970–71 season, and he continued to be one of the club's most consistent performers. He had chalked up a then-record of 607 first team appearances when he left Arsenal in 1977 to rejoin McLintock, who was manager at Leicester. After a handful of games for Leicester and a season at Stockport, Armstrong began a coaching career that took him to Aston Villa, Middlesbrough, Enderby, Norway and Kuwait. In July 1990,

Geordie returned home, being appointed Arsenal's reserve team coach. His enthusiasm for the game had never faltered and he approached his job as a coach with the same energy that had worn down opposition full-backs for so many years.

Arsenal and England left-back Ashley Cole recalls, 'When I joined Arsenal, Geordie was my first coach. His great strength when dealing with us as kids, which was true of his reserve team training sessions too, was that he knew how to make training fun. He was able to get his ideas across while keeping smiles on our faces. His enthusiasm was infectious. I remember that I used to run home from school buzzing at the idea that I had to go training and Geordie was taking the session. Geordie was a friend to us all and like all good friends he was always honest. He'd let us know our faults or mistakes but his message, even when he was letting you know how badly he thought you'd done, always had a positive tone.'

Armstrong was still imparting his enthusiasm and wisdom to Arsenal players when, on 31 October 2000, he suffered a brain haemorrhage and died at the age of 56. 'I couldn't believe it when I heard Geordie had died,' says McLintock. 'If there was someone you thought was going to live to be 100 it was Geordie. He was so full of energy. As a player he would play every game as though it was his first game.'

Peter Simpson was one of Armstrong's best friends during their playing days. 'We roomed together when we travelled and we were great mates even though we were total opposites,' he says. 'He loved training and did exercises at night when we were in the hotel, while I was having a cup of tea or smoking. He only ever had the occasional beer and would never get pissed. He was too generous and I think he had a few hangers-on who took advantage of him. It was a shame because he was just a nice genuine lad.

'He was a typical northerner and would speak his mind, although he was not clever with words. I always thought of a coach as someone with the gift of the gab, who could explain things easily, and I didn't think George was up to it. I think he was good at it because of his confidence and his enthusiasm for the game. Last time I saw him all he wanted to do was talk football, football, football – I had to walk away in the end.'

McLintock concludes, 'Off the field, he would moan about everything – the biggest moaner you could meet. But we all loved him. He was the most generous person you could ever meet. He'd always be saying, "It's my bloody round, you bought the last one." In fact, he'd bought the last two. You could never get to the bar with him around. If your car broke down, he would be round to pick you up. He gave his heart and soul to everything.'

Arsenal took a break from League action to draw 0–0 at Ipswich in the second round of the League Cup. Sammy Nelson was enjoying another game in place of Radford, while McLintock further aggravated a hamstring injury he had picked up against Spurs. Ipswich were the better team, with their South African-born midfielder Colin Viljoen heading just over and Wilson being called into action to deny Peter Morris and ex-Gunner Jimmy Robertson.

Despite their solid start to the season, Arsenal's management was concerned about their lack of creative options. Jon Sammels was still a long way from fitness, as was Charlie George, who could play up front or drop back into a midfield role. In the middle of the park, the Gunners were clearly more artisan than artist. The solution that Bertie Mee and Don Howe hit upon was a £125,000 bid for West Bromwich Albion's Scottish international Bobby Hope. 'I hope we get him because I regard this as a very rare chance to improve the overall quality of the squad,' said Mee. 'Inevitably, people will say that bidding for an outsider is a criticism of the players we have here, but that simply isn't realistic. The players have been marvellous, but why should I be satisfied?'

Albion turned down Arsenal's offer when it became clear they could not persuade Sunderland's young star Colin Todd to move to the Hawthorns to fill the first-team space that would have been left by Hope's departure for Highbury. So it was with a still Hope-less midfield that Arsenal travelled to Burnley.

The Lancashire town had enjoyed First Division football since 1947, but since the club's FA Cup final appearance in 1962 fortunes had been on the wane and the precarious financial position at Turf Moor led to the sale of the club's best players. Winger Willie Morgan went to Manchester United for £100,000 and the bald centre-forward Andy Lochhead to Leicester for £70,000.

The club did win the FA Youth Cup in 1968 and many of those boys were quickly given their chance against the grown men of the Football League, reeling off a magnificent run of eight victories early in the 1968–69 season. They reached the semi-finals of the League Cup and even thrashed champions-to-be Leeds 5–1. The 'Burnley Babes' were born, delivered by their managerial team of Harry Potts and Jimmy Adamson. They included Martin Dobson, an elegant midfield player, the powerful Steve Kindon and an elusive winger in Dave Thomas. The catalyst for much of their exciting football was Ralph Coates, a versatile forward from Durham.

But, unable to maintain their momentum, Burnley found themselves seven games into the 1970–71 season without a win and rooted to the bottom of the table. Adamson was fighting to stop the players deserting the club, with Coates, who narrowly missed making the World Cup squad for Mexico, a prime target. Looking considerably older than his 24 years, thanks to thinning hair that was given the Bobby Charlton treatment, Coates was a man for whom the top clubs were willing to pay £200,000. 'If I sold Coates I would be signing my death warrant,' asserted Adamson. 'He's not for sale at any price.'

A crowd of less than 13,000 sighed in resignation at another defeat when Kennedy headed Arsenal into an early lead. But a Burnley side that had not scored in its previous five games tore back at the Gunners. Wilson had to be at his best on his 100th League appearance, but he was finally beaten when John Roberts diverted a Thomas effort into his own goal. Radford was on hand with ten minutes remaining to secure another Arsenal win, the grateful Roberts being the one to set him up. The result left Arsenal tied with the surprising Crystal Palace for third place in the table, two points behind leaders Leeds, with unbeaten Manchester City occupying second place.

5

FIGHTING IN THE STREETS

ARSENAL'S TRIUMPH IN THE 1970 FAIRS CUP FINAL IS CREDITED BY THEIR players as the springboard to the achievements of the following season. Defender Peter Simpson says, 'The Fairs Cup was the biggest thing of all, because it was our first trophy and Arsenal had not had any success for so many years.'

Without the ability to foresee the events of the 1970–71 season, the defence of their European crown was a high priority as the new campaign kicked off. Yet it was only two weeks before the beginning of the season that UEFA decided to bring the Fairs Cup into line with the European Cup and Cup-Winners' Cup by giving the holders entry to the next year's tournament. For most of the summer it seemed that Arsenal – who had finished out of the European qualifying places in 12th place in Division One – would have to surrender their trophy without kicking a ball.

On their return from the pre-season trip to Scandinavia, Arsenal heard the good news. Bertie Mee greeted the decision by saying, 'They changed the rules to bring them in line with other tournaments but we had one other thing in our favour. All last season we stayed out of trouble in the Fairs Cup. Arsenal were a credit to the competition. I think we gained a lot of sympathisers all over the continent with the way we approached the job. I think the committee has seen sense.'

Mee could not have imagined how severely Arsenal's powers of self-restraint would be tested when they were drawn to face Italian club Lazio in the first round, with the first leg to be played in Rome. There was no doubt that it would be an intimidating experience. Lazio were coached by Uruguayan Juan Carlos Lorenzo, who led the Argentina team described as 'animals' by Alf Ramsey during the 1966 World Cup. Lazio's players had been involved in a brawl with their Wolves opponents during the summer's Anglo-Italian Cup. 'You must smile and walk away,' was how Bertie Mee prepared his team for the provocation.

It was to be the first time Mee's team had come up against Italian opposition. Even though Lazio were certainly not in the same class as teams like Juventus and the two big Milan clubs, Bob Wilson explains that English players held all the Italian teams in high esteem. 'We were playing at a time when foreign players had infiltrated Italian football, including British boys like Joe Baker, Denis Law, John Charles, Jimmy Greaves and Gerry Hitchens. For this to happen in a country's domestic game was then virtually unheard of in football anywhere. Italian football was attracting all the best players because they paid them phenomenal money and their clubs won a lot of things. The only country that matched them for winning European trophies at that time was England. But there was a suggestion of English teams being in awe. What became almost mythical was the defensive strategy of Italian football. They built up this thing about the sweeper system and the *catenaccio* and I guess that was also part of the myth. But I think that because Jimmy Greaves and company didn't do particularly well over there we were under the impression that their football was a much higher standard. Gerry Hitchens and John Charles, who was an absolute god at Juventus, were the exceptions.'

Before tackling the on-field threat, there were concerns about getting the Arsenal players to their destination. On the day the team was due to fly to Rome, eight British people were among fifty being held hostage by Arab terrorists in Amman, the capital city of Jordan, following the hijacking of a BOAC VC-10, the latest in a spate of such events.

Arsenal chose to reduce the odds of becoming involved in another political incident by changing their usual practice of splitting the players between two different planes. Club secretary Bob Wall explained, 'It was uppermost in our minds that planes were being hijacked left, right and centre. We knew, too, that Rome is on the main air routes to the Middle East and has been the centre of hijacking in the past.'

The journey proved uneventful, but the game itself lived up to all the predictions. The Gunners were greeted by fireworks, flares and all manner of missiles from the fans, while the Lazio players had their own hostile welcome for their opponents. 'They were treading on us and elbowing, and they would spit in your face at a corner,' recalls Wilson. 'And they went up to the younger players and pulled their hair just in order to provoke them. It really was horrible stuff.'

For most of the game, the good guys looked like emerging victorious. John Radford, big, brave and made for occasions like this, muscled his way onto the end of an Eddie Kelly cross to score the first goal minutes after half-time. Before long, Kelly supplied Radford again and Arsenal were 2–0 ahead. That was when things began to get really nasty, says Frank McLintock. 'We went two–nothing up and they started to put the boot in. They had a left-back who was half English, Guiseppe Wilson, who nearly chopped George Armstrong in two, and there were one or two other nasty fouls.

'In those days, the difference between Italian football and English football was remarkable. In our opinion they would be sly. They would fall over looking for free-kicks and spit on you – all that stuff. We would tackle from behind and go in with big crunching tackles that they thought were unfair, so the ideologies of the two camps were poles apart.'

Kelly adds, 'What they were so good at was when you went down after they had tackled you they would help you up and pinch the skin under your arm. You would lash out and people would think, "Look at that nasty bastard." They were intimidating all the time.'

The best player in a Lazio team destined to be relegated was their Welsh-born Italian international Giorgio Chinaglia, who had played four League games for Swansea six years earlier before being given a free transfer. Having threatened little all game long, the former teammate of John Roberts scored twice in the final six minutes, the first a clear-cut shot past Wilson, the second a controversial penalty. Wilson was given a telling off for the first goal by Howe, who felt the goalkeeper was at fault for coming out and leaving a gap at the far post instead of letting McLintock or Roberts deal with the danger. Moments later, McLintock appeared to have preserved the Gunners' lead when he dived to head a goal-bound effort by Chinaglia off the line, but the West German referee pointed to the penalty spot.

At the end of a bad-tempered game, both teams were invited to attend a banquet. The Arsenal players were presented with the kind of leather handbags that were fashionable among European men but considered effeminate by a bunch of English lads. There was some sniggering during the formal speeches and some of the handbags were tossed around.

McLintock takes up the story. 'We were in this restaurant and Peter Storey was just growling at the Italians, who were sitting only about ten yards away. It was very hot in the restaurant, no air conditioning, and Ray Kennedy went outside for a breath of fresh air. I think one of their centre-halves and a couple of the supporters went past and said something to Ray and he said something back. Even though he was young he was a big lump and he wouldn't take anything from anybody.'

Sammy Nelson, the full-back from Belfast, had accompanied Kennedy outside. 'We were just standing in the street when these three fellows came down. The guy who had been playing against Ray tried to knee him as he was passing. Ray just went "Smack!" and splattered him. I couldn't believe it. The others lads were coming out and there was shouting and screaming. It was like a comedy film, with people being thrown over Fiat 500s. People were opening their shutter windows and looking out and shouting and then the police arrived. It made me homesick for a while!'

Reports spoke of McNab being pinned against an iron grille by up to six assailants and almost pushed through a large plate-glass window, while Armstrong was slammed against the side of the team bus. Witnesses described as many as five groups of players fighting. McLintock continues, 'A couple of the other lads had gone out and Bob Wilson came back and said, "There's a fight outside." Well, you shouldn't tell a Scotsman that and quick as anything Eddie Kelly, Jackie Carmichael and myself were out there. I don't think George Graham was – he wasn't much of a fighter. When I got out there someone was throwing Peter Marinello over a car. Someone jumped on my shoulders and he was there for two or three minutes punching the back of my head while I was punching this other guy. It went on for five or ten minutes until the police came and pulled their guns out.

'Their manager picked up Bertie Mee by the lapels and stuck him on the team bus. I nearly got the guy who was punching me on the back of the head. There was about five minutes of shouting and bawling and then I've seen the guy, I recognised him by the brass buttons he had on. I sidled up to him about 15 or 20 yards along the wall and just when I was going to pull the trigger and whack him in the mouth, someone grabbed me from behind. It was John Roberts and he dragged me with my heels scraping along the ground for about 20 yards. I gave him such a volley. I said, "Where were you when the fighting was going on?"

'Of course the next day there were about 200 cameras at the airport. The funny thing was, on the bus back Bertie had said to us, "I don't want you speaking to any reporters, I want this kept under wraps!" I don't think it was our fault. We were just defending our teammates.'

Even Mee, strict disciplinarian and fierce defender of the good name of Arsenal, said, 'I am proud to be the manager of these players. They withstood terrible provocation during the match. It was asking too much of any group of men to then resist defending themselves when they were provoked again, and more seriously, some time after the match. I cannot condone fighting but the players all have my sympathy.'

The repercussions included calls for English teams to withdraw from

European competition, although the economic realities of big nights in Europe meant that it was never considered as a serious option. Ironically, Arsenal chairman Denis Hill-Wood had three years earlier expressed the view that it might be better for English teams to steer clear of the Fairs Cup because of its history of conflict. The immediate concern was the return game one week later and the threat of vendettas being carried on to the field. Bob Wall warned, 'If any man takes the wrong sort of action on the field he will not remain an Arsenal player for more than five minutes after the game.'

Lazio left behind Guiseppe Papadopulo, identified as the instigator of the fight, although the Italian club officials said he was being punished for being first to succumb to Arsenal provocation. The coach, Lorenzo, claimed his team was one of the best behaved in Italy and accused the British press of inflaming the situation. 'My players have been told to think of nothing but football,' he said when Lazio arrived in London.

'It was a fantastic boost for ticket sales for the second leg,' says Nelson, and a crowd of 53,000 turned up at Highbury expecting to see fireworks. But UEFA had appointed a referee, East Germany's Rudi Glockner, who appeared determined to rid the game of even an acceptable level of passion. The night passed off without incident and with a satisfactory result for Arsenal, a 2–0 win. Glockner, the World Cup final referee, booked five of the Italian players, although only Guiseppe Wilson's foul on George Graham was truly worthy of a caution. The press, denied a better story, accused Glockner of being overbearing and ruining a potentially dramatic cup-tie, but Arsenal were content enough with the events of the evening. Radford scored his third goal of the tie to give Arsenal an aggregate lead after only ten minutes, Peter Storey the supplier. The second goal had to wait until fifteen minutes from time, Storey once again the provider and George Armstrong the unlikely person heading home his cross.

It was almost a month before Arsenal resumed their defence of the trophy, by which time it was clear where the club's priorities lay. On the eve of the tie against Austrian team Sturm Graz, Mee said, 'Things are very different this season. Last year it was the Fairs Cup or nothing. This season the League title is the only thing. There is tremendous emotion about doing well in these competitions, but there may come a time when I have to curb it.'

Arsenal were due to play the home leg first but the Austrians requested a switch because of doubts about the weather by the time the second leg came around. Mee described the opposition as being little better than Second Division standard, but in front of 20,000 enthusiastic home fans they stunned the Gunners with a 1–0 win. The game was a disjointed affair, with the referee blowing frequently for offences and Arsenal, who conceded a goal early in the second half, struggling to find any rhythm.

The Gunners were still fully confident of overturning the deficit at Highbury, and it took only eight minutes before Kennedy found the net. From then on, however, the night turned into one of frustration as chance after chance went begging. The Dutch referee had played almost five minutes of injury time at the end of the second half when Graham beat the goalkeeper with a volley and the Graz defender Reiter stopped the shot on the line. Not for the last time during the season, Peter Storey stepped up in a moment of high pressure and stuck away the spot-kick.

The third round, played early in December, paired Arsenal with Belgian part-timers Beveren-Waas, and this time there were no scares. Storey was, for once, off target with an early penalty in the home leg but a couple of goals by Kennedy helped to see Arsenal through to a 4–0 win. The second leg was drawn 0–0 and the holders were safely through to the last eight as the European competitions went into their three-month winter break.

Back in the League, the drama of the brawl in Rome clearly had no immediate ill-effects. Two days after arriving back battered and bruised, the Gunners played host to West Bromwich Albion and rattled in six goals, although they did concede their first two home League goals of the season.

Bobby Hope, the subject of Arsenal's interest a few weeks earlier, was absent through injury from the Albion side and his place went to Asa Hartford. The 19-year-old Scot would play in every game for the remainder of the season and would hit the headlines the following year when his £170,000 transfer to Leeds was called off at the last minute after he was discovered at the Elland Road medical to have a hole-in-the-heart condition.

In front of the watching Scotland team manager, Bobby Brown, George Graham gave what was considered one of his finest performances in an Arsenal shirt, rounding off his display with a goal that showcased his balance and skill. With his back to goal he controlled a high ball with his right foot and in one swift movement fired home a blistering shot on the turn, his second goal of the game. Ray Kennedy scored twice, George Armstrong added another and Albion midfielder Len Cantello scored an own goal. One of the Albion goals was scored by Tony 'Bomber' Brown, who would finish the season as the First Division's top scorer with 28 goals. He would also earn his first England cap and play a big part in one of the incidents late in the season that helped to determine the destiny of the championship.

Despite a haul of six goals, coach Howe was more concerned about Albion becoming the first away team to score twice at Highbury. 'Don slaughtered us,' says McNab. 'We got destroyed because two guys about 4 ft 9 in. had scored! We had a crisis meeting on the Monday and we had just won 6–2!'

If Howe had been worried about a fall-out from the Lazio affair, his fears proved well-founded four days after the second leg, when Arsenal visited Stoke. Tony Waddington's side had given plenty of warning of their ability to upset the leading teams only two weeks earlier when they overcame Leeds 3–0 at the Victoria Ground. In fact, Waddington would become the first, and only, manager to deliver a major trophy to the Potteries when his team won the following season's League Cup. As Arsenal were to discover, they came close to breaking their duck one year earlier.

Waddington, a former Crewe Alexandra wing-half, arrived at Stoke in 1952 to take up the position of coach. Five years later he became assistant manager and in 1960 ascended to the manager's office. Within three years he had steered the club back to the First Division, boosted by the shrewd £3,000 re-signing of a 46-year-old Stanley Matthews. Waddington added to his reputation for financial cunning by acquiring, relatively cheaply, established forward players like John Ritchie, Peter Dobing and Jimmy Greenhoff. They teamed up with locally-developed players like John Marsh, Mike Pejic and Mike Bernard and by 1970 Stoke were ready to move into the big time.

They were set on their way towards an impressive double – first Leeds, now Arsenal – with a first goal that was alarmingly simple. Roberts was all at sea and guilty of ball-watching at the far post as centre-forward Ritchie headed in a right-wing cross from the ginger-haired Irishman Terry Conroy. The second goal was a defensive shambles. McNab played an ill-advised short pass to McLintock, who mis-controlled the ball and then under-hit a pass to Roberts, allowing Ritchie to steal possession. Ritchie strode past the Welshman's lunge and, despite being driven wide by Pat Rice, beat Wilson with a low left-foot shot.

Two–nil down at half-time, there was little Arsenal could do when Conroy received a return pass from Dobing and walloped the ball in from 25 yards. Wilson contributed to the fourth goal, failing to gather an awkwardly bouncing ball when Conroy overhit his pass into the box, allowing Greenhoff to clip the ball over a couple of yellow-shirted defenders on the line. The fifth came when Wilson parried an effort from full-back Marsh and another defender, Alan Bloor, smacked in the rebound. As well as the loss of two points, the result had a damaging effect on Arsenal's goal average, the ramifications of which would be felt later in the season.

Possible explanations for the setback ranged from the fact that the team had travelled on the morning of the game instead of staying overnight, to revelations that Mee and Howe had not issued their normal pre-game team talk. But Wilson says, 'Sometimes teams just have days when everything goes in. After the game Bertie said to us, "You have just had a great run of seven games unbeaten. Now you are going to start another run." He didn't hold a big inquest into it.'

Instead there was a team meeting where the players had the opportunity to talk about the embarrassing defeat. Howe explains, 'We used to have regular team meetings if things were not right. We had a little room halfway down the tunnel at Highbury, on the way out to the pitch. We called it Halfway House. It was a tactical room with a blackboard. We used to have real ups and downers in there. We'd had a real beating but the players responded the right way to criticism flying around. It really was a slating match but it was a man's way of dealing with it.'

Eddie Kelly recalls, 'I think Bertie and Don felt we might be fed up with listening to them and thought it would be better for the lads to have a chance to say how they felt. Frank led the meeting and he insulted a few of us. I remember thinking, "Bloody hell, Frank, you are putting yourself up against the wall here." He was just going through the whole team and criticising how I was playing, or how Pat Rice was playing, or whoever. One or two had a go back. It was a vicious meeting but it was really good, much better than if the manager or coach had taken it. If they had taken it then it would just have been Frank or Bob McNab answering back but this way everybody had their say. Frank slaughtered me and in the end I had to say, "Yes, you're right."'

Ipswich, due at Highbury for the League Cup second-round replay, were the unlucky opponents who would find themselves in the eye of a Highbury storm. McLintock recalls, 'Stoke was a freak result but maybe the best thing that could have happened. We wanted to make sure it didn't happen again. We were shit that day and it was a good way to get back to basics quickly. We didn't mess about talking about trifling things. The attitude for the next game was, "This is our pitch, if anyone is going to get knocked over it is going to be them. First tackle you make in the back four, make sure you come out with the ball. Win the first header. When they get the ball I want you closed in within two yards – if you can win it, good; if you can't, make them pass it across." So we made sure the tempo was set for the whole team. It was back to basics, no niceties, and let the football take care of itself.'

Ipswich were returning to London two days after being the victims of a curious incident that made even bigger headlines than Arsenal's humbling experience at Stoke. At Stamford Bridge, Chelsea's Alan Hudson was awarded a decisive goal after most of the 30,000 crowd had seen his shot clearly go into the side netting. Television news footage and still photographs confirmed what everyone inside the ground believed – everyone, that is, except referee Roy Capey. Ipswich manager Bobby Robson unsuccessfully demanded a replay.

Amazingly, the reverse was happening on the same day in a Division Two game at Leicester, where a shot from Portsmouth's Jim Storrie bounced off the stanchion at the back of the net after beating Peter Shilton on its way into the goal. The referee, believing the ball to have struck the post, waved play on. Leicester went on to win 2–0 and Shilton admitted, 'I was amazed – it was my lucky day.'

Ipswich needed more than luck against a determined Arsenal side and were never in the game. Roberts' towering header opened the scoring and Radford converted a Kelly free-kick into the second goal. Kennedy added two more, the first set up by Radford for a 3–0 half-time lead and the second arriving in the dying seconds.

It was the perfect way for the players to get the Stoke result out of their systems, although events at the Victoria Ground were about to rear their ugly head once more. Mee may have been philosophical about the Stoke result but he was unhappy the following Saturday when Wilson, already establishing himself as a television pundit, bravely talked the BBC's Saturday lunchtime viewers through Stoke's goals. Mee felt it was akin to giving away inside information, and was especially displeased as he himself had deliberately avoided public recriminations.

Wilson explains, 'I had been involved in the BBC's World Cup coverage. When I got to the studio for the first time there were about eight of us, including people like Brian Clough, and it was ridiculous. I suggested I spend several hours each day in an edit room putting together analytical pieces, which had never been done before. Jimmy Hill would talk and analyse the game on *The Big Match*, but no one had ever cut special pieces and laid down a voice track.

'They were successful pieces and the BBC asked if I would continue doing one each week during the season. Bertie said it was fine as long as it didn't interfere with my commitments to Arsenal. On the Thursday I went into the BBC and cut a piece looking at the five Stoke goals. Well, Bertie went apeshit when he saw it. He thought it was unprofessional to be talking about our own team like that. I suppose he was right but at the time I felt that I couldn't go on and talk about how we had beaten teams without talking about it when we got beaten as well.'

Wilson took the field for the home game against Nottingham Forest with Mee's anger ringing in his ears. If it was any kind of distraction, then it hardly mattered as the Arsenal goalkeeper was little more than a spectator as Arsenal took their tally of goals to sixteen in the last four games at Highbury with another 4–0 victory.

It was hardly a surprising outcome. Forest, four seasons removed from being runners-up in the League and semi-finalists in the FA Cup, were struggling in the lower half of the table. They had won only two out of ten games and were without their best player, winger Ian Moore (who until this season had used the distinctive surname of Storey-Moore). Strong and skilful, he had earned his first full England cap a season earlier in a friendly against Holland but had then torn ligaments in his right ankle and missed the rest of the season, and with it a chance of World Cup selection. Now he was missing in action again after damaging ligaments in his left leg playing for the Football League against the Irish League. Without him, Forest had little to offer going forward, despite the presence of Scottish schemer Peter Cormack.

At the back, they quickly proved themselves to be equally out of their depth. Sixteen minutes had elapsed when centre-half Bob Chapman failed to control a bouncing ball and saw it spin off his boot to Kennedy, who scored from close range with his left foot. After 46 minutes Kennedy and Radford found themselves homing in on McLintock's through ball and, ignoring his teammate's plea to 'leave it', Kennedy swept the ball into the net.

Forest goalkeeper Jim Barron temporarily denied Kennedy a hat-trick, but in the 59th minute the young striker harried two defenders into letting him in for his third, making him the First Division's leading scorer with nine goals. Radford set up a fourth for Armstrong, but it was Kennedy's day, even though he was denied the match ball when referee Leo Callaghan nabbed it as a memento of his last game at Highbury. Kennedy had to make do with praise such as that which came from the pen of Alan Hoby, who wrote in the *Sunday Express* that he was 'a latter day Ted Drake, only with better ball control'.

The player's reaction to his first senior hat-trick was to question whether he would still find a place in the team when Charlie George eventually returned, arguing, 'When Charlie is fit he'll get back in, so it will be John Radford or me to go out.' Time would prove that Kennedy could not have been more wrong and George would have to be accommodated elsewhere in the team. For now, the Radford-Kennedy partnership was here to stay.

6

A PERFECT MATCH

JOHN RADFORD HAD BEEN AN ARSENAL PLAYER FOR EIGHT YEARS – including five as a first team regular – by the time Ray Kennedy burst onto the scene. He had seen his share of strikers come and go since establishing himself as the spearhead of the attack during the 1965–66 season. Some, like Joe Baker, had been star players when Radford first signed as a professional. Others, like Tommy Baldwin, had come through with him before moving on to fresh pastures. George Graham, signed from Chelsea, had made a successful conversion from front man to midfield schemer, while Bobby Gould had arrived in a £90,000 transfer from Coventry and been sold to Wolverhampton in the summer of 1970.

By that time, Radford, 6 ft of solidly built Yorkshireman, appeared to have found the regular striking partner for whom he had been waiting. Over the second half of the previous season, including the latter stages of the Fairs Cup run, Charlie George had established himself as Radford's running mate. 'We were in transition for many years and it wasn't until I started playing with Charlie that things started to develop, but all that went to pot in the first game of the new season,' says Radford wryly. 'I felt we were developing a very good partnership. Charlie was such a great player, he could do anything on the ball. Everything was going so well through pre-season in the summer of 1970 and then he breaks his ankle in the first game.'

Arsenal turned to Kennedy, a 19 year old from the North-east who had teamed up with Radford on two occasions the previous year and scored one goal in a total of four League appearances. But it was in the Fairs Cup final where Kennedy had made a name for himself, grabbing the all-important

71

away goal in the first leg at Anderlecht after coming on as substitute.

Steve Burtenshaw, who had been coaching Kennedy in the reserves, recalls, 'Bertie Mee and Don Howe did what they would always do with a young player they were thinking of moving up. They asked me, "Do you think he can handle it?" I would always just give them a straight "yes" or "no" and if I said "yes" you could bet your life they would give him his chance. I was absolutely 100 per cent sure Ray had enough ability.'

At first glance, Kennedy's 13½ stones, coupled with his ability in the air, suggested he was too similar to Radford to form an effective partnership. But by the time the players left the field after the demolition of Nottingham Forest, the pair had shared 17 games in all competitions. So much for theories. 'Ray stepped almost straight from the youth team into the first team,' says Radford. 'It worked right away, even though I had hardly ever played with him or had the chance to train with him. Right from the first game I knew it would work.'

The natural rapport between the two was complemented by a lot of hard work during demanding training sessions. 'We used to come back and work in the afternoons, it wasn't just off the cuff,' Radford continues. 'Don Howe would come and do a lot of work with us, showing us the kind of movement he wanted. It was all in and outs – one player going for the ball and the other making a run in behind him. We also did a lot of coming towards the ball and spinning off. We used to work endless hours at that. At the time, teams weren't playing with sweepers. We used to try to draw defenders in and then spin off them and play balls over the top. People used to say we were just knocking balls over the top but it wasn't like that.

'There were lots of different ways of doing it, it was not just straight balls. You could play different angles, or have one man going for the ball and another spinning away – me blocking Ray's defender, him blocking mine, to get people away and to get a yard of space. We did a lot of near-post ball work, where the first one is spinning off and getting in the way of the centre-half as the other is coming past. We scored a lot of goals at the near post.'

As Kennedy began to attract the attention of the football world, he explained, 'John and I have hit it off on the field and off it and we are great friends. We did not play a lot beside each other before I came into the side, yet we hit it off from the start and it's almost telepathic. Neither of us cares who gets the goals. I think a lot of our strength lies in the fact that we are perfect foils for one another. We can read what the other is going to do and act the best way for the other one. For instance, I will work my way out on to the wing taking a defender with me. This will open up the way for John to whip though on goal. And it works the other way.'

Bob McNab recalls the exhibitions the duo used to put on during training. 'If people could have made videos of them playing up front in practices with Don Howe, they would be used as coaching videos. You couldn't believe what they did. It was a nightmare when Don used to go two-on-two and change defenders every few minutes. They were both so big and quick. It was mesmerising. They would dummy it, flick it through and side foot it into the goal. You couldn't defend it. I'll never forget a session after they signed Jeff Blockley a couple of seasons after the Double. They never failed to score. Fifteen goals in fifteen attempts. We were killing ourselves laughing. Poor lad, if he'd been a horse they would have shot him.'

Peter Simpson learned enough from facing the pair in those training sessions to sympathise with defenders at other First Division clubs. 'John and Ray were difficult to play against. They could hold the ball well and tuck it away and it was very difficult to get it off them. They could put their bodies in the way and I wouldn't have wanted to mark them. Playing up front is far harder than playing in midfield because you have your back to where you are going, but they were lethal.'

Jon Sammels adds, 'I couldn't believe some people criticised Ray and Raddy for being cumbersome. Raddy was very nimble and Ray had a fantastic first touch. Because they were big lads, people had this picture of them being immobile. They had a sixth sense about where the other would be on the field. You would very rarely get them both flat. One would be a little bit withdrawn and the other further forward, and it was all done without a lot of shouting and bawling at one another.'

Colleagues remember how the success of the new double act up front made things easier for the rest of the team. Frank McLintock says, 'Ray and Raddy were made for each other. They had great touch and they were strong and big. When I was receiving the ball and my eyes were down, I knew exactly what they were going to do, maybe running away and checking at the last minute to come short, or turning and spinning. They were both very mobile and could run all day and they shared an interest in hard work. Any of the back four could hit the ball up to their feet, up to their chest, and they would flick it on to each other. Or they could come short and receive it and then lay it off and make a run. It was a pleasure to play in the team with them. They would do crossovers and that would leave a gap. Other teams weren't like us, they would mark man-for-man and follow them, which meant you could hit the ball into the gap. Because of their movement they created so many chances for other people, George at the far post or Charlie running through the middle.'

Bob Wilson adds, 'As a goalkeeper, I was pretty accurate with the ball out of my hands so I would either hit space or I would hit the player. If it was Ray I would try to knock it in front of him because he was so good at holding it up for other players. If it was Raddy on a spin, I would hit the space.'

Radford recalls that the development of his partnership with Kennedy was a learning experience for the other players. 'The hardest part is getting understanding from the people who are delivering the ball. In training sessions, people were knocking it in as we were spinning and it looked bad. Eventually they got the understanding. They knew they could hit the channels. Obviously if they had time on the ball you got a better pass, but if they were under pressure they knew they could just hit the channel and one of us would be there.'

Radford's Arsenal career had blossomed in the latter years of the '60s, finishing as the club's top scorer in two successive seasons and earning the first of his two caps for England. Born in the Yorkshire town of Hemsworth, not far from Pontefract, Radford grew up watching Barnsley but considered himself a Manchester United fan. 'Funnily enough my dad was an Arsenal fan for some reason, but that wasn't why I went there. I would have gone anywhere to play professional football. I was playing for Bradford City while I was still at school and there was a connection there because Roy Ellam, their centre-half at the time, came from Hemsworth as well. I actually signed the professional forms for Bradford City. Well, I signed them at home and put them in a drawer for three or four days. Suddenly, I got the knock from Arsenal. I had an aunt who lived in Wembley so we came down for five or six days and played a couple of games, and the Bradford forms just got left in the drawer.'

Like so many players who were feeling their way into the Arsenal set-up in the early 1960s, Radford was not over-impressed with what he saw on the field. 'They had a very good forward line but it didn't seem like anyone at the helm could organise things defensively. Obviously things were going downhill. Billy Wright gave me my chance in football, but looking at it as a kid he didn't seem to have the strength to handle the senior players, even though at youth level he signed about five of the Double side.'

A first team debut against West Ham came Radford's way in the spring of 1964, the result of Joe Baker's sending off against Liverpool. 'It was only one game, but it gave me my chance. The season after, I played half a dozen games or so and the next season gradually got into the side.'

Graham shakes his head to emphasise his perception of an injustice when he says, 'What an underrated player John Radford was. The caps he should have won. He was a strong runner, great in the air, very brave, could hold up the ball. What would he be worth today?'

Despite Arsenal's success and Radford's rich vein of form, it was another north London-based centre-forward, Martin Chivers of Tottenham, who was pushing more serious claims for a place in the England team during the 1970–71 season. For now, Radford would have to be content with the challenge for club honours and the enjoyment of his blossoming partnership with a young player whose career had almost been brought to a premature end by an English football legend.

Sir Stanley Matthews, England's first footballing knight, was manager of Port Vale when he visited the Kennedy home at Seaton Delaval near Whitley Bay to sign young Ray. But only one year later, Matthews wrote to Kennedy's parents to inform them that Ray would 'have difficulty in making the grade'. Matthews added that Kennedy was 'sluggish' and 'would be wasting his time here'.

Matthews followed up his letter to the Kennedy home by breaking the news to Ray himself. 'At the end of the year, Sir Stanley came up to me and told me I'd had it. I was out. You've no idea how I felt about that. I was shattered. My whole world just collapsed. I can't think of anything worse to happen to someone of my age than to be told you haven't got it to survive. I was back home, right back where I started, and extremely deflated.'

In later years, Matthews claimed the decision had been a financial one, that Port Vale could not afford to retain a promising group of youngsters. McNab suggests, 'Managers often look for players who are like themselves and don't like anyone who doesn't play like they did. Perhaps that's why Stanley Matthews said Ray couldn't play.'

Faced with life back in the real world, Kennedy got himself a job in a local sweet factory and began playing again with his old amateur team, New Hartley. But when the whispers went round that Arsenal were interested in one of the team's young strikers, Kennedy assumed it was his partner, Ian Watt, who had scored 60 goals in a season. 'I'd got stuck in and began to enjoy the football I was playing, but I never thought about myself for Highbury,' he said modestly.

Burtenshaw, a long-serving player for Brighton and Hove Albion, who had taken the job of reserve team coach following Howe's promotion, remembers Kennedy's arrival at Arsenal. 'Ray came down after being released by Port Vale and at the trials he played left-wing. I remember thinking that, with the way the ball stuck to him, it would be a shame to have him stuck out on the wing when it was obvious he would be an exceptional centre-forward. When you ally that ability with the pace and strength he had, it made you wonder why someone had let him go. In general he was a damn good player, although it was not obvious to everyone.

'Charlie and Ray could play in the same side as a twin spearhead but one was completely different to the other. You could tell Charlie something a couple of times and he would practise it and he would get it, and he'd know when to put it into operation. Ray needed a bit more work to get something into his mind, but when it was in there it stuck and he could react to situations without any problem at all.'

Kennedy received extra coaching as part of the regular routine of Burtenshaw's reserve team. 'We would get the younger players in the reserve team back for extra work in the afternoons,' Burtenshaw explains. 'They would come back in small groups, six to eight sometimes, other times twos or threes, and sometimes individuals. They all had their turns but Ray had that at least twice a week. We felt he needed to really tune in to what we wanted of him so we worked with him specifically for a couple of afternoons a week. He was maybe 18 months behind the other boys but he soon caught up because he was willing. We worked on quickening his running and thinking and we started to see the results on a close season tour to Holland and Germany. We all knew he had the ability to make it.'

Despite his vital role in the winning of the Fairs Cup, the 1970–71 season appeared to offer Kennedy only the hope of the odd game here and there and another few months of patiently learning his trade. 'I thought I was going to be the odd man out again. But I was told to watch everything the other lads did so I would know what was expected of me if I was called on to play in the first team. It was then I knew I had a real chance to gain a regular first team place.'

Howe, realising that Kennedy was being rushed along in the absence of George, devised even more training sessions. 'I hated them,' Kennedy admitted. 'But I realise that if Don had not taken that trouble I wouldn't have had such a good season. It was sheer murder. They came after I'd done my regular stint with the rest of the lads. I'd have a spot of lunch then Don would say he wanted me back for an extra workout. They would go on for two hours sometimes. It was repetitious, with Don lobbing high balls over for me to head. They'd come time after time. I used to get dizzy standing there waiting for them, looking up and then nodding them down, to the right, to the left. If I'd had a choice I would have done anything else but that. The goals I scored with my head were goals I almost certainly wouldn't have notched up had it not been for those dreadful extra stints.'

According to Howe, the young striker was 'a coach's dream'. He explains, 'Ray listened and acted on advice. You could make constructive criticisms and he'd take them on board. He was told he was not good enough so he set out to prove them all wrong. He was a very phlegmatic character who seemed to take the game in his stride. Ray and John were big powerful boys, down to earth, called a spade a spade. I used to keep them both out practising when the others had gone home and they'd never complain.'

The first impressions of Kennedy as just another big target man in the best traditions of English centre-forwards were quickly dispelled. It would certainly be no surprise to his teammates when, several years later, he found success for Liverpool and England on the left side of midfield. 'What a footballer Ray Kennedy was,' says McNab. 'He never mis-controlled a ball in his life and he was the consummate team player.' The hard-tackling full-back even appears teary-eyed by the time he has finished recounting how Kennedy used to look after him on the field. 'Ray was so brave. I would be stuck in a corner being pressured and Ray would come 15 yards away from me down the line and let me roll him a little under-weighted ball. He used to stick his great big backside in and the centre-half would be kicking him and Ray would win a throw or flick it back to me. And he'd look at me and go, "All right, little man?" He would do for me. I would have sold the North Bank before I sold Ray Kennedy. That is how good I thought he was.'

Sammels describes Kennedy as 'a very mature boy', adding, 'For a midfield player like me he was a dream. You could knock the ball up to him and if you weren't in a position to receive it, he could hold on to it, hold off the centre-half and allow you to get in position. Then he'd knock a lovely weighted ball into your path. Like all great players, he knew when to hold it and when to lay it off and he would never use you to make himself look good. If he thought a teammate should have the ball he would give it to him, he wouldn't just use that runner as a decoy. He didn't need a lot of room to score goals or get a shot in. He had a short backlift and he could get in a shot that would go through people's legs, but only because he had hit it slightly quicker than anybody else would. I remember him having small feet for a big man and he was very nimble when the ball was around.'

Kennedy learned quickly to take the knocks that came with life in a First Division forward line and McLintock says, 'Ray could never get a penalty. If you whacked him from the back he never toppled over. He had concrete legs. The modern-day players would be doing somersaults, but for Ray it was a matter of pride that he didn't go down and wouldn't be knocked about.'

Nor would Kennedy retaliate in the face of the kind of sustained provocation that was part of so many defenders' gameplan. 'I was always frightened to strike back in case I got sent off and lost my place in the side,' he said. 'In any case I always found it much more satisfying to beat my marker with skill than by fouling him.'

Off the field, Kennedy and Radford developed a close bond. Kennedy and his young wife even bought the house next to Radford in New Barnet and would often go next door for dinner. 'I think Ray looked up to me a bit,' says Radford. 'We were very close and I even took him for a few driving lessons. I think there was a lot of respect there and if you are friends off the field you work better on it.'

Kennedy confirmed, 'Raddy is more than just the bloke up there at the front with me. He's my mate and I am grateful to him for so many things. He sort of adopted me, which was a great help to a youngster, especially on away trips when you felt inhibited and out of place. There seemed to be an immediate chemistry between us and we developed a special understanding. Raddy is pretty stubborn, though, and I would hate to argue with him because I know I'd always lose.'

Sammels echoes that view by remembering Radford as a 'typical Yorkshireman', saying, 'If you asked Raddy what he thought he would tell you. You knew where you stood with him. He would never give you any bull and you knew he wasn't waffling you. Everything was black and white with him.'

Radford still wonders how different history might have been if Gordon West had not landed on Charlie George's ankle, but ventures, 'I think things would have worked well. I would have been doing my thing and Charlie would have been doing his. Charlie was a little bit different, had a little more movement than Ray, and he could do the unexpected. He was a bit of a genius. At the time, I thought there were a lot of goals coming. It might have developed into a great partnership, maybe better than Ray and me. We'll never know. But the way it happened, everything fell into place. It would have been hard to leave Ray out and you knew you could play Charlie anywhere when he was fit again.'

Kennedy returned to Tyneside for the game against Newcastle, but this time failed to get on the scoresheet. Arsenal almost fell behind early in the game when Terry Dyson headed over with Wilson stranded, but once Bryan Robson's effort from a free-kick had been ruled out, because the referee wasn't ready to resume play, Arsenal began to take control. Newcastle goalkeeper Iam McFaul, the long-term understudy to Pat Jennings in the Northern Ireland team, was called upon to save from Armstrong and Storey and it was against the run of play when the home team went ahead eight minutes after half-time. The prodigious head of Welsh centre-forward Wyn Davies was first to a Frank Clark free-kick and 'Pop' Robson grabbed his chance in the six-yard box. Arsenal ensured the point they deserved, however, after 69 minutes when George Graham seized upon a mistake by the centre-back Ollie Burton to net the equaliser.

Back at Highbury a week later, it was business as usual for the Radford-Kennedy partnership, who proved too much of a handful for the weakened defence of League champions Everton. The Merseysiders' team included Henry Newton, the midfield player they had just signed for £150,000 in a deal that prompted a wave of protest from Nottingham Forest fans. Faced with accusations of lack of ambition at the City Ground, Forest manager Matt Gillies said, 'We let him go because of his attitude. Once Sir Alf Ramsey had passed him over for the World Cup he believed he had no further opportunity of getting into the England team. The thought dominated him and he never played his best for us again.'

Newton, who had been in the Forest side thrashed at Highbury two weeks earlier, took his place in an Everton team that was missing veteran Brian Labone and had Andy Rankin in goal in place of Gordon West. The front-runner a year earlier for the role of Gordon Banks' deputy in the England team, West had chosen to remain at home with his family during the summer instead of travelling to Mexico to be a World Cup bench-warmer. That decision left the way clear for Peter Bonetti to feature in the ill-fated quarter-final against West Germany after Banks went down with food poisoning. Now West had created more controversy by being spotted on television giving an obscene gesture to fans at Blackpool during an Everton victory.

Rankin came into the line-up just in time to be the victim of one of the most-repeated goals in BBC television history. A rather nondescript 3–1 defeat at Coventry was guaranteed lasting notoriety when the home team won a free-kick on the edge of the Everton area. Standing with the ball between his feet, Willie Carr, the slight, ginger-haired midfielder, kicked up his ankles behind him, flicking the ball into the air for Ernie Hunt to volley past the flailing left hand of Rankin into the top corner of the net. Had the ball ended up in the stand, as the odds favoured, few would have remembered it. But the incident, as well as winning BBC's Goal of the Season prize, led to the banning of what quickly became known as the 'donkey kick'.

The television cameras were clearly becoming an unkind presence for Everton goalkeepers, and so it proved at Highbury. Without a victory in their first six games, and with only four wins from twelve League games, Everton proceeded to offer another performance that left *Match of the Day* viewers pondering the whereabouts of last year's Championship-winning team. Attempting to shield his eyes from the sun, Rankin's first error was to don a cap that looked, both in colour and style, frighteningly like something Donny Osmond would wear to trill out 'Puppy Love' to a nation of screaming teenaged girls. His second mistake was to make a half-hearted attempt to reach George Armstrong's left-wing corner, finding himself in no-man's land as Graham helped the ball on to the back post for Kennedy to score.

It was soon clear that, once again, the aerial route was Arsenal's most direct path to success, especially given Everton's defensive shortcomings. As well as missing Labone, the visitors were without John Hurst, the man who always wore the number 10 shirt but played beside England's World Cup centre-half in defence. Radford had a shot turned round the post before Pat Rice hit a long diagonal ball to the far post, where a complete mismatch saw the tall figure of Kennedy outjump Howard Kendall, a 5 ft 8 in. emergency central defender, to head home the second goal. It all seemed too easy, prompting only a half-hearted celebration from Kennedy, who three days earlier had been in the England Under-23 team that beat West Germany 3–1 at Leicester.

The second half brought two more goals. The first, 20 minutes after the interval, resulted from a long throw by Radford, cleared by Kendall and Roger Kenyon to the edge of the penalty area and returned with interest by the right boot of Eddie Kelly. The final goal of the day was a penalty by Storey after Kenyon, who had been lucky to get away with a first-half challenge on Kennedy, used his hand to prevent McNab getting in a cross.

How the paths of these two teams had diverged since the opening day of the season. Everton manager Harry Catterick offered a rather bizarre explanation for his team's disappointing start; the fact that four players, including Joe Royle, Colin Harvey and Howard Kendall, had got married during the summer. 'I've seen it happen time and again,' said Catterick, who at least offered up his own post-nuptial form as an example. 'We measure the form and sharpness of our players in training and the stopwatch checks show that the newly-weds are down on the times they were setting last season. They tend to be a little sluggish until they have settled into their new life.'

Up next for Arsenal were a Coventry team whose defence included centre-half Jeff Blockley, an ill-fated Highbury signing a couple of years later, and a 19-year-old reserve goalkeeper in Eric McManus, deputising for the injured Bill Glazier. Four days before facing Arsenal, they had conceded six goals against Bayern Munich in the Fairs Cup. It took only 11 minutes for Arsenal to find their way through to the home team's goal when Radford's right-wing cross was headed in by Kennedy at the near post. A good fingertip save by McManus kept the score down and Coventry could even have equalised just before half-time when Wilson had to push the ball over the bar as he collided with forward Brian Joicey following a header from Neil Martin. For the most part, though, McLintock and McNab comfortably patrolled the Arsenal back line.

Two minutes into the second half, Armstrong twisted past right-back Mick Coop to set up Radford at the far post for the second goal, although the striker did break a bone in his wrist in the process. Martin pulled one back for Coventry after Arsenal failed to deal with a corner, but Graham made the game safe four minutes from time when he pounced on a mistake by former Arsenal player Geoff Strong after good approach work by Radford. The points won, it was Kelly who was singled out for praise by Bertie Mee for his return to form in midfield.

One week later, while Geoffrey Boycott was celebrating a century in the MCC's first game of their Ashes tour of Australia, the man who was to become one of the Yorkshire batsman's biggest pals, Brian Clough, was taking his Derby County side to Highbury. Clough had risen to prominence as much through his brash, outspoken, made-for-media image as for his achievement in returning Derby to the forefront of English football. However, Clough was more than mere talk. His freely-dispensed opinions, delivered in a nasal tone that made him fodder for the likes of television impersonator Mike Yarwood, carried the weight of considerable achievements as both a player and manager.

For goals per game, no post-war striker in the Football League had ever been more lethal. Clough scored 197 goals in 213 League games for Middlesbrough, his home town team, and 54 in 61 games for Sunderland before his playing career effectively ended at the age of 27 on Boxing Day 1962 in a collision with Bury goalkeeper Chris Harker on a muddy pitch at Roker Park. The result was a torn cruciate knee ligament. Two years and three unimpressive first team games later, Clough was persuaded to turn to coaching the youth team, quickly gaining his FA coaching certificate and helping the club to the semi-finals of the FA Youth Cup. Two years as manager of Hartlepool followed, before Clough left the North-east in 1967 to become manager of Derby, fourth from bottom in Division Two. With him to the Baseball Ground went Peter Taylor, a friend from his Middlesbrough days, summoned from non-league Burton Albion as his assistant.

Clough inherited a club that had achieved nothing of note since the first season of football after the war, when a team spearheaded by Raich Carter lifted the FA Cup. During the summer of 1968, Clough made one of the most influential signings of his career, buying the ageing Scotland half-back Dave Mackay at a knock-down £5,000 from Tottenham. A little overweight maybe, yet far from over the hill, Mackay was a proud, combative figure who had fought back from twice breaking his leg. He provided the leadership and inspiration on the field that Clough was providing on the training ground and his performances saw him share the 1968–69 Footballer of the Year award with another veteran defender, Manchester City captain Tony Book, as Derby won promotion to the First Division. Mackay's influence was considerable on young players like Roy McFarland, a stylish young centre-half signed from Tranmere after a midnight visit from Clough, and forwards John O'Hare and John McGovern, signed from Sunderland and Hartlepool respectively and destined to become talismens for Clough throughout his career. The final piece in the promotion jigsaw was Alan Hinton, the blond winger with the sweet left foot.

Clough had gone into his first season as a First Division manager with typical confidence, saying, 'You either have the right players or you don't. We have them.' The players, with Welsh half-back Terry Hennessey arriving from Nottingham Forest to add versatility and experience, proved Clough right by finishing fourth in the First Division. Derby were denied the place they had earned in Europe and fined £10,000 after being charged with 'gross negligence' in administrative matters. That included a payment of £2,000 to Mackay for writing programme articles. Small consolation came in the form of a place in the first Watney Cup, which Derby won by thrashing Manchester United in the final.

McLintock recalls, 'You wanted to shut a guy like Brian Clough up. But you also had great admiration for him. He was so big-headed and so arrogant, but his players never knew if he was going to give them a kick up the backside or a pat on the back. You have to have great confidence to not care if you are liked, and he didn't give a monkey's.'

While Arsenal sat in second place in the table, Derby were in the bottom three after a season of injury problems. Predictably, therefore, the home team were quickly on top, although they struggled to create many openings against McFarland and the nearly 36-year-old Mackay, whose performances as sweeper had Clough claiming he was good for another 300 games.

At the other end, McLintock was turning in another composed performance against centre-forward O'Hare, thought to be on the verge of a Scotland call-up, and the livewire Kevin Hector. McLintock recalls his relief any time he managed to keep Hector off the scoresheet. 'I found Kevin Hector very difficult to play against. He would go deep and come straight at you from a deep position. I used to like to make players go one way or another, I didn't like to give them options. He was a bit like George Best, light on his feet, and he wouldn't have to put his foot down hard to change direction. He would sway and when I had got him in a position and was ready to tackle he dipped his shoulder and got me spinning. There might have been better players than Kevin Hector at that time but I found him particularly difficult to play against because he was quick and had a terrific change of direction.'

It was the Derby defenders who had the greater problems at Highbury, and it took four of them to halt Rice after he took it upon himself to launch an attack. The ball broke for Kelly and he took the opportunity to test the handling ability of goalkeeper Les Green, who stood less than 5 ft 9 in. tall. After a quiet spell it was Kelly who put Arsenal ahead when he made the most of an uncharacteristic slip by McFarland. The man widely tipped to follow Brian Labone and Jack Charlton into the England number 5 jersey was alert enough to get to Radford's nod down before Armstrong, but the quick-thinking Kelly anticipated McFarland's attempted back-pass and stole in to beat Green with a neat first-time finish.

The second goal, in the second half, was simplicity itself. Graham received McNab's throw-in and hoofed the ball hopefully into the penalty area, where Radford rose high above McFarland and forced home a header that Green may have struggled to stop even if he hadn't been floundering around needlessly at the edge of the six-yard box.

Derby did, however, begin to play more like the team that had finished in the top four the previous season than a side occupying a place in the bottom three. At something like full strength after a series of injuries, they forced John Roberts to head Alan Hinton's free-kick off the line and saw O'Hare head past the post. Arsenal, too, had opportunities to add to the score but Mackay swept a Graham effort off the line and then denied his fellow Scot again with a timely tackle after a free-kick.

A two-goal win was more than enough for Arsenal and the following day Armstrong, looking rather camera shy on *The Big Match*, said, 'This is the best Arsenal team I have played in. The secret is the spirit in the team. Everyone is fighting for one another, everyone has faith in each other and there is a lot of skill in the team. Every team has room for improvement but at the moment I can't see anyone getting in our team.'

7

THE ARSENAL WAY

ARSENAL ENTERED NOVEMBER WITH HOPES OF FOUR TROPHIES. A CHALLENGE for the League Championship was taking shape, with Leeds only two points ahead after the first 15 games, while the Fairs Cup had been won once and could be won again. The FA Cup lay in the future, but the early rounds of the League Cup were gathering momentum.

These were the days before English teams' money-driven obsession with the Champions League, when the League Cup was still a major prize. Although the competition was considered important enough to offer its winner a place in the Fairs Cup, fans of even the top teams regarded any piece of domestic silverware worth winning in its own right – not just because it represented entry into the lucrative world of European football. The League Cup had come a long way since being introduced ten years earlier and its place in the sport's pecking order had been cemented when it was decided that the tournament should reach its conclusion at Wembley. In 1967, the first time the final was played at the home of English football, a Rodney Marsh-inspired Queens Park Rangers, then in the Third Division, beat West Bromwich Albion 3–2.

Having disposed of Ipswich in two games in the second round, Arsenal had journeyed to Second Division Luton's Kenilworth Road, where they encountered a packed ground, an old friend in former Gunners striker David Court, and future Highbury favourite Malcolm Macdonald. Macdonald's reputation as a phenomenal goalscorer was growing as quickly as his dark mutton-chop sideburns. Already he had scored ten goals in the season, a total that would reach thirteen just four days after the Arsenal game when he struck a hat-trick against Sheffield Wednesday. Goals had come easily to Macdonald ever since Fulham, his local team, were struck by an injury epidemic and forced their young full-back into emergency service as a centre-forward. Macdonald, who had gone to Fulham from Southern League Tonbridge, scored five goals in ten starts for the west London club before being transferred to Luton for £17,500. While failing to meet manager Alec Stock's semi-serious target of 45 goals in a season, he would eventually manage to score 49 League goals in 88 appearances before a £180,000 transfer to Newcastle in the summer of 1971.

'I don't consider I've had a good game unless I score,' he explained at the time. 'To be brutally honest I'd rather have a stinker and score two goals than a blinder and not get on the scoresheet. It's the only way I can measure my contribution. Some strikers get involved in midfield play. That's not my game; I do all my work in the 18-yard box. Even if the ball goes in off your backside it's a good goal. I'm a bit of a glory hunter, I admit that. I consider myself an extremely limited player as far as some of the skills go. I have strengths and weaknesses. Of course, I train to improve the weaknesses but I don't let them worry me. Instead, I concentrate on the strengths – speed, the ability to take the ball round the keeper and keep a cool head in tight situations. I still feel I lack the stamina to run and work all the time.'

Macdonald's only real rival for the title of the most colourful character outside the First Division was Marsh at Queens Park Rangers. In fact, one week after Macdonald's hat-trick, Marsh would score one of the most spectacular televised threesomes of the age against Birmingham City: a thumping header, a dipping volley and a sublime exhibition of ball skill on the edge of the box. Like Marsh, Macdonald revelled in, and added to, his image of confidence and arrogance, claiming to have been disappointed since the age of 14 whenever an England squad was announced without his name in it. To prove his ability at self-promotion he would announce his eventual arrival at Newcastle by turning up at his new club in a Rolls-Royce.

Macdonald, who could have ended up at Manchester United had the club not waived Luton's promise of first refusal, was clearly the biggest threat to Arsenal's progress and he forced a save from Wilson after 18 minutes. But eight minutes later the Gunners were ahead. Court gave away a free-kick and Arsenal's aerial power was once again decisive, George Graham the scorer of the game's only goal with a near-post header. Macdonald was denied a headline-making upset, but there were to be plenty more headlines coming his way, including a British record £333,333 transfer to Arsenal at the start of the 1976–77 season.

The team that now stood between Arsenal and a place in the quarter-finals was Crystal Palace, one of the surprises of the season. Promoted to the top flight for the first time in their history at the end of the 1968–69 season, Palace were clearly determined to improve on a debut season that saw them finish one position and one point out of the relegation places. Manager Bert Head proved it by spending £100,000 on the blond midfielder Alan Birchenall, surplus to Chelsea's FA Cup requirements, and £41,000 on his former Stamford Bridge colleague Bobby Tambling, the west London club's record goalscorer. In addition, full-back Peter Wall arrived from Liverpool for £35,000. 'We've bought instant footballers, instant goals and instant ability,' said Head confidently. 'It's like putting the milk and butter into the pot to get mashed potatoes.'

Palace had made front-page headlines on the eve of the season with a pay scheme that promised to make its players the first £300-a-week men in the game, their reward for winning two games within a week. To remain at that level of earnings the team would have to remain in the top five and have a good Cup run, but the thought that the Selhurst men could top the £14,000 annual salary of Prime Minister Edward Heath made for good copy. New signing Birchenall gasped, 'I could not believe my eyes when I saw the terms Palace were offering. The money here is out of this world.'

A year earlier, Palace had money available but chose to spend £300,000 on improvements at their Selhurst Park ground. 'We could have spent £200,000 on players and gone down,' explained Head. 'That would have put the club back years. So we decided to sweat it out and wait. Now we have the horse facing the right way.'

The horse was quickly away from the stalls, too. Seven wins and only three defeats in the first fourteen League games found Palace in the top four when they were drawn to play at home to Arsenal in the fourth round of the League Cup. More than 41,000 saw the home draw against West Ham three days before the visit of Arsenal. The Cup draw had led to some controversy among the Palace fans as the board decided to raise prices by four and five shillings. Head defended the decision on the grounds that all it did was restore the prices of the previous season before they were lowered during the summer.

A thrilling game surprisingly ended without goals. One day after Muhammad Ali made his boxing return after a three-year absence by quickly dispatching Jerry Quarry, Arsenal and Palace traded punches for 90 minutes without either being able to administer a knockout blow. Palace had more of the possession but their enthusiasm and energy could not break down an Arsenal side who created more chances. Kelly, Armstrong and Radford came close and Palace keeper John Jackson saved well from Storey and Kennedy, who also lobbed just over the bar late in the game.

By the time the replay came around, Arsenal had followed their defeats of Everton, Coventry and Derby with their fourth successive League win, a 1–0 success at Blackpool. Wearing unfamiliar navy blue shirts – both their red and yellow strips were too similar to the tangerine of Blackpool – Arsenal adopted a cautious approach at Bloomfield Road. 'Dully unambitious' was how one newspaper described it. In Tony Green, a skilful young Scottish midfielder who had at times been linked with Highbury, Blackpool had a player capable of turning a game, while winger Tommy Hutchison was also a threat. And even though they had won only two League games so far, and would win only two more throughout the remainder of the season, the memory of their FA Cup victory against Arsenal a few months earlier was still fresh in the memory. But Arsenal coped easily with Blackpool's greater share of possession, Wilson's afternoon amounting to a few crosses and a save at the feet of Mick Burns. Late in the game Arsenal killed off the home team with a header by Radford from a George Armstrong cross. It was a classic Arsenal performance, the kind that 20-odd years later would have the North Bank fans bellowing 'One–nil, to the Ars-en-al' in ironic appreciation of their team's ability to eke out narrow victories.

Peter Storey admits that Arsenal's tactics could make them unpopular when they ventured outside north London. 'Our attitude in away games was always, "Right, we have got one point, let's keep it," and try to nick a goal and get a 1–0 win. It was good for those days but it didn't make for good spectator sport sometimes. It is better now with three points for a win, but in those days if you drew your away games and won at home you would probably win the League. That made football a bit negative. You have to do a bit more today because if you keep getting one point you get nowhere.'

Two days after Arsenal's trip to Blackpool came the unfinished business with Palace. Unbeaten at Highbury since a 3–0 defeat to Chelsea ten months earlier, the Gunners named an unchanged team, which meant no return for Peter Simpson, Jon Sammels or Charlie George, all three of whom had just played in a 6–0 reserve team victory. Arsenal fell behind when Wilson could not hold a shot from Jim Scott and the rebound was converted by Gerry Queen, but Palace still seemed ill-equipped to hang on for victory. Their midfield was without its linchpin, Steve Kember, while a defence already missing Mel Blyth, lost captain and full-back John Sewell after only 20 minutes. Arsenal missed chance after chance, Kennedy, Kelly, Radford and Graham all guilty, before Palace scored again after 75 minutes. It was a moment of madness by John Roberts that put paid to Arsenal's chances. Wilson won a high ball cleanly, but Roberts took exception to the way Queen had challenged with his elbows. The Welshman chased down the Palace striker and shoved him to the ground, giving referee Norman Burtenshaw, a recurring figure in the quest for the Double, no choice but to award a penalty. Tambling converted the chance.

Palace were the opponents again when Arsenal resumed League action and Bertie Mee sent the team out with instructions to 'spread it around more and keep it low as well'. On a day of torrential rain in London, it was another entertaining contest, with Storey squandering a chance to score on the volley as early as the second minute. After 16 minutes, Kelly's shot was blocked by a defender and Radford scored on the rebound, only for Palace to hit back immediately. A short pass by Queen caught Roberts off balance and the defender failed to cut out the ball before it found its way into the penalty area. The slip allowed Birchenall to score. Jackson made a couple of saves and got away with his mishandling of a Kelly shot, while Blyth turned away an Armstrong cross after a great dribble by the Arsenal man. Jackson saved again from Kennedy following a poor back-pass by Birchenall, Graham shot over from 18 yards and Arsenal were frustrated in their quest for two points.

Four and a half hours of football against Palace had brought only one goal, while the one intervening game, the victory at Blackpool, had seen Arsenal's performance come in for much criticism. The methods of attack that had been serving the Gunners so well suddenly began to be questioned. In a less than scientific study in *Goal* magazine it was suggested that the inventive midfield influence the Gunners had failed to find was missed more than ever. The survey's author suggested that Arsenal had 'allowed themselves to be kidded into thinking that twenty-nine goals from nine wins and one draw in their first ten home games had signalled a new golden era'. He went on to suggest that 'defenders have come to terms with marking two big, brave front-runners out of the game'.

The survey revealed that in the draw at Palace, 50 per cent of the passes out of defence were played direct to Radford or Kennedy, while the majority of short passes were merely to set up the long pass. It added that the big men would more often than not turn and try to beat a defender when they received the ball. At Palace, said the report, the front men laid the ball off for a midfield player only five times and never once knocked the ball out to the wings. It also suggested Armstrong spent too long reinforcing the midfield instead of attacking down the wings, leaving full-backs Pat Rice and Bob McNab to supply the width. Eddie Kelly, meanwhile, was 'overworked'.

It was all flimsy, of course, but it did illustrate the way in which critics of the Arsenal methods were quick to speak up when a couple of results went against the team. The cries of 'I told you so' could be heard from Highbury to Hillsborough. In attack, said the so-called experts, Arsenal were predictable and in approach they were defensive.

'We did hit it long sometimes,' admits Radford, 'but we had two players up there you could hit it long to. Look at Liverpool 30 years later. There is no point in hitting long balls if Robbie Fowler and Michael Owen are up there; it is going to come right back to you. But when you have got two big guys like me and Ray up front and guys like George Graham, Jon Sammels, George Armstrong and Charlie George who can come through from midfield, there is nothing wrong with long balls like that.'

McNab claims that being forced to play on some of the mud heaps that passed for First Division pitches made the ability to hit the long ball a tactical necessity. 'What we did away from home on a bad field was play it over defenders' heads and make them face their own goal. The fields were so bad you couldn't afford to play football sometimes. We had to allow for bad bounces. I would be running down the line and get slagged off for crossing the ball behind the goal but people wouldn't have seen the ball stick or bobble.'

Criticism of the Arsenal methods is, of course, shrugged aside by the man responsible for devising the Gunners' style of play. 'It was that jealousy of Arsenal that still exists today,' Don Howe asserts. 'You are always going to get people who criticise you for the way you are playing and the success you are having. If you get to the top in any sporting life people want to find things wrong. It is professional jealousy, but it never affected my way of thinking. If people wanted to join in the criticism then I looked at it as them not having the knowledge to know what was going on. It is a shame for them. People don't know what they mean when they talk about defending or defensive football. I know I am good at defending but that doesn't mean I am defensive. People were very inquisitive about what we were doing. It was a busy time at the training ground at London Colney, we had a lot of people coming from abroad to look at how we were doing things. We were quite open about it, we never closed our doors.'

Graham is quick to come to Howe's defence. 'I think Don has been very badly portrayed in England. Everyone associated Don with defence but that is untrue. He was not only a good defensive coach, he was a good offensive coach. He got a reputation that I think was unfair. He made sure he got things right at the back first. I got the same reputation as a manager.'

Arsenal's football under Howe may have had its detractors, but McNab believes it was a product of the times. 'If people thought our games were not exciting then it was a condemnation of what was going on at the time. Only four teams scored at Highbury that season. Well, it takes two to tango. If teams come to play you'd get four penalties during a season! It was an indictment of what was going on at the time. Teams would even put on someone to mark me, and I couldn't run that season. We had some bad games that season where, if people had come to play, they could have taken us.'

In any case, McNab contends, Arsenal's aim was always to get as many men forward as possible. 'When we had the ball, we had only three at the back because Pat Rice or I would go forward. Geordie would make a run and clear space for me and I would be like a midfield forward. People had never seen that. It just evolved, we never really planned it, although we did a lot of practice at getting out of the back into midfield with the ball.'

Howe's system also saw the use of the famous Arsenal offside trap, another piece of frequently used anti-Gunners ammunition. McLintock explains, 'When forwards used to make their runs we bent our run with them, and I haven't seen anyone recently doing it the way we did. We used to make a run with them and when they thought they were going to be okay, then we would step up a yard. Norman Hunter, for example, would bring his foot back and you'd get the call, "Hold, Frank," and Allan Clarke or Mick Jones would be ten yards offside. When they started the run they thought you were trying to catch them up, but you were just pretending, not going as fast as you could. In the meantime, the full-backs were taught to stay two yards ahead of us centre-halves because we might come up quickly and catch them off guard. We played the offside trap with just the two of us, keeping the full-backs slightly ahead of us, and it really worked great.

'Tactically, as a team we were so aware, so knowledgeable. Bob Wilson was a sweeper behind us and we used to fox teams. When their right-back or right-half was going to put the ball into the box and someone like Derek Dougan was about to start his run, one of us would shout, "Hold your line," and the forward would hear that and put on the brakes. He would start coming back and Bob would pick up the ball 15 yards from goal with no challenge at all. So then they would try to get the ball to the forward's feet because they couldn't get it behind, and that was when we caught them offside. Instead of marking directly behind we would mark on the side, so when the ball came up we could see it all the way and nip in front. We had a great defensive record and we knew how to protect any weaknesses.'

The architect of the Arsenal system arrived at Highbury in the spring of

1964, a skilful former England full-back signed from West Bromwich Albion for £35,000. Even as a 28-year-old player, coaching was already in Don Howe's thoughts. 'When I was in the England team, the manager Walter Winterbottom said to us that we would be better players if we took a coaching course. As a player of 21 or 22 I thought it wasn't a bad idea, so I did the course and passed my exams and became qualified, with the idea that playing does not last for ever.'

Two years after his Arsenal debut, Howe's foresight paid off when his playing career was brought to a premature end after breaking his leg in a collision with Blackpool goalkeeper Tony Waiters. Sammels recalls, 'It was the worst break I have ever seen. Waiters' head hit him right in the shin. I was the first one there and Don had hold of my arm so hard I thought he was going to break it, he was in that much pain. The bone was sticking through his sock.'

Howe comments, 'I don't know whether I was lucky or unlucky. I had a compound fracture of the right leg and they decided to give me a new operation and insert a plate in my leg, a new thing they had been doing with skiers. I was never the same and Bertie came to me and said, "Would you like to be manager of the reserve team?" I had already done some coaching in amateur football in the Midlands, coaching a steelworks team, and I realised that after my injury I would have to drop down the divisions if I was going to carry on playing. So I agreed to do it.'

The decision was no surprise to Sammy Nelson, who remembers early signs of Howe's interest in coaching. 'They tried to introduce a provisional coaching badge for the players and we had these coaching set-ups every Monday for about six to eight weeks. Dario Gradi ran the course and most of us just thought it was a joke. This is how you trap a ball, this is how you head a ball, teaching schoolkids. But Don really enjoyed it. He was very keen.'

By the time first team coach Dave Sexton moved across London to Chelsea, Howe had done enough to convince Mee that he was ready to take over the first team squad at the age of 33. McLintock explains, 'When Don was 28 he was like 35. He was that kind of father figure. I love him and have great respect for him. He won us over, made us such an efficient team. We could play against anyone and they would be huffing and puffing and we never felt we were in any danger.'

McNab used to go with Howe to watch games. 'I loved being with Don. I wasn't afraid of people thinking I was creeping, I was just very comfortable with him. I liked to sit and talk to him about the game. I see practices now and some of them are Don's from 30 years ago. George

Graham's practices when he was manager at Arsenal? Don's practices. There is no great mystery to it all.'

Kelly adds, 'Don was an excellent coach. He was always one for a good kick up the arse, but he was someone you could talk to. Don's knowledge of the game was superb and he could talk to you. He had been at the top. The whole system was top notch.'

Wilson explains, 'It is not only that Don can read the game so well, he can read it through the eyes of every player on the field. You could stand eye to eye and argue with him and there would be spit flying everywhere, but we always had great respect for him.'

The selection of Howe as the man to build upon Sexton's foundations may have been Bertie Mee's most significant contribution as Arsenal manager. Mee certainly never professed to be a footballing genius himself, but he had been around the changing-room long enough to know footballers and coaches. The son of a Nottinghamshire miner, his modest playing career at Derby and Mansfield had been followed by six years in the Royal Army Medical Corps, which led to a position overseeing the rehabilitation of disabled servicemen. Six years after being appointed Arsenal's physiotherapist, a surprised Mee was installed in the manager's office.

Polite, genial, shy and with an elocution style straight from the officer's mess, Mee set about reorganising the club, although he insisted on the option to return to his previous role after a year if things didn't work out. 'Bertie had a good track record in administration and that's what was needed,' says Nelson. 'Someone to administer and run the club properly.'

Mee himself admitted, 'The first thing I realised was that I knew nothing about the job even though I had practically been the right-hand man to George Swindin and Billy Wright. I took my time before accepting it because I didn't want to let down a club with great traditions.'

McLintock recalls, 'It was a big surprise when Bertie got the job. He was a very pompous little man and he'd say, "It's Mr. Mee to you." He was like Captain Mainwaring in *Dad's Army*. But he was very disciplined and had the intelligence to get Dave Sexton in there and let him get on with the coaching because he didn't have a clue. I remember Dave having to miss training one morning and Bertie had to take it. He said, "I'm sorry, lads. I am sure you are aware I can't do it very well so I'll just run you this morning." He was very good at that, he knew all about pulses and times and was very strict. Dave and Don were superb coaches so Bertie let them get on with it.'

By the time he became manager, Mee had already earned the respect of the players for his abilities as a physiotherapist. 'He was brilliant, probably the top one in football,' says Sammels. 'If you were injured when Bert was physio you used to train a lot more than when you were fit to play. If you were fit enough to get your basic strength back again he would make you piggy-back guys up the East Stand. And if there were two of you injured, he would set one of you off on the track at the bottom of the North Bank and you'd have to run all the way round the pitch. Your partner would be seeing how many times he could run up and down the terrace. Then you'd change over and keep going until Bertie thought you'd done enough. He'd test your pulse and if it wasn't up enough he'd send you round again. I always had a low pulse rate, so I always ended up having to go round again.'

Mee's experience with injured footballers, along with his close contact with seriously wounded troops, had helped him develop an understanding of players' sometimes fragile mental state. Sammels says, 'Bertie knew more about the players than we did ourselves. When you have treated people for broken legs and torn ligaments, when you have nursed them through lonely hours of rehabilitation, taught them to run and kick a ball again, you are bound to get to know them pretty well. Bertie knew us through our most defenceless moments.'

The level of esteem in which Mee was held by his squad varies from player to player. Kelly, for example, remembers a caring man away from the football pitch. 'I know a lot of people were a little bit indifferent to him and Charlie George hated him, but I liked wee Bert. He did all he could for the younger lads. I got married and I went to see him a couple of times for advice about getting a house and the club couldn't have looked after me any more than they did. And Bert was brilliant in the Double season when I was up before the FA after the Bremner thing. He stood up and said, "Eddie has just got into the first team and just got married. He is a fiery chap and he has got to curb it and he knows it." The good thing about Bert was that he would support you if he knew you were right.'

George, meanwhile, declines any opportunity to expand on his colleagues' comments about his relationship with his authoritarian manager, but McLintock reveals, 'Charlie couldn't stand Bertie. With Charlie you are either a diamond geezer or you're a cunt, no in-between. "Don't like the little cunt," he'd say.'

Simpson adds, 'Charlie didn't have much respect for Bertie because football-wise he was limited. He respected Don so he got the best out of Charlie. Bertie was a disciplinarian and Charlie is not the sort of person who takes to that very easily.'

Howe says, 'I don't know what it was between Charlie and Bertie, I never got caught up in any of that. But Bertie was the boss, the disciplinarian, and that is never easy. He never flinched from his responsibility. One or two would have a moan back but most of the players respected it. Bertie was strict about the way they behaved in training, starting with punctuality. If you weren't on time he let you know where you stood. He was keen to make sure the players behaved the right way on the field. "No vendettas," was one of his great sayings. He would tell them to forget it and get on with the game. If we lost he expected us to lose with dignity, and to behave the right way if we were invited anywhere. He used to say, "Remember who you are, what you are and who you represent."'

Mee reinforced the status of his club by frequent use of the definite article before the club's name, especially when emphasising the status of the club with outsiders. 'I can recall a time on a tour to Japan when we were being held up at the ticket counter,' says McNab. 'Finally, Bertie went over to the people behind the desk and said, "Do you not realise that this is The Arsenal you are holding up?" The people there had no clue who we were and only spoke about three words of English. "The Arsenal" was said in a very pompous and arrogant manner and the players started to mimic him. Don't forget that, apart from Bob Wilson, most of the lads were from poor working-class backgrounds.'

Another of Mee's comments became something of a catchphrase among the squad and was used to poke fun at their manager. After losing 1–0 at Everton to finish the 1968–69 season fourth in the League and qualify for Europe, Mee gathered the players together for a meal in a private room in an intimate country hotel just outside Liverpool. The players were in an end-of-term mood, feeling good about a season in which they had achieved Arsenal's best League position for ten years and reached a Wembley final. But Mee killed the party atmosphere with a speech in which he warned that fourth place was not good enough. 'Some of you may fall by the wayside, but we are going to the top,' he barked. The players may have agreed with the sentiment but did not appreciate the timing, and stories circulated later that Mee's ire was due to the fact that he would have been paid a bonus for a place in the top three.

None of Mee's team has a greater appreciation of the job that faced him than George Graham, who would go on to win two League Championships, two League Cups, the FA Cup and the European Cup-Winners' Cup as manager of the club between 1986 and 1995. Graham credits the discipline and mental durability of the side – subsequently mirrored by his own teams – to the manager's insistence on a high level of professionalism. 'Bertie was a great one for standards,' he says. 'That is the word that sums him up best.

Everything was done with a bit of dignity. Bertie was very business-like, not like Tommy Docherty, who I had worked with at Chelsea before I joined Arsenal. Tommy was wise-cracking with one-liners and loved a joke with the lads, while Bertie was a total professional, total businessman.

'I didn't appreciate Bertie when I was a player, but when I went into coaching and management I realised what his assets were. He was tough, strong, authoritarian. I did a lot of learning from Bertie about management, not necessarily about coaching but about handling people and groups of people. An important part of being a manager is an eye for detail. It is many, many little things that make you successful as a manager, like time-keeping for instance. If you are asked to be ready to start training at 10.15 in the morning that is not such a terrible time to ask anyone to go to work. There is no excuse for people being late. He believed in a dress code and I have always been a stickler for that, even though I know it has become unfashionable.'

As a manager, Graham has become a great student of the cerebral element of succeeding in football, reading and digesting books by some of America's most successful sports coaches. Relating his findings back to Mee's squad, he says, 'Leeds may have been a better side than us technically at that time, but where we had it over them was that we were so mentally strong. That comes from the day-to-day workings of the people in charge. The way they make you do things in training, the way they make the time count. I am always suspicious when people say training is fun. It can be fun when you are doing some shooting, some crossing and heading, but when you are doing tactics and trying to build up a team I want people to take things seriously. That means when we take it into a match we know how to handle it. Don't mess around with me when I am coaching because my time is valuable. That is what I believe in and that is what all my sides have had. I'll hold my hands up and say they could have been more technically gifted but my teams very rarely got down. We were among the mentally toughest sides around, both the Double team and my teams that won the Championship.

'There are a lot of players and ex-players who don't understand what I'm talking about, and most of them have never won a championship. In every sport, a group of people always gets to a certain level and then what happens is that the mental side kicks in. There are a lot of people and teams in sport who never fulfil their potential because of a lack of mental toughness. In any team, you need those strong players to carry the ones who are less mentally tough because sometimes your technically best players are not the ones who have this mental strength. You have got to have a blend. For example, Peter Simpson was very laid back, cool and relaxed, but he and Frank were a great unit because Frank was the motivator.'

Graham continues, 'The other great thing about Bertie was that he was excellent at delegating. He delegated and let people get on with it. He knew his job was not on the training pitch, although he would turn up every day in his tracksuit and just stand and watch. He would be perfect in today's game. I think he would have been a successful manager today and a strong manager. I think the more successful and wealthy the players become, the stronger the manager needs to be. If the players today think you are a weak manager you have got no chance. When I went into coaching and management I would often go to see Bertie to talk about football and life and he was a great help to me. I think all this stuff about foreign coaching is nonsense. What the majority of managers now do is hire a coach, discuss tactics with him and then stand back and let the coach get on with it. That is what Bertie did 30 or 40 years ago.'

Howe endorses that view, insisting, 'I never had any problems with Bertie. He gave me my head to work with the players, which was hard to do when he knew that if I didn't get them playing well it could be him who was out of work. He was straight down the middle and he knew how he thought players should behave. But there was another side to Bertie. We used to go off to Blackpool, where his brother had a little hotel, for two or three days now and again and we had a great time. Bertie would let his hair down. But on the bus ride back he would change and became the boss again.'

Wilson recalls, 'The more success Don had, the more Bertie gave him his head, but you still knew Bertie was the boss. He had a very strict disciplinary code, right from the dress code he insisted on for travelling to away games. On the training ground it was mostly Don doing the coaching. Bertie was standing behind me one day at training with a folder and a pen. He said something like, "Bob, that is 184 times you've hit the ground today." I don't know what that was for.

'Bertie and Don had a good working relationship, but I do remember one game at Ipswich where we were getting murdered and were lucky to be only one down. Bertie always insisted on having the first word in team talks and he came in and said something like, "Keep going, be patient and we will be all right. Don?" Don just starts yelling, "Fucking all right? You lot are rubbish." And he really laid into us.'

Tactical discussions before games were designed not to overload the Arsenal players with details about the opposition. There were none of the dossiers for which Don Revie became famous, particularly after he ascended to the England job. Peter Simpson explains, 'We had a way of playing and we stuck to it. Gordon Clark, the chief scout, would do a file on the teams and come back and give us a rundown on their players and their playing system, but we didn't actually change our style of playing. It was more like individual things: this guy's a good player, so you have got to keep tight to him, don't let him do this or that.'

Kelly adds, 'Bert used to take the team meetings and tell you what he expected from you, especially the youngsters. With the senior players like Frank, he knew what they could do so he let them get on with their job. Don wasn't afraid to give you a kick up the arse, but Bertie wasn't a bawler and a shouter. He would take you to one side to give you a bollocking, whereas Don would give you a bollocking in front of anybody.

'In the team talks, Don would say, "You know who you are playing against and you know what type of player he is and what he likes to do, but don't let that stop you playing your own game. Let him deal with you." Don was great at motivation, and then you had Frank and Bob McNab as well. Don would tell us, "For the first ten minutes, don't go mad. Just settle down, make sure you get your first tackle in and get your first pass in." It was good for young players, you never felt you were under pressure to do this or that. Don knew he had a great squad of players. He knew the senior pros would help out the young players and that a lot of the players were at the peak of their careers.'

Howe trusted the senior players in the team to do much of the talking themselves. 'Don and Bertie would slaughter us after a bad result but we were very honest as a team and we would be hard on each other,' says McLintock. 'Don would let me go into them at half-time if things weren't going well. He would let me go for a couple of minutes and then he'd say, "OK, Frank, you've made your point, now calm down." And he'd tell the players, "What he's saying is right and this is what we are going to do."

'Bob McNab and I did a lot of changing things around on the pitch. Sometimes you would see little things, like Geordie Armstrong having the beating of their full-back, and I'd say, "Let's just give it to Geordie every time." I remember one game at Carlisle, Geordie ended up playing against John Gorman, who was a great attacking player. Wee Geordie ended up inside our 18-yard box every time and was forever getting pinned in. I told him, "Never mind about coming back with him. We will shove the midfield across and you just stay on the halfway line and when we get the ball we will give it to you." We ended up winning 2–1 but in the first half we had hardly got the ball out of our half.'

Howe says, 'It really was a blessing to have players like that. It is a terrific thing if you have confidence in players to adjust things while the game is going on. I never thought the manager ought to wait until half-time, the game could be over by then. It's great if you have someone you can just give a quick signal to and they can get on with it.'

Training sessions under Howe encouraged the players' competitive spirit, as well as being masterpieces of organisation. Kelly says, 'Don always liked a lot of competition in training, defenders against attackers, midfield players against midfield players. It was always very tactical and had a purpose.'

McLintock adds, 'People think Don was boring. Jesus, he wasn't boring. When I see some of the defences playing in the Premiership and see the mistakes that they make, I find it amazing. Don used to work us one against one in the whole half of the pitch and then two against two – Peter Simpson and me against John Radford and Ray Kennedy. If you dived in he would make you do press-ups, to make you stay on your feet and close in and wait for your teammates to help. Then it would be six forwards against the back four so you would be overloaded. It was to make you hold your line and win your tackles. If it didn't go right he would reproduce where it went wrong and show you where you should have been and what you should have done.'

And as hard as the players would work for Howe, the tempo was always that much higher when Mee was on the training ground. Radford says, 'Bertie would be out there at training most days and when he wasn't you could tell that the lads were taking it just a little more easy, even with Don out there. When Bert was out there things went up ten per cent.'

With Mee's influence and background, Arsenal were destined to become one of the fittest teams in the game. 'We had a very athletic side,' says McLintock. 'We could run all day. No one competed like we did. We actually trained probably three times harder than the modern Arsenal team. Looking back we probably trained too hard. We did 800-yard runs and 440s and 220s, carrying each other up the terraces. Liverpool and Manchester United always used to train lightly, just five-a-sides, and kept their energy for Saturday.' But Mee's heavy training schedule would eventually reap its rewards.

8

ACCIDENTAL HEROES

TWO DISAPPOINTING GAMES AGAINST CRYSTAL PALACE PERSUADED BERTIE
Mee and Don Howe that it was time for some changes. The news from the
medical room was that Peter Simpson and Jon Sammels were ready to step
up from the reserve team for their first games of the season and both were
included in the side to play at Ipswich. George Graham was relegated to the
substitute's bench to make way for the Ipswich-born Sammels, while John
Roberts was about to pay the price for his gaffes in the games against Palace.

Hailing from a small mining village in South Wales, Roberts worked on
the railways until joining Swansea at the age of 18. After three modest
seasons, he moved on to Northampton, where he became a Jack-of-all-
trades and spent most of the 1968–69 season as centre-forward. But
Arsenal's chief scout, Gordon Clark, had been impressed by Roberts as a
centre-half when he came up against him as manager of Peterborough, so it
was for defensive cover that Arsenal paid £40,000 to Northampton at the
start of the 1969–70 season. When Simpson twisted his knee and suffered
cartilage damage in the final game of Arsenal's pre-season trip to
Scandinavia a year later, the investment paid off. 'John played a great part
early in the season in keeping the team up there,' says Sammels. 'If it was a
backs-to-the-wall job, John would put his body in the way or head the ball
away. He did a terrific job.'

Eddie Kelly agrees, adding, 'A lot of people don't mention John when
they talk about that season but he was absolutely brilliant for the first few
months. I think Frank McLintock enjoyed playing alongside a big man who
was good in the air. I think John was the unluckiest man in football to lose
his place and I don't think he ever got the pat on the back he deserved.

Peter was fortunate to get back, but that shows how much Bertie and Don thought of him as a player. Nobody else would have got a place.'

However, Bob McNab, who played alongside Simpson on the left side of the Arsenal defence, was pleased to see his more experienced colleague return. 'John was a bit nervous. He was good in the air and he was a hell of a jumper so at set plays he was more of a threat coming up than Peter. He had a good left foot, but he wasn't a great passer. He was better away from home, when we would be battling, than he was at home, when we had to play. He was not so good at coming into midfield and creating an extra player. That wasn't his cup of tea, so we missed that without Peter.'

Simpson's return meant that, after 17 games in the League and nine more in various cup competitions, Roberts was destined to become a mere footnote to the Gunners' campaign, playing only two more games all season. 'Poor old John. I feel absolutely gutted for him because he played really, really well,' says Simpson. 'I didn't think I had any chance of getting back in because he was playing so well. They very seldom changed the team unless we were doing badly, but then John made a couple of errors and I got in. But I don't think it was so much because of the way he played that I got back – I was just lucky that Don wanted me in the team.'

With Simpson back alongside McLintock at the heart of the defence, Arsenal were to embark on a run that would leave no one in any doubt about their resolve and their resilience, keeping clean sheets in eight of their next ten games. It underlined Simpson's importance to the team, although his admission of fear about regaining his place comes as no surprise to his defensive partner.

'Peter was the most negative person off the field you have ever met in your life,' says McLintock. 'I used to argue with him all the time and tell him to shut up. Derek Dougan of Wolves would come and see us before the game and Derek always looked 7ft tall because he was so skinny and angular. As soon as he had gone Peter would say, "You pick him up at corner kicks." I said, "Bollocks. You pick him up if he is on your side. You're the same height as me – you can do it." On the pitch he was a different man, but off the field you had to shut him up.'

Simpson responds, 'Oh, Frank, he gets on my nerves – he tells everyone that story. But I suppose I didn't have enough belief in myself. I have always been a pessimist, still am. I always took the easy route, still do. It's just my personality. No belief in myself. I hate to fail but I am scared to try in case I fail. It's ridiculous – I don't know how the missus has put up with me.'

Peter Storey recalls, 'Peter didn't like playing football. He would rather have been playing golf.' And with a slim cigar in one hand, coffee in the other, and golf, his sport of choice, on television in the background, Simpson tells the story of a reluctant footballer. 'I am not a great lover of football, it is just something I did pretty well. I played a lot of sports at a reasonable standard and football was the one I went into. When I was a kid in Norfolk, football was something you did because it was cheap. You only needed a tennis ball, and we would play one against one and two against two. My parents didn't have a lot of money so it was what you did.'

Arsenal's scouts saw Simpson playing on the wing for the Norfolk Schoolboys team and asked him to attend a trial. 'I had a couple of other teams watch me but I knew nothing about them at the time. They talked to my father and he knew Arsenal was the team I wanted to play for. I think Leeds watched me, but not Norwich, funnily enough.'

There was also an offer to sign for Crystal Palace. 'I had a game for Yarmouth Boys against Croydon at Crystal Palace's ground. Arthur Rowe, the Palace manager, came along and watched and asked if I fancied signing. I told him I had a practice match for Arsenal the next night and said I obviously wanted to play. He said, "If you don't succeed, let me know," so I was on a winner either way. I played well in the game and Arsenal signed me straight away. They had a good batch of youngsters. The youth team had five or six youth internationals. George Swindin signed me, but I got into the team when Billy Wright was manager. He was too nice to be a successful manager; he wasn't hard enough. It was not always easy to get guys like Joe Baker and Geoff Strong to do what he wanted. They were difficult people.'

Simpson made his debut as an 18 year old in the spring of 1964, coming into a team that was beaten 4–2 at home by Chelsea and staying for five more matches. 'It was difficult, but obviously if they were putting people like me in there then they had problems at the back.'

As surprised as anyone else by Bertie Mee's appointment as manager, Simpson quickly responded to the presence of Dave Sexton as coach. 'When Billy was manager there were no real tactics and the training was totally different, a bit of running and five-a-side. I was disappointed when he went because as a young player you are not aware of everything that goes on, so we were just disappointed that someone we liked was going. But if we were going to be successful changes had to be made. Dave Sexton was fantastic. He was one of those coaches who encourages you so much. I remember one game when I was playing inside-forward and I was having a nightmare. After the game I was sat there with my chin in my hands. He asked what was wrong and I said, "I had a stinker out there." He went through all the good things I had done in the game and I thought that perhaps I hadn't played that badly after all. He geed you up, I loved him. I thought he was a terrific coach.'

Despite such encouragement, Simpson's natural pessimism made him question whether he would ever oust club captain Terry Neill or Scotland international Ian Ure for a regular place in the team. 'I never felt as if I deserved to be playing in front of people like Ian Ure, who was a big signing. I suppose I didn't have the confidence to think that. There were times when it didn't look like I was going to make it and Bertie Mee said to me, "Do you want to play football or not?" I got married, and that made a difference. Things happen, you have a few good games and you start enjoying the games more.'

Simpson, named 'Stan' by his teammates after the quieter half of the Laurel and Hardy partnership, steadily established himself as a regular, although he admits that motivation was often a problem for him. 'Don Howe would scream and shout if you weren't doing what he wanted. I always thought I responded to the likes of Dave Sexton more than Don because I didn't like people shouting at me. But, there again, I needed a gee-up sometimes. Frank and Bob McNab could give you an earful if you weren't doing what you were supposed to and I needed it because I was very lax at times and found it difficult to concentrate. Sometimes before a game I would have to go in the boot room and start talking to myself to get geed up. I always felt I could play against anyone and the confidence was there on the park, it was more off the park that I was lacking confidence.'

Sammy Nelson states, 'Peter is the only man who takes prunes with his All-Bran, he is so pessimistic. I met him recently and he looked like he had just been let out for the day from an old people's home. He could have gone to the Mexico World Cup but he didn't think he was good enough. He didn't want it; he just did what he needed to do. If he pushed himself the way Pat Rice pushed himself, he could have had more. But he didn't want the limelight.'

Kelly remembers, 'Peter and Geordie Armstrong were great mates and I remember once Geordie saying, "You could be a great player if you put your mind to it." Peter looked up and said, "George, you do your job, and I'll try to do mine."'

Simpson's pre-match routine was a source of amusement among the team, as John Radford explains. 'Peter would be in the cubicles smoking until five minutes before the game. You'd see this cloud of smoke coming up from the toilet and Bertie would say, "Somebody go and get Peter." You'd shout, "Come on, Stan, we're going," and you'd hear that one last drag and "pssshhhh" as he threw the fag in the toilet.'

But there was no suggestion of nerves in Simpson's performance on the field. Sammels, who came through the ranks with Simpson, says, 'He had a great left foot and never gave the ball away. He was unruffled and calm and very consistent. He could also come forward and make passes and he read the game well. He was not the quickest of runners but he used to compensate by being shrewd and holding the line and knowing when to let the opposition run into offside positions.'

Simpson's chances of an England cap were blocked by Bobby Moore's presence, although some observers felt he deserved to rival Norman Hunter for the job of backing up the England captain. McNab remembers his dominance of the five-a-side sessions during training and says, 'If you'd seen Peter play five-a-side you'd have said he should have played 60 times for England. He had unbelievable ability. He read the game like *The Beano*. He would get the ball off the keeper and beat five people. Peter gave us the opportunity to break teams down and act as a spare man in midfield. Peter could dribble and beat people, while Frank would commit people and pass the ball. Those two, pushing into midfield, making an extra man and committing people, were vital.'

Typically, Simpson scoffs at his colleagues' endorsement of his England potential, even though he did make Sir Alf Ramsey's preliminary squad of 40 for the 1970 World Cup finals. 'I was surprised I was in there. I had made a few squads and trained with them, but I always felt as if I was a kid when I was up against Jack Charlton and Bobby Moore and I didn't feel like I should be there. There was no way they were going to take Bobby Moore out. There were times when I was in the papers and people would say "Simpson should be in," but I felt that was why I was in some squads – because of the press. I just didn't have the belief I suppose I should have had. Some players are cocky and confident but I am not that sort of player. I might have seemed that way on the park because I was slow. They used to say I was cool and calm and casual, but I was just slow for Christ's sake!'

Simpson believes his best years were already behind him by the time Arsenal were competing for the Double. 'I found it tough getting fit after my injury and getting back into the groove. My best years, I think, were 1968 to 1970.' That period, of course, culminated in the winning of his first winner's medal in the European Fairs Cup, a competition in which Simpson felt he played some of his best football.

'I loved playing in Europe because the games were all evening games. I loved playing in the evening. I couldn't stand playing on sunny days, I still hate them even now. With evening games, there was always a great atmosphere under the floodlights. The crowd doesn't matter, you can't see them. And my brain functions better at night. When I get up in the morning it's no good talking to me. I have to walk around for an hour and a half drinking coffee and having a smoke before I can do anything.'

European games also meant a break from facing the typical First Division target man that gave Simpson, at under 5 ft 11 in., the most trouble. 'The awkward ones were the straightforward ones. Someone like Derek Dougan, who was big and gangly and could knock you about. They were all bigger than us. You had to use your arms and bodies to make sure they didn't get the ball. But we weren't frightened of anybody.'

There appeared little reason for the returning Simpson and the rest of Arsenal's back four to be scared at Portman Road. Ipswich, who went into the game well below the halfway mark in the First Division, were without first-choice centre-forward Frank Clarke and had already failed to breach the Gunners' defence in two League Cup ties. Bobby Robson's team had, however, won three of their previous five games and gave further evidence of their improved form by dominating the action and bombarding the Arsenal goal. Bob Wilson saved well from Mick Hill, who was playing in a central role instead of his usual wide position. But even in his excellent form, the keeper was relieved to see a 30-yard effort from full-back Mick Mills hit the post.

Sammels missed the chance to score on his return to the side when he lashed the ball over from Armstrong's cross and the home team seemed to have gained a creditable point as the game entered injury time. But then Armstrong swerved inside a defender and struck the ball solidly at Laurie Sivell. The little keeper, only 5 ft 8 in. and 19 years old, allowed the ball to drop behind him and failed in his scramble to keep it out of the net, losing his appeal that he had done enough to keep the ball from going behind the line.

Armstrong deserved to be the matchwinner, having been Arsenal's most consistent forward, but it was a day when the Gunners knew they were fortunate to return to London with both points. Mee admitted, 'We were not settling for a draw but Ipswich were pressing so hard it looked like it was all we were going to get. We were lucky.'

Ipswich manager Robson fumed, 'Arsenal should be ashamed to walk away with the points,' and responded to the suggestion that it had at least been a moral victory by commenting, 'If we get three more moral victories like that I'll get a moral sacking.'

On the morning of Arsenal's next game, against Liverpool at Highbury, stories in the newspapers reported the feel-good manner of the previous day's annual shareholders' meeting. It had been a far cry from the same meeting 12 months earlier, when Bertie Mee had been given a grilling by supporters impatient for success. The meeting, held three weeks after the club announced an annual profit of £56,000, was, according to an official quoted in newspapers, 'very smooth and pleasant'. Adding to the relaxed atmosphere around the club was the fact that the players had just returned from several days in Jersey. However, there would soon be tension on the pitch.

Try as they might, Arsenal could not make their early pressure pay off. Alongside the battle-hardened features of Tommy Smith, the young centre-half Larry Lloyd stood firm and upright, and behind the two of them was Ray Clemence, already emerging as Peter Shilton's challenger for the task of eventually succeeding Gordon Banks in England's goal. Arsenal had scored only five goals in their previous six games and a midfield quartet of Kelly, Storey, Sammels and Armstrong was not seen by some as likely to rectify that. 'Hard working but guileless,' said one newspaper report.

Arsenal's first glimpse of an opening resulted from a right-wing cross by Radford, prompting a clumsy attempt at a clearance by Smith in the six-yard box. But before the lurking figure of Kennedy had a chance to add to his one goal in seven games, Lloyd put the ball out of harm's way. It was Lloyd who was manning the Liverpool area when Armstrong chipped across a free-kick from the left, but the big defender's headed clearance landed at the edge of the area, where it was met by Storey with a piledriver of a shot that ricocheted for a corner. The Gunners continued to rely on long-range efforts, two coming from the feet of Sammels. First McNab's cross was headed away by Liverpool's blond left-back Alec Lindsay and Sammels returned it just over the crossbar with a right-footed half volley. Moments later the Arsenal midfielder shot low and wide of Clemence's left post with his left foot after the visitors' defence had again only partially cleared.

At the other end, McLintock and Simpson were efficiently marshalling Liverpool's newest signing, John Toshack, signed for £110,000 from Cardiff. The tall Welsh international striker was playing his third game for his new club, having ensured a rapid acceptance from the Liverpool fans by scoring in a 3–2 win against Everton a week earlier.

With 20 minutes to play, and Graham on the field as substitute in place of Kelly, the game turned in the space of 30 seconds. Storey took a short pass from Simpson but in casually pondering his options was robbed by Steve Heighway. The leggy forward with the university degree raced at the Arsenal goal, holding off the challenge of Rice, and fired in a shot that the standing figure of Wilson managed to block. Down to the other end went the ball. Graham harried Smith, Sammels dived in quickly to tackle Ian Ross and between them they caused possession to break to Graham. A quick one-two with Sammels found Graham 12 yards out and in place to execute a murderous left-foot volley on the run that flashed past Clemence and threatened to break though the net into the North Bank.

The relief around Highbury was even greater nine minutes later when Armstrong helped the ball forward from the left and Graham flicked it on towards Kennedy. Clemence and Lloyd ushered the ball away from the Arsenal man, whom they clearly felt was offside, but only into the path of Radford. It was an easy task for the number 9 to slide the ball in for the second goal.

Two stories kept the journalists busy after the game. For those writers more interested in the Liverpool angle, Anfield manager Bill Shankly provided meaty copy. 'If I said what I thought about the officials in this game I'd go to jail. Both goals were offside, make no mistake about that,' he argued, although television evidence knocked down his claims about the first goal and was inconclusive about the second.

For those servicing the London papers, the story was Graham, out of the starting line-up for the past two games, but now back in emphatic fashion. 'I was dropped after being told that I was not scoring goals recently and my passing was off,' he told reporters. 'But I thought seven goals from a midfield position this season was fair going. I am not bitter, but when you are dropped there are two things you can do. You can sulk or you can go out there and show them. I decided that when the chance came the best thing I could do was to get out there and prove my point to the manager.'

Simpson explains that Graham's goal after coming off the bench was typical of his teammate. 'He needed reminding of his ability every now and again. He would play five or six terrific games and then he would start pondering on the ball. Occasionally he used to get dropped and then he would get put back in and he would have another nine or ten games where he was excellent again. He would score goals, be buzzing around and then he would start getting lax again.'

Looking back, Graham accepts that assessment. 'I was very inconsistent. There is no question about that. I was day or night. I was outstanding or I was crap. I had to be good on the ball and when I was bad I was very bad. I look back and wonder if there was a way I could have become more consistent, but that was just the way I was. I can understand Bertie thinking, "I'll drop George because that will upset him and he will come back and play better." He dangled the carrot and I was the donkey and I went for it. I remembered things like that when I was a manager, not to let players get too confident or too depressed.'

Graham, like Simpson, could often appear like someone for whom football was of secondary interest. 'He had no interest in the game,' says McNab. 'No interest in football whatsoever. But necessity being the mother of invention, he couldn't do anything else. We would do a cross-country and I would be out of the shower going to the tea room before George had finished. And he was the laziest bloody defender you ever saw in your life. I used to scream at him. He used to throw himself into a tackle because he was tired. Instead of staying up in a crouched position and doing the work, he would hit the floor. I would be standing behind him shouting, "George, don't dive!" and he would do it. You can't kid players and I coated him. In fact, he once tried to butt me on the field and I put my head down just in time.'

It was not Graham's defensive abilities, however, for which Arsenal gave Chelsea £50,000 plus striker Tommy Baldwin in the autumn of 1966. Graham had been banging in goals, many with his head, since he was a tall-for-his-age teenager in the Scottish town of Bargeddie. He had signed as a teenager for Aston Villa and played eight first team games before transferring to Chelsea in 1964. At least by the time Graham signed for Arsenal a couple of years later he'd had time to learn the geography of London. 'When I moved to Chelsea from Aston Villa, I was living in a hotel for quite a few months,' he remembers. 'One of the people working at Chelsea realised I was looking for digs and said, "Why don't you come and live with me in Stamford Hill?" I thought that was terrific because it must be next to Stamford Bridge. I didn't realise it was the other side of London. What a shock I got when I found out.'

The Chelsea team in which Graham played reached a pair of FA Cup semi-finals, won the League Cup and earned a reputation for flashy football under their young Scottish manager, Tommy Docherty. 'I was very happy as part of what had become a very good Chelsea team. But it looked as though the team was going to break up. Terry Venables had moved to Spurs and there were other players ready to get away. The writing was on the wall and I thought it was the right time. I had already worked with Dave Sexton, who was a Chelsea coach when I first joined them. I thought he was one of the best people I have ever worked for, so when Arsenal came in with an offer for me, I joined them.

'It was a culture shock. I had been 19 or 20 years old when I joined Chelsea. It was the King's Road, it was the '60s and it was an exciting time. We had very funny, comical players at Chelsea. When I joined Arsenal everything was so professional, and I thought, "What have I done? Have I made a mistake joining this club?" You noticed it in the training and the way you did things at Arsenal. It must have taken me two years to understand what the club was all about. The Arsenal way of doing things. But joining them helped me grow up and I became a fan of the club and began learning its history.'

Graham's scoring rate at Chelsea – 35 goals in 72 games – did not continue at Arsenal, where he was one of several players given a chance to play alongside John Radford. Says McLintock, 'When Raddy used to play alongside George, he thought he was a lazy bastard because he didn't like the running. George wasn't a very energetic player, he was a very skilful player. Raddy and him didn't quite see eye to eye. Raddy would come short, play it off, spin and make runs, whereas George was a more stable player, a touch player rather than a runner, so he went into midfield. The move definitely suited his game much more. He was facing the play rather than having his back to goal the whole time.'

Graham explains that the switch came about by accident, a short-term solution to cover for an injury to McLintock during the 1968–69 season. 'Don said, "We are going to try you on the left side of midfield." I remember we played Sheffield Wednesday away, won 5–0 and I had a fantastic game. Next week, Frank was back and I was dropped, but it gave Bertie and Don an idea. I could play there and come late in the box and maybe get a few goals. So I took on a new role and enjoyed it.'

There was plenty of vociferous advice for the rookie midfielder, much of it offered by McLintock. 'I would slaughter George a lot, even though he was my best mate and we roomed together. He was slightly on the lazy side, he was more artistic. If he lost his man I would go up to him at half-time and tell him, "I'm trying to cover my centre-forward and your midfield player is making runs through the middle so fucking pick him up." But George was a terrific technician and he didn't score many scruffy goals. There was nothing scruffy about him, everything was immaculate. His passing was classy and he had a good football brain. The bigger the game, the better George played.'

Sammels, the kind of player who could run all day, admits to initial doubts about Graham's potential in midfield, but says, 'George would arrive at the right time and prove you didn't need to be covering every blade of grass. He didn't give the ball away and he would arrive in his own time at the far post. He scored some incredible goals with his feet and his head. He was great in the air, had a great spring and scored a lot of goals at the far post. He didn't have a threepenny bit head. It would always go where he directed it.'

It was Graham's spectacular goals that earned him most of his headlines during the Double season and McNab describes him as 'one of the best headers towards goal I have ever seen – as long as there was no contact, because he was a bit too good looking'. But the full-back also remembers his colleague's immense contribution to the left side of the Arsenal team. 'I never got a kick after George left Arsenal. He could deliver me a ball like it was a free-kick; it had almost stopped running as it reached me. He knew I didn't have a Rivelino left foot, but I could deliver it all right. George could make me sing going forward and when they sold him it broke my heart. He would always pick up my runs.'

Fellow midfielder Kelly adds, 'George had a lot of great players beside him who did the donkey work. He knew that as well, because he wasn't a tackler and wasn't aggressive. If he got the ball in a good position, he was likely to score a good goal. He was a man who could put his foot on the ball and slow the game down to his pace.'

Graham's nickname of 'Stroller' was a perfect reflection of his seemingly relaxed approach to the game. On the practice field Graham was, he admits, 'a terrible trainer'. He contends, 'Some people are lucky to have this natural fitness level. They can run for fun. It is not an effort because they have been blessed. I was not associated with that level of fitness so everyone looked at me as lazy. If I could have run a lot faster, I would have done. I was extremely one-paced. If you introduced a ball I loved training; it was all about making decisions. But if there wasn't a ball I hated it. When it came to the running day, usually on a Tuesday, Don would absolutely hammer us physically. We would be at Highbury running up and down the terraces. It killed me. There was no point in getting me chasing shadows all day and closing people down. I just wasn't that kind of physical animal.'

Graham would be sold to Manchester United midway through the 1972–73 season, the first of the leading players in the Double-winning team to depart. 'That's what happens. It's called expectation. Once you get to a certain stage and are winning things, then people start casting doubts as soon as you don't win. I was always the one in and out of the team so I realised when things were slipping I would be one of those on the move. But once again Bertie handled it brilliantly. He got me into his office and said, "George, we are accepting bids for you and we have set a price of £120,000. Three clubs have matched our offer, West Ham, Everton and Manchester United. I have organised a room at the White House Hotel in Euston Road so you can meet the three managers at your convenience." Class, absolute class.'

After teaming up with Docherty again at United, Graham moved on to

Portsmouth and wound up his playing career at Crystal Palace, where his relationship with manager Terry Venables drew him into the world of management. His former teammates would never have guessed that he would end up as one of Arsenal's most successful managers and earn a reputation as an intimidating disciplinarian. 'I had no interest in coaching when I was playing for Arsenal. I was an intelligent player and I knew my capabilities. I knew I had the technical ability to spray passes around and come in late on the back post, but I probably wasn't an infectious player on the field in the coaching sense, not like Frank and Bob. It's strange that it was me who went on to become a successful manager.'

McLintock says, 'George never looked like a captain or a manager in a million years, but he became a better professional through guys like Bob McNab and myself. He must have absorbed a lot, although it didn't look like he was absorbing too much at the time.'

The man himself admits that the George Graham of 1971 would never have earned a place in the teams he has managed. 'I wouldn't pick me in my team now. I couldn't get around the field. In today's game the players are far too quick. You need a midfield player who can carry his ability to three thirds of the pitch – the defensive third, the midfield third and the attacking third. That is the modern midfield player, someone like Patrick Vieira. That is who we are all looking for. That wasn't me.'

9

COURAGE IN A DUFFEL COAT

UNBEATEN IN THE FIRST EIGHT GAMES OF THE SEASON, INCLUDING A RUN of five consecutive wins, Manchester City found themselves in great need of a victory when Arsenal arrived at Maine Road on the first Saturday of December. Defeat by a single goal at First Division leaders Leeds a week earlier meant City had won only twice in the eleven games since the flurry of their opening burst and were nine points off the pace in fifth place. What City did not need was to run into an Arsenal team at their stubborn best, inspired by the excellence of Bob Wilson in goal.

A City forward line spearheaded by Francis Lee and Mike Summerbee and supported from midfield by England's Colin Bell suffered a frustrating 90 minutes. Bob McNab subdued the right-wing menace of Summerbee, while McLintock kept the bustling Lee in check. When Arsenal's unruffled defence did allow a sight of goal, Wilson was unbeatable. Such doggedness laid the foundation for another Arsenal 'smash and grab' victory. Only 15 minutes remained when the Gunners broke swiftly from defence to win a corner on the right. Sammels, retaining his midfield place in preference to Eddie Kelly after George Graham was restored to the starting line-up, sent over the place-kick and the big City keeper Joe Corrigan fumbled, allowing George Armstrong to score with a neat chip. A minute from time, an incisive move involving Graham, Ray Kennedy and Armstrong was capped when Radford headed home.

The game, however, had been dominated by a heavy Maine Road playing surface that did nothing to promote the kind of attractive football for which the home team had earned a reputation. City manager Joe Mercer admitted, 'The pitch was a disgrace and it was entirely our fault.'

The most notable example of the problems faced by the players came when City defender Derek Jeffries saw a back-pass stick in the mud, offering a golden opportunity to Radford. The big Arsenal striker promptly slipped over. 'It was not a pitch for flamboyance,' said Gunners coach Don Howe. 'We decided to do the simple things accurately.'

For the seventh time in ten League games since they conceded five goals at Stoke, Arsenal's defence had remained unbeaten. While the organisation of Howe's back four, bolstered by the return of fit-again Peter Simpson, could not be understated, events in Manchester offered further evidence of the importance of Wilson between the sticks. 'It was the best I had played in my career because I was reaching a greater level of consistency than ever before,' says Wilson. 'I finally felt that I was up there alongside the likes of Gordon Banks, Pat Jennings and Peter Bonetti.'

Teammate Simpson recalls, 'Bob was having a brilliant season and I always felt comfortable with him behind me. All keepers make mistakes, but Bob didn't make that many.'

It had not exactly been a story of overnight success. Already 29, Wilson was in only his third full season as Arsenal's first-choice goalkeeper and there had been times since his arrival at Highbury in 1963 when he wondered whether he had a future at the club. In fact, he had even walked out on the club on one occasion. Having played a handful of first-team games during his first full season at Highbury, Wilson saw manager Billy Wright sign goalkeeper Jim Furnell from Liverpool and had begun the 1964–65 season in the reserves. A 3–2 defeat against Hendon saw the team eliminated from the London Challenge Cup and the following day Wilson received the news that he had been demoted to the third team. He headed straight to the manager's office.

'In there were Billy Wright, Bertie Mee and some of the coaches, Alf Fields and two or three others. Billy said he felt I was largely to blame for the defeat and went round the room asking the others what they thought. Bertie said nothing, while the others agreed with Billy. But Alf said he thought it was the team that was at fault. That was what I felt as well and I could feel myself getting more and more angry and upset. I was close to tears and didn't really know where to look. I tried to avoid looking at Billy and kept turning away. There was a mirror on the wall in there and I must have looked in that direction. Billy shouted, "For God's sake, stop looking at yourself in the mirror."

'Well, I just went into a violent rage and there were all kinds of swear words coming out. I stormed out and thought, "Right, that's it. I have no future here." I knew there was a job opening at Loughborough University so I thought I'd apply for that. Alf came after me and stopped me. He said, "Listen, you have something special. If I didn't think there was a chance for you I would tell you to go, but you have a real chance here." I went home and talked it over with my wife, Megs, and decided to stay.'

Wilson's alternative job option, a teaching position at his former college, was indicative of a background that was far from typical for a professional footballer. An England international at schoolboy level, he could have joined Manchester United in 1957, the era of the 'Busby Babes', but his father had turned down the opportunity on his behalf. Instead Chesterfield-born Wilson ended up studying physical education for three years at Loughborough, where he gained a reputation as one of England's best amateur goalkeepers and relished the opportunity to turn out for Wolverhampton Wanderers' second and third teams. As his stint at Loughborough drew to a close, Wilson borrowed a car from a fellow student and drove to London to accept an invitation to visit Highbury. 'I remember the first time I went to the stadium. There I was, being met by Billy Wright, 105 caps for England, and the place was like a cathedral. I fell in love with it straight away and I am still in love with it. I was there for a couple of hours and I left convinced that Arsenal was my club.'

Wolves had different ideas, though. The Midlands club held Wilson's registration and manager Stan Cullis was keen to retain his services as a part-time professional. Wilson, however, needed to teach for a year to complete his qualifications, while Megs planned to work as a drama teacher. A move to London fitted their plans perfectly but the Wolves board decided that if Arsenal wanted Wilson's registration they would have to pay and demanded a £10,000 fee. 'When I signed an amateur registration with Wolves I had been assured it was not binding. Wolves hadn't paid me, apart from my rail fare from Loughborough, but because the board had made me an offer to turn professional they felt it meant that I was their player. That would never have held up in court.'

Wilson wrote to the Football League to put his case and met with the Wolves board, who he felt misinterpreted his motives as an attempt to prize some kind of signing-on payment from the club. His temporary solution was to sign for Arsenal in August 1963, not as a professional, but as an amateur. In the meantime, the story hit the newspapers and Wilson was unhappy at implications that he had been 'tapped up' when Football League secretary Alan Hardaker was quoted as saying, 'He had been happy with Wolves until something happened and then he suddenly wanted to join Arsenal.'

Training in the mornings and teaching in the afternoons at Rutherford

School in Paddington, Wilson had played six games in Arsenal's first team by the time the issue with Wolves was resolved in February 1964, giving him the freedom to sign as a professional. 'Arsenal handled it in their typical way. They felt they were above getting dragged into something like that so they quietly agreed to pay £7,500. My dad wanted to go to court because of the principle of the thing.'

On the October day in 1963 that Wilson's first-team debut against Nottingham Forest was announced, the local newspapers ran pictures of 'Mr Wilson' in the playground with his pupils. It was clear that the new goalkeeper in the squad had a certain novelty value. Frank McLintock says, 'He was different from us. He was one of the few who could do joined up writing! He only occasionally came down the pub with us. He would rather go home to Megs. We were all comparatively scruffy and not had the same education as he'd had. But he was very easy to get on with because he was a lovely man, a very nice, humble person. We recognised him as different and went our separate ways.'

Jon Sammels adds, 'Bob was a very likeable man. He used to turn up at the club in his duffel coat and it would be a freezing cold day and he'd be in his open-top Sprite.'

Wilson smiles at the memory and concedes, 'I was just someone trying to establish a place in the team, but I was a little strange to them. Yes, I came down in a duffel coat and as for the car it was a Ford Prefect first and then an Austin Healy Sprite. I had that for a couple of years and then got rid of it. If I'd hung on to it, it would have been worth thousands now. But the thing about our team, and all of football for that matter, is that people only care about what you can do on the field. Once you have earned people's respect by convincing them you can play, nothing else matters.'

Wilson was convinced that he would soon win over those at his new club. 'I went there with the attitude that I was the number one. I had always been number one wherever I had played, Chesterfield Schoolboys, England Schoolboys, wherever. I was pitched straight in at the deep end. They said Ian McKechnie had a weight problem and Jack McClelland was injured, so I was straight in. I did pretty well for six games and thought I was in, but then they went out and bought Jim Furnell for £16,000 from Liverpool and I was out.'

Having decided not to quit the club after his bust-up with Wright, Wilson settled down for what turned out to be a long wait in the wings. 'In hindsight, maybe it was better that I was not a regular in the team around that time. Arsenal were one of the most entertaining teams in the country. They could score three or four goals a game, but then they would let in four or five. I think any goalkeeper in the team at that time would have struggled.'

Continuing to combine his football with the required year of teaching, Wilson had plenty to keep him busy and distracted from the fierce goalkeeping competition he faced at Highbury. 'Every second Arsenal player seemed to be a goalkeeper in those days. There was Jack McClelland, Tony Burns, Ian Black, Ian McKechnie and myself, and when Jim signed he brought the total to six.'

McClelland was sold to Fulham and McKechnie went to Southend before eventually establishing himself as the number one at Hull City. That eased the congestion somewhat, but Wilson still had to be content with the less than glamorous lot of a reserve team player. 'For a first-team match at Arsenal we reported to South Herts Golf Club in Totteridge in the morning, had lunch together and drove to Highbury in a coach. You could feel the atmosphere before you were within a mile of the ground. The streets were lined with cars, there were police, flags, scarves and the whole approach to Highbury had a buzz about it. The club entrance in Avenell Road was always jam-packed and there seemed to be hundreds of people in the Marble Hall and perhaps television cameras as well. For a reserve match we simply reported to the ground an hour before kick-off. Few people were around. You had to convince yourself you had come to the right place at the right time, and when anyone walked across that Marble Hall you could hear the footsteps echo. I had to create my own atmosphere, to forget that I wasn't playing in the First Division and tell myself it was a vital match that could make or break my career.'

Wilson believed he was better than Furnell, the man in possession, but when he did get a brief chance during the 1965–66 season, a dislocated arm in a game at Fulham kept him out of football for three months. To pass his spare time, he began teaching in the afternoons at Holloway School, where he remained for more than two years. The turning point came in the fifth round of the FA Cup against Birmingham during the 1967–68 season, when Furnell's mistake allowed the opposition to force a replay. Wilson was picked for that game and, despite an Arsenal loss, was in the team to stay.

A League Cup final appearance and a Fairs Cup victory followed and the re-emergence of Arsenal as a force in English football brought attention to their goalkeeper. Wilson was finally earning greater renown for his unique and effective style of keeping than his untypical footballing background. His calling card was the manner in which he threw himself head first at forwards' feet to deprive them of possession as they bore down on goal. It was a vastly different approach to most goalkeepers, who would slide towards the attacker with their bodies spread horizontally, or someone like Tottenham's Pat Jennings, who would stay on his feet as long as possible and use legs, torso or any other available body part to block the shot.

'It was a style that worked for me,' Wilson says. 'I had seen Bert Trautmann play that way for Manchester City but it wasn't something that I really worked to develop, it was just God-given. My theory was that any time a forward came through on you one-on-one, unless he was George Best or had the ball tied to his boot, there would be a time when he pushed the ball a few inches too far forward. When that happened I would just dive head first with my arms outstretched and take it away from him. People called it courage, but it wasn't to me – it was just natural. I had been a good 400-metre runner at Loughborough and I was quick on my feet. That was one of my greatest strengths. I remember Don Howe saying to me, "You are going to get hurt like that." I had received a broken arm, a dislocated arm, had my ear half ripped off, although not necessarily from diving at people's feet. One day in training we worked on what we called "hedgehog rolls" where I would get the ball then tuck myself up into a ball and turn my head away. After a while I gave up on it because it just wasn't working.'

Sammels says, 'Strange for such an intelligent bloke to be so willing to throw himself at blokes' feet like he did. You'd watch him and think, "What are you doing there, Willow?" We had enormous respect for him. To force his way through four established goalies takes some doing. He had strong opinions and had the respect of the lads because they knew when it was muck and nettles he would be in there.'

Courage is a recurring theme among teammates when asked about Wilson. 'He was very, very brave, almost to the point of being foolish,' says full-back Sammy Nelson, a colleague in the reserve side for several seasons as both men strove for a first-team place. 'He was fearless at a time when forwards didn't mind putting their boot in.'

Simpson reveals some early doubts about the potential of the man who 'spoke a little better than most of us'. He says, 'Bob didn't start off as the best of keepers. He wasn't great with crosses and things like that. I thought he was perhaps a little bit afraid of making mistakes, so he didn't come for many balls. But he worked at it and he became a brilliant keeper.'

Many was the day when Wilson would ask teammates to stay out on the training ground to help him practise different aspects of his game. 'I think he made himself a good goalkeeper,' says Graham. 'When I became a manager my appreciation of Bob increased because I admire people who get the most out of their ability, even though that talent may not be the best.'

These days Wilson's life is a whirl. As well as presenting football on ITV, for whom he ended his long-standing relationship with the BBC in 1994, he has duties as Arsenal's goalkeeping coach and helps wife Megs run the Willow Foundation. The charity was set up in 1999 as a memorial to their daughter, Anna, who died from cancer a year earlier, and raises money to organise days out for terminally-ill young adults. 'He has even more respect from us now because of all the things he does,' says Simpson, whose home in the Hertfordshire village of Cuffley is only five minutes from Wilson's in Brookman's Park. 'He is always there for the lads, as busy as he is. All the functions you go to, he is there.'

As Arsenal prepared for a visit from Wolves, one of Wilson's closest friends in football was planning to prove a point. A £90,000 signing from Coventry midway through the 1967–68 season, Bobby Gould had been sold to Wolves for £55,000 during the summer after losing his place in the forward line in the wake of Charlie George's arrival on the scene. While at Highbury he had scored 23 goals in 72 games, including Arsenal's only goal in the Wembley defeat against Swindon.

There was obvious bitterness in Gould's pre-game comments. 'This is my big match, a comeback against the team who tossed me into the reserves and left me on the transfer list for nine months without explanation. I am an honest chap and I give 100 per cent on the field. I expect honesty in return and one day I hope someone will come up to me and say why Bobby Gould was not the Arsenal success he would have liked to have been. Had the manager and coach been more frank it might have helped me in my career. I can't wait to get on the pitch and prove they were wrong to let me go. I think I've proved in the short time I have been with Wolves I am no scrubber. I can still get goals. I improved on my skills at Arsenal and became a better player but in the end Bobby Gould the goal-getter became Bobby Gould the goal-maker and that's not my game.'

The media latched onto the story of the relationship between Wilson and Gould, who visited his friend's house on the Thursday before the game and was photographed having a kick-about in the garden. He was even interviewed by Wilson for the BBC. 'If there were prizes for effort and enthusiasm the name of Bobby Gould would be written large in gold,' said Wilson. 'I suppose this is why I admire him. He has this uncomplicated love of the game that overrides everything. He was always cheerful and chirpy at Arsenal when things weren't going his way, even when he was dropped, on the transfer list and, it seemed, ignored by other clubs. He played 22 reserve matches and scored 32 goals during that period when lesser men would have gone into a corner and complained about their luck.'

Wilson adds, 'Bobby loved the game so much and was so enthusiastic that when he scored in the reserves he would run behind the goal and salute the North Bank even though there was no one on the terraces.'

The passing of time has softened Gould's feelings on the subject of his departure from Arsenal and he says, 'I think the unfortunate thing for me was that people simply didn't think I was good enough, that I didn't have the ability. I didn't think Don Howe fancied me, not with Raddy there at centre-forward and the likes of Charlie George and Ray Kennedy on the up and up. I just had to take it on the chin and go away and prove myself, as I did the next season at Wolves. I don't think I played as well as I could have while I was at Arsenal. I was just a country bumpkin when I joined them from Coventry. It was a dream to be transferred to a club like that, I felt like Dick Whittington coming to London. But I don't think I had the chance to play my natural game. I was a natural predator and goalscorer but I was used more as someone who would be a provider.'

Gould's first season at Wolves was going well, both for him and his new club. After a poor start that saw them lose four of their first five games, Bill McGarry's team had lost only two of fifteen League games. They had also advanced to the semi-finals of the inaugural Texaco Cup, where Gould's 15th goal of the season had given them a 1–0 win at Irish club Derry City in the first leg.

Perming two strikers from the trio of Gould, Derek Dougan (the new chairman of the Professional Footballers' Association) and the Scot Hugh Curran, Wolves had scored 32 goals in their previous 15 League games, including a Gould hat-trick that secured a 3–2 win against Manchester United at Molineux. 'When I arrived, the boss made it clear that I did not just get a place because I had cost a fee,' said Gould. 'I had to compete with Derek Dougan and Hugh Curran for two places. That's not bad competition in any language. I recovered my zest and enthusiasm in the box and this has made a great difference.'

The Highbury crowd had to leave their lunchtime pints prematurely so as not to miss an early kick-off, the consequence of nationwide industrial action by power workers. The dispute had already led to midweek matches, including Arsenal's scheduled home game against Burnley, being postponed because of fears of floodlight failures. The cancellation irritated Arsenal manager Mee, who could already see fixture congestion looming down the road of a busy season. The FA issued instructions that midweek cup replays should kick off at 2.15 unless local power companies could guarantee floodlighting, while all Saturday League games were ordered to kick off at 2.30.

It meant an earlier than usual surge of fans up Gillespie Road from the Arsenal tube station and an early performance for the Metropolitan Police band, providers of the traditional Highbury pre-match entertainment. No sooner had the vocals of Constable Alex Morgan faded into the distance, than Wolves were under siege with Kennedy hitting the bar and defender Francis Munro clearing off the line. Sammels was twice denied by Phil Parkes, the man who challenged Manchester City's Joe Corrigan for the title of the First Division's tallest goalkeeper, and it was some surprise that the first goal had to wait until the 22nd minute. Munro's clearance smacked into Sammels' midriff and ran free for Storey to clip to the left edge of the box, where Graham ran in to nudge the bouncing ball past Parkes.

Arsenal squandered chances to move further ahead before half-time, but had to wait only a minute after the interval before doubling their advantage. John McAlle carelessly put the ball out for a corner and Armstrong curled his cross out towards the edge of the box. Sammels' diving header was blocked by McAlle and Radford picked up the pieces to fire in from close range with his left foot.

The return of Dougan to the side had meant Wolves went into the game with a three-pronged strike force, but were missing the influence of their injured skipper, Mike Bailey, in midfield. They did pull a goal back in the 65th minute when Dougan headed past Wilson from a David Wagstaffe free-kick, but for Gould there was to be no revenge and Arsenal played out time for another two points. 'I felt my own performance left a lot to be desired,' Gould admitted.

Having played one game less than the leaders, Arsenal's victory left them only two points behind Leeds, who were surprisingly held 0–0 at home by Ipswich. It was a rare disappointing result for Don Revie's team, whose September loss at Stoke was still their only League defeat in 22 games. Leeds had coped with the three-game suspension of skipper Billy Bremner and the early season absence of Johnny Giles, who missed eight games with a fractured cheekbone. Now winger Eddie Gray, who missed five games in the opening weeks of the campaign, would be out until the final weeks of the season with a broken ankle. The versatile Paul Madeley had begun the season at right-back while Paul Reaney completed his recovery from the broken leg that had kept him out of the previous year's FA Cup final. Then he had switched to midfield to take Gray's place, scoring four goals in five games. Allan Clarke had bagged eight League goals for a team whose only other setback had been a surprise League Cup defeat at Sheffield United, although they had also wasted a point at Crystal Palace when the error-prone Sprake dropped a hopeful shot by full-back John Sewell.

Tottenham, who embarked on a ten-match unbeaten run following their September loss at Highbury, occupied third place in the table. However, a 3–1 defeat at West Brom meant they had not won in four games and had allowed a six-point gap to develop between them and their London rivals. The Championship already seemed destined to be contested by the top two teams only. As always, Chelsea, level on points with Spurs, had been fun to watch. Former Millwall forward Keith Weller, a £100,000 addition to their Cup-winning squad, was picking up the goalscoring slack for Peter Osgood, who had found the net only twice in the First Division. The problem for Dave Sexton's team had been consistency and not once had they won more than two consecutive League games. Liverpool, struggling with injuries, were unbeaten at home but had been able to win only two of ten games away from Anfield, scoring just five goals in the process. They shared fifth place with Manchester City.

The Lancashire duo of Blackpool and Burnley were three points adrift at the bottom, while the struggles of West Ham, stuck in 19th place, had taken some of the gloss from Jimmy Greaves' achievement of scoring his 350th League goal, which he managed at Stoke in October. There had been a classic 'what happened next?' moment in the Hammers' game against Wolves in November, when Bobby Moore stepped in to stop play by blowing the whistle after his clearance had knocked out referee Lewis. Two days later, Moore's testimonial against Celtic, sponsored by Esso, raised £19,000 for the England skipper.

League champions Everton had become the first English team to be involved in a penalty shoot-out in Europe when they squeezed past West Germany's Borussia Moenchengladbach. However, their hopes of advancing further in the European Cup were destined to be dashed in the spring at the hands of the surprising Greek team Panathinaikos, coached by the great Hungarian, Ferenc Puskas.

10

UNITED THEY FALL

WHEN ARSENAL ARRIVED AT OLD TRAFFORD ON THE FINAL SATURDAY before Christmas 1970, they found a club in disarray. Two years earlier, United had been the reigning champions of Europe. On a day when attendance was traditionally hit by the demands of Christmas shopping, a crowd of 33,182, United's lowest of the season, was as much a sign of their problems as evidence of families at the stores buying Spacehoppers and Subbuteo teams for the kids.

United had won only five First Division games all season, and their last League contest had hurt them deeply – a crushing 4–1 home defeat against their greatest rivals, Manchester City. There had been a chance for redemption four days later with a home leg in the semi-finals of the League Cup against Third Division Aston Villa. A year after losing at the same stage to City, United were heavily favoured to put their problems behind them and advance to Wembley, but could only manage a 1–1 draw. A week later they would lose 2–1 at Villa Park.

In between the semi-final ties came the game against Arsenal. Charlie George was left at home three days after his first competitive appearance – substitute in the European tie in Belgium – since the opening day of the season. Arsenal's resounding win against United in their first home game of the season had centred around their aerial attack, and once again it was United's inability to deal with a corner that saw the Gunners take the lead after 15 minutes. With the ball untouched by a United player, Ray Kennedy, Bob McNab, John Radford and George Graham all took turns at getting their head to it before it fell for an unmarked Frank McLintock, who controlled on his chest and fired into the net from the edge of the six-yard box.

Within five minutes it was 2–0, another Armstrong corner from the left finding Graham on his own 12 yards from goal. The only movement the midfield man had to make was to pull back his head and direct his header past the United defenders on the line. As a contest, the game was over after 35 minutes when yet another Arsenal man was left unmolested in the box. This time it was Kennedy who benefited, heading home Pat Rice's left-foot delivery. Even allowing for a high wind that made defending awkward at times, United's defensive shortcomings had been savagely exposed. In particular, young centre-half Steve James endured a horrible afternoon.

Shortly before half-time George Best wriggled into a dangerous position and the ball ricocheted to Carlo Sartori. The ginger-haired midfielder of Italian descent duly scored, but Arsenal never looked like letting a commanding lead slip in the second half. Bob Wilson was on hand to make outstanding saves from Best and Bobby Charlton while Willie Morgan shot wide on the run. Wilson's biggest headache, literally, came from the Stretford End fans, one of whom threw a coin that struck the goalkeeper's head and caused a stitch to be inserted. This was just one week after Manchester City keeper Joe Corrigan had been the intended target when a pair of scissors was thrown. Wilson requested that the referee did not mention it in his report, saying, 'It's a pity that two or three lunatics should get the rest into trouble.' Such feelings of sympathy extended to the playing field. Asked about United's plight, McLintock said, 'I feel sorry for them. We were in a similar state three years ago.'

The result left United with only four teams below them in the table and, off the field, things were getting just as turbulent. Denis Law, one-third of the Holy Trinity with Best and Charlton, had been on the transfer list early in the season, while goalkeeper Alex Stepney was demanding a move after losing his place to Jimmy Rimmer following his injury early in the season. Bob McNab recalls an incident that made him doubt the team spirit and commitment at Old Trafford. 'I remember coming in two goals up at United. Willie Morgan comes down the tunnel at half-time singing and pretending he was playing the guitar. "I can't get no, da-da, da-da. Sat-is-fac-tion." I said, "Whatever you do, Willie, don't let this result worry you, son." The veins would have been popping out of our necks in that situation. Frank would have been grabbing somebody by the throat.'

And then, of course, there was George Best. Earlier in December, much had been made of his failure to report in time to travel with the team to a game against Tottenham, arriving on his own in London two hours after the rest of the squad. A week later, the loss to City had ended in controversy when rival defender Glyn Pardoe broke his leg in a tackle with Best, who was booked for the incident although later exonerated by Pardoe. Earlier in the year, Best had served a six-week suspension after knocking the ball from referee Jack Taylor's hands and had been sent off when playing for Northern Ireland for tossing mud at the match official.

At the eye of the United storm was Wilf McGuinness, promoted from youth team coach to chief coach at the end of the 1968–69 season, at the age of 31. His task had been an impossible one: to take over from the man who had effectively made the club what it was, the most famous name in English football. With his 60th birthday approaching, Sir Matt Busby had chosen to 'move upstairs' after finding that administrative matters were taking him away from the club's training ground at The Cliff with increasing frequency. No more was he able to rush through his paperwork by 11 a.m. and change into his tracksuit. At one point during their season as reigning European champions, United had even been in danger of descending into the pit of a relegation struggle.

Such a plight would have been unthinkable earlier in the club's 24 years under the wing of the genial son of a Scottish miner. A childhood star in his Lanarkshire town, Busby achieved his dream of becoming a professional footballer when he signed, ironically, for Manchester City in 1928. Six years later, he helped them win the FA Cup. A wing-half of grace and dignity, he later played for Liverpoool and captained the Scotland side on several occasions during the war. Invited to become Manchester United's manager at the end of hostilities in Europe, Busby set about the tasks of lifting Old Trafford out of the shadows cast by the achievements of their Maine Road neighbours. He also endeavoured to free the club from the state of confusion in which it had existed for many of the previous 20 years. He made it clear he would do things his own way rather than serve as a tool of some faceless committee, as was common in football at the time. His methods quickly paid dividends, with the FA Cup arriving at the club in 1948 and the League Championship following, after years of narrow failure, in 1952.

But it was the team that carried off the title in 1956 and '57 that earned the club and its manager worldwide renown. The 'Busby Babes', a side comprising almost exclusively of home-grown talent – most notably the prodigiously gifted Duncan Edwards – played an off-the-cuff style of football that produced goals by the sackful, captivated crowds around the country and struck fear into opponents. They seemed destined to bring the European Cup to Britain for the first time when tragedy struck on the afternoon of 6 February 1958, as United journeyed home from a quarter-final victory against Red Star Belgrade, the champions of Yugoslavia. On its third attempt to take off after refuelling at Munich, Flight 609 crashed. When Edwards lost his fight for life two weeks later it took the death toll among the United players to eight. In one savage act of fate a team with an average age of 21 and limitless potential had been wiped out. In all, 23 people died, leaving the football world shocked and grief-stricken. As Manchester prayed for his recovery, Busby lay critically ill in hospital after suffering multiple injuries.

Miraculously, Busby lived, despite twice being administered with the last rites. Once his physical recovery was assured, the process to rebuild the club began. To lesser men it would have been a battle for which they had no heart, especially after losing a group of players he regarded like his own sons. Yet a new generation of Red Devils blossomed under Busby's careful nurturing. This time the manager's skill in the transfer market was used to bring in men like Denis Law and Paddy Crerand to complement Old Trafford products like Bobby Charlton, a Munich survivor, and Nobby Stiles.

The '60s brought another FA Cup victory, two more League Championships and, finally, the biggest prize of all, the European Cup. Ten years after costing Busby his team and almost his life, the greatest of all club competitions – the driving force behind Busby's physical and emotional rehabilitation – brought him his finest moment in football. While the team of the late '50s performed in stark contrast to the mood of post-war bleakness that pervaded Britain, Busby's European champions of the '60s – including the young Irish genius Best, dubbed 'The Fifth Beatle' – were a perfect symbol of such an exciting decade.

Busby's recipe for success, according to those with the good fortune to work with him, was the special relationship with his staff, his feeling for the way the game should be played and his ability to recognise players capable of playing in accordance with his vision. Famed for knowing everyone at Old Trafford, his memory and courteousness also left an impression on players from opposing teams. Jon Sammels recalls, 'I was invited up to Arsenal a couple of times before I signed as an apprentice. I had been to see them play Manchester United and I was invited into the Marble Hall and the restaurant. I met Tommy Docherty, who was playing for Arsenal then, and I also met Matt Busby. I saw him again two years later when I played at United as a 17 year old. He pulled me aside as I was walking into the dressing-room and said, "I hope you have a good game today, Jon." He said he remembered meeting me in the Arsenal restaurant. I thought that was fantastic.'

Sir Matt was a straightforward man with simple pleasures: his family and children, and a game of golf with the lads. He was awarded a CBE, a knighthood and the freedom of Manchester, yet other things meant more to him, like when his players surprised him by presenting him with a cut glass vase to mark his 20 years as a manager. He had to leave the hotel room in which the ceremony took place in order to compose himself for the pictures. His charisma and paternalism left the players in awe of, yet also in love with, the man. Law explained, 'The great thing about the boss has always been his warmth. You could always go to him with any kind of problem and know that he would offer some sort of answer.'

Charlton added, 'That charm and courtesy is not a façade. It is only part of his immense personality. If he had gone into politics, he would be Prime Minister by now. He has this amazing ability to make people work harder for him. The youngest apprentice, the washerwoman, he knows them all by name. He is kind, tolerant, patient, but he can be ruthless too.'

Such was the enormity of the man into whose shoes McGuinness stepped in April 1969. Many had expected Busby to abdicate after United's European Cup win. Surely there was nothing left to strive for after the fulfilment of his greatest ambition. Yet Busby continued at the helm, explaining that football was too much part of his life. Midway through the 1968–69 season, however, he announced that he would shortly be giving up the handling of team affairs. After three months of speculation, during which Burnley's Jimmy Adamson, Celtic's Jock Stein and even Leeds manager Don Revie were touted for the job, McGuinness was revealed as the man Busby had decided would be his successor.

McGuinness, who received confirmation of his new role only two hours before the scheduled media announcement, was a surprise choice to those who thought United would go for a personality to match the stature of the club, someone who would be undaunted by the likes of Charlton, Best and Law. McGuinness had been at the club since signing as a 15-year-old schoolboy wing-half. He went on to win two England caps before his career was ended by a broken leg in a reserve game against Stoke in 1959. He stayed at the club to become youth team trainer and even played a full season for the reserves during a brief comeback to the playing field in 1966. As youth team coach, he set up a steady supply line of talent to the first team and was eventually rewarded with the title of first team coach, although not manager, when Busby moved on to the post of general manager.

McGuinness was placed in charge of team selection, coaching and tactics, although it quickly became apparent that he was unsure of exactly where the demarcation line was drawn between the training ground and the general manager's office, notably in the area of transfers and players' contracts. Another problem facing McGuinness, a man of passion and a fierce temper, was the balancing act required to negotiate the tightrope separating the players – with their drinking sessions and card schools – from their bosses.

His first season brought another disappointing League campaign and two cup runs that ended one tie short of Wembley. In the League Cup, United fell to neighbours City in the two-legged semi-final, their exit hastened by a first-leg penalty conceded by centre-half Ian Ure. Arsenal's fall guy in the same competition against Swindon a season earlier had been a surprise £80,000 purchase by general manager Busby in the early days of the season. United's run to the semi-finals of the FA Cup brought some refuge from their League problems, featuring a revenge victory over City and an 8–2 victory over Northampton Town in the fifth round. Best, in his first game back from his one-month suspension, scored six goals, his control on a heavy pitch and his instincts for goal being quite breathtaking. Hopes of a place in the final ended with a 1–0 defeat to Leeds at Bolton's Burnden Park in the second replay of a semi-final that had previously produced four hours of goalless football. In truth, a place at Wembley would merely have created a false impression of the club's health under their new team leader.

There were signs once the European Cup had been won of ambition sighing out of the club. Instead of signalling the beginning of a great new era, as would Liverpool's triumph in the competition nine years later, United's realisation of the Busby dream precipitated a slump. An injection of new players eager to live up to the standards of illustrious predecessors might have helped. World Cup hero Alan Ball and Wales centre-half Mike England might have ended up at Old Trafford rather than Everton and Spurs had United adopted a more aggressive attitude in the transfer market. United also failed to sign Luton striker Malcolm Macdonald, stylish Sunderland defender Colin Todd and young Ipswich full-back Mick Mills. Instead, the old guard of Busby's side, notably defenders like Bill Foulkes, Shay Brennan and Tony Dunne, saw their places going to untested youngsters. Players like midfielder Sartori and defenders Paul Edwards and Steve James began to prompt doubts about the quality of player being produced by a nursery that had once harboured the talents of Best, Stiles, David Sadler and Brian Kidd.

The only big signings in the two years following victory over Benfica were Ure, who did have a reasonably solid first season at United after being virtually laughed out of Arsenal, and Burnley's Morgan, a talented player whose favoured position on the wing and his long, dark hair helped to promote unfair comparisons with Best. A newspaper survey confirmed that United had spent less money on transfers in that period than any other First Division club.

McGuinness's inexperience was evident to close observers and stories emerged of his problems in handling some of the players. On the field, McGuinness assigned specific roles to players, instead of taking the free-and-easy approach that had been the hallmark of Busby's teams. It was, of course, the modern method, but his diagrams on blackboards proved less effective than Busby's ability to inspire players to give their best effort. McGuinness simply lacked Busby's mystique and the players did not have the same unquestioning attitude towards McGuinness and his ideas that his predecessor had enjoyed. At least the new man could not be accused of lacking in bravery. How many managers, after gaining only one point in his first three games in charge at the start of 1969–70, would have dared to drop Charlton, Law and Foulkes for a tough trip to Everton? United lost 3–0, but McGuinness probably felt he had made another kind of point.

The FA Cup semi-final replay at Villa Park was played out with most people unaware of an intriguing incident involving Best and McGuinness earlier in the day. Staying in a Worcester hotel, McGuinness, acting on information received, used a hotel pass key to discover Best in the room with a businessman's wife 30 minutes before the team were due to leave for the stadium. 'I'll be downstairs in the bar,' the dumbfounded coach told Best and left the room. McGuinness warned Best that he had better play well, but the Irishman went out and gave one of the worst performances of his life, more because of the pressure he felt to please his boss than the effects of any alleged pre-match exertions. Interestingly, such was the reputation of Leeds and their manager at the time, that several people suggested the woman in the hotel had been planted by Don Revie.

Perhaps McGuinness could have played it differently. But he was feeling the burdens of the job becoming heavier as the season progressed, he had seen cliques forming and the harmony of the club disintegrating. Winning a trophy seemed like the only way of reversing the trend. McGuinness had been so worked up after the fourth round victory against Manchester City that he vomited on the boardroom floor. Victory over Arsenal in the closing weeks of 1970 would not necessarily have saved him. But a place at Wembley might have, so when United lost at Villa Park the die was cast. Two days after a 4–4 Boxing Day draw at Derby, United announced that McGuinness would revert to reserve team coach with Busby back in charge of the first team. In fact, within nine weeks, McGuinness would quit the club completely.

Busby announced his return by stating, 'This is going to be one of the great challenges of my career. I have to say it is a formidable and worrying one. If I have built my managerial career on anything it is the ability to make players feel good, feel important. I'm hoping now this gift has not left me. Obviously the confidence of the lads is right down. For myself, the limit of ambition now is that in the next few months they begin to play again, that the mood of the club is changed and bright again when a new man comes in the summer.'

Busby's first test would be the FA Cup third-round tie against Middlesbrough, a contest that did nothing to lighten the mood around the club. Following a goalless draw at Old Trafford, a strike by Best was not enough to prevent a 2–1 replay defeat at Ayresome Park. And by the time that replay came around Best was in further trouble with the authorities, having kept an FA disciplinary committee waiting ninety minutes after missing his train to a hearing to discuss his three bookings in the previous twelve months. Best eventually showed up in time to be fined £250 and receive a suspended six-week ban.

Four days later, with United out of the FA Cup, Best's train timetable let him down again. This time Busby announced that Best had failed to make the journey to London for the game at Chelsea. Sir Matt explained, 'We've heard no message or reason for his not being with us. He hasn't been doing it for us lately. I don't know what is wrong with him. We encourage George to discuss his problems with us but he seems to bottle everything up inside him.' Two days later United announced that Best was being suspended by the club for two weeks, a punishment he accepted by admitting, 'I was wrong'.

It transpired that Best had stayed in London with actress Sinead Cusack. In his autobiography *The Good, the Bad and the Bubbly* Best revealed, 'I was completely screwed up and I wanted someone to talk to.' He likened the experience of losing to teams that United would have demolished three or four years ago as 'like being in a bad dream' and described the dressing-room atmosphere as 'like a morgue'. Best confessed that he would leave the ground on his own, go and get drunk for a couple of days and miss training on Monday mornings. 'The whole thing became a vicious circle,' he said.

Busby's suggestion that Best seek psychiatric help was not welcomed by someone who admitted that he 'tended to keep my worries and thoughts locked up'. When United arrived in London for the Chelsea game, Best ventured to the team hotel in order to speak with his manager. 'I wanted to talk things over with Sir Matt,' he wrote. 'But when I got to the hotel in Russell Square where he was staying and saw the cameramen and photographers waiting outside I decided I couldn't face it and told the taxi driver to keep going and drive me to Sinead's flat in Islington.'

Best would serve his two-week suspension and return to the team, turning in a typically brilliant goal-scoring performance against Tottenham. He would finish the season as the club's top scorer with 18 First Division goals as United won 11 and lost only 5 of their 19 games following Busby's return, climbing to the respectability of 8th position. For Best's future career, however, the writing was on the wall. As he explained, 'the disappearances became a habit,' and by 1973, at the age of 26, he had played his final game for United.

On a brief return to League football with Fulham during the 1976–77 season, Best would find himself playing alongside an old nemesis, Peter Storey. The ex-Arsenal man recalls, however, that Best was not exactly a changed man. 'Rodney Marsh had left earlier in the season but Bestie was still there. We never used to see him. One of the last games we played that season was at Oldham and we went up on the Friday afternoon and stayed in Manchester. We had a mid-evening meal and most of the players were just going to bed or watching television. We got up on the morning and no one had seen George. He had been out in Manchester and hadn't come back. So we are going to the game and getting on the coach and he still hasn't shown up. We are just pulling away from the hotel and someone says, "Hang on a minute, here's George." He is running down the road so they stopped the coach and let him get on. "Hello, George," we all say. Well, they let him play and he just stood out on the wing and didn't kick the ball.'

While United had been playing their final game under McGuinness, Arsenal were entertaining Southampton on a snow-covered pitch at Highbury. The continuing restrictions on the use of electricity meant that the undersoil heating was not allowed to be switched on, but Bertie Mee said later, 'The pitch was soft underneath with a light covering on top. It wasn't dangerous. This is what English football is all about.'

Arsenal took to the field in unfamiliar red shorts in order to make the players more clearly visible against the white backdrop. But against a Saints team that had won only once away from home since the start of the season, their only noteworthy move of the first half was when Graham nodded Kennedy's chip back to Radford and his header went straight into the grasp of the visitors' keeper, Eric Martin. The young Scot was to enjoy an outstanding afternoon, plucking the ball off Radford's head after good work on the left by Armstrong and clinging on to the ball after Radford met Storey's clipped delivery with a right-foot volley. Graham grazed the top of the crossbar with a header from Rice's cross, and Radford's suspicions that it was not to be his day met with further proof when his low volley from the edge of the box was turned against the post by the groping figure of Martin.

When Armstrong dispossessed Saints full-back Joe Kirkup on the right edge of the box his cross found a diving Radford at the near post, but yet again Martin was equal to the task. With the snow driving and the minutes ebbing away, Arsenal had the ball in the net. Armstrong banged in a cross from the right, Kennedy jumped against Martin and defender Jimmy Gabriel – who made as though he'd been impeded by the big striker – and when the ball dropped Radford swung a leg and toe-ended a shot that bumbled over the line. Referee Sinclair from Guildford agreed that Gabriel had been shoved in the back and ruled out the goal, despite furious protests from Radford and his colleagues.

Sammels was twice denied by the goalkeeper as the Gunners mounted a final charge, Radford shot low into the side netting, and McNab's right-foot drive was blocked by a diving Martin at the edge of his six-yard box. More than 34,000 frozen fans left Highbury bemused at how their team had failed to gain both points, while Radford complained, 'I don't think I've ever had so many shots in one match and failed to get a goal.' And even after seeing the disallowed goal on television, he said, 'It was a harsh decision.'

Meanwhile, McNab lamented, 'I've damaged my right ankle again, and all for that. I think it's ligaments. I had a plaster on after the United game and it only came off on Thursday. If we had won 15–0 you couldn't have argued.'

So it was that 1970 ended with Leeds three points clear at the top of the First Division. But with Arsenal still having a game in hand, maybe it was the Londoners who sprang to the minds of Leeds players whenever Radio One pumped out the Dave Edmunds song that had spent the final two months of the year at number one, 'I Hear You Knockin''.

11

SOMETHING IN RESERVE

THE NEW YEAR BEGAN WITH THE COUNTRY MOURNING THE DEATH OF THE 22-year-old Olympic athlete Lillian Board from cancer; The Beatles squabbling over their millions; and headlines screaming – a few years prematurely – of a new National Lottery, with prizes to match pools wins and the money raised being used to fund worthy causes. While Coventry City were asking unsuccessfully for permission to play a League match on a Sunday in April, football was fighting to stage games in the wake of heavy snow all over the country.

Scottish football, meanwhile, had more serious concerns following the events at Ibrox on New Year's Day. Sixty-six people died when Rangers supporters among the 80,000 crowd for the game against Celtic attempted to get back inside the stadium at the roar of an equaliser by their team. One person slipped, panic set in and steel railings on the seven-lane exit stairway buckled under the human avalanche. 'It was hell. I am lucky to be alive,' said one of the survivors. 'Suddenly there was chaos and we swept forward. We were standing on people and there was nothing we could do about it.'

Another fan said, 'I remember going down. People were flailing their arms and screaming hysterically, kicking and pushing. All they did was end up with the rest of us. I passed out and my legs had been crushed. I rolled over to ease the pain and looked straight into the face of a dead man lying alongside me.'

The incident had taken place on Terrace 13, at almost the same spot where a staircase had collapsed in 1961, killing two people. As the investigations and inevitable recriminations began, it was asked why no compulsory certification of clubs' facilities was required in Scotland, as it was in England. Within two weeks of the tragedy, one in five Football League clubs reported that they had made safety-related improvements at their grounds, including the addition of new handrails on staircases at Old Trafford and the planning of 'pens' to keep rival fans apart at Maine Road. Arsenal's response was to introduce a taped message to be played over the public address system as the fans exited the ground. As they headed into the night, Highbury spectators would hear the voice of club secretary Bob Wall advising, 'Please walk. Do not push. If you can not see ahead, please wait.'

On the field, Arsenal's first challenge of 1971 was a third-round tie in the FA Cup at Southern League Yeovil, a club famed for a pitch that sloped 12 ft from side to side and a history of embarrassing professional teams. The most talked about day in their history was their upset of First Division Sunderland in 1949. Arsenal prepared for the task ahead by braving the elements and training outdoors to simulate game conditions instead of using the comfort and warmth of their indoor gymnasium.

Yeovil were in the third round for the eighth time, a record for a non-League team. Their place had been achieved with victory at Bournemouth, who boasted the Football League's top scorer in Ted MacDougall. He had scored six goals in a second replay victory against Oxford City and a year later would hammer a competition record nine goals in an 11–0 rampage against Margate. Yeovil, however, shut him out in a 1–0 victory and now prepared for their windfall by putting up terrace tickets from four shillings and sixpence to 15 shillings, which a few weeks later would become 75 new pence. Seats were increased from six shillings and sixpence to 30 shillings, or £1.50 in new money.

The Somerset club was one of the nation's wealthiest part-time outfits, owning their own 14,500-capacity ground and nine club houses. But it was the notorious slope at The Huish for which they were best-known. 'Don Howe had been to see them play and he said that the pitch had a little bit of a slope,' says Jon Sammels. 'When we got there we had to be roped together!'

Yeovil's 29-year-old manager, Mike Hughes, looked forward to his club's big day by warning, 'The slope definitely gives us a bit of an advantage. I think Arsenal may have a bit of trouble with it until they find their feet. And we might be a goal up by then. Playing on it for the first time can be a bit unnerving, especially in a cup game where one slip can prove fatal. Goalkeepers find it most tricky in judging centres from the top slope. As you drop back, the ground seems to fall behind you.'

Concerned about the game being scheduled for 2 January, Bertie Mee considered taking his players away for two days to distance them from the temptations of New Year's Eve. 'He decided to put us on our honour,' says Wilson. 'I had a glass or two of wine at home and then went to bed. The other lads did pretty much the same. Bertie watched us training the next day and knew no one had taken advantage of him.'

It transpired that conditions made it impossible for the game to go ahead as planned on the first Saturday of the year. Having looked at the icy pitch, referee Bill Gow warned, 'The players might break their legs – and so might I.'

Yeovil, sensing that the snow and ice could have helped narrow the gulf between the teams, were angry at the postponement. 'Bertie Mee wants to wrap his players in cotton wool,' complained home captain Cliff Myers. 'The pitch was playable in our opinion. Had it been a Southern League match it would definitely have been on.' Yeovil chairman Norman Burfield added, 'When the referee announced his decision Bertie Mee was the first one to pat him on the back. It was obvious Arsenal didn't want to play.'

Arsenal didn't help relations between the two clubs when they refused Yeovil's request to stage the rearranged tie the following Thursday, early closing day for the town's shops. Mee felt it was too close to the weekend's League programme and insisted on a Wednesday afternoon date. Having made their second journey of the week to Somerset, the Arsenal players were sent out half an hour before the scheduled kick-off time in order to get a feel for the eccentric playing surface and to test Wilson with crosses from the top end of the slope. Preparations complete, the Gunners peeled off their tracksuits and quickly snuffed out the part-timers' challenge.

Dominant in the air once again, the Gunners were two goals up and had the game in the bag before half-time. Jon Sammels created the first, racing forward and clipping the ball on to the head of John Radford, who scored with a simple finish from the middle of the penalty area. Sammels began the move that led to the second strike when he spread the ball out to Armstrong on the left flank. Armstrong cut inside to fire a shot that was deflected by one defender and blocked by another, only for Kennedy to pounce on the loose ball. Yeovil did manage a couple of attempts on goal in the second half and Arsenal had to wait until a minute from time for their third goal. Substitute Eddie Kelly fed Armstrong and his cross to the far post found Radford looping a header back over the keeper and under the crossbar.

At the other end, the threat caused to Wilson by the slope was easily dealt with. 'I decided not to try to catch any crosses coming from the up-side but to get a hand to them and flick them on. Just a touch and they were in the bottom stand. I had only one awkward save.' Overall, it was a thoroughly professional performance by Arsenal, who could now look forward to a trip to Portsmouth.

Elsewhere in the third round, West Ham crashed out 4–0 to a Tony Green-inspired Blackpool. But the result was merely the forerunner of the real story. England legends Bobby Moore and Jimmy Greaves, plus forwards Brian Dear and Clyde Best, were revealed to have flaunted the club's 'honour system' and broken the players' curfew the night before the game, staying out in Blackpool until 2 a.m. The club announced that the four players had been fined 'as a result of a breach of disciplinary rules'. Then came the bigger bombshell that the club captaincy had been taken from Moore and that he and Greaves would not play in the forthcoming game against Arsenal at Highbury.

Bertie Mee, ever the disciplinarian, used the incident to remind his players about the responsibilities of representing Arsenal Football Club. 'He told us, almost in passing, that fines would not be the Arsenal way,' says Wilson. 'He didn't need to spell anything out. If any player was caught letting down the club in this way I don't think he could expect to play for Arsenal again.'

Against West Ham's weakened team, the Gunners launched into attack mode and for the first 15 minutes the Hammers looked like a team in disarray. Sammels tested the defence from long range and McLintock came close on two occasions before the visitors gradually settled into the game and created a chance of their own through Best. It was little surprise, however, when George Graham opened the scoring after 40 minutes following a free-kick by Rice.

There was a strange incident in the second half when Sammels drove the ball into the side netting and, as he turned to trot back to await the goal-kick, saw referee Jack Taylor awarding a goal. The ire of the West Ham players, followed by consultation with the linesman, corrected the error. Hammers goalkeeper Bobby Ferguson did well to delay the second Arsenal goal until 10 minutes from time but was beaten when Radford touched on a cross for Kennedy to head home from no more than a couple of yards.

There had been few problems for Arsenal's defence, even though they were unable to include Bob McNab. His right ankle had been in plaster between games, allowing the patient Sammy Nelson to step in for only his fourth game of the season. Despite establishing himself as a regular in the Northern Ireland team, Nelson was still waiting for the door of opportunity to open at Highbury, where he had arrived from Belfast in 1966. 'We used to call him "Squiggly",' McNab recalls. 'He was a great lad and our relationship was very good. He was my understudy but he never made me feel uncomfortable with him. I would never want to argue with him. He is a real wit and a very bright boy. He was always supportive of me and it must have been difficult, considering he was playing international football.'

Ironically, McNab had been pressing the Arsenal management for some time off because of his pelvic injury. 'Sammy could have taken my place in that team that year and to be honest I wouldn't have minded. I wasn't happy because of my injury. I didn't enjoy the Double season much because I was injured all the time. It was drudgery. I would be popping pills and it would be three days after each game before I could stand up straight. I was like one of these high-energy kids, and the club decided that when I was injured they would put me in a plaster because I would still want to go in the gym and play head tennis or something. The best thing they could do was immobilise me.

'The biggest thing I was worried about was not letting anyone down because I couldn't play the way I wanted to. I did ask Don and Bertie if I could be left out because I was not doing my job. I couldn't kick a ball or sprint, it was like someone digging a knife in me. I was used to being a significant player, someone who has carried players, not someone who is being carried. I had a meeting with Don, but he told me to stay in the team to talk to the players and organise.

'Nobody knew about this injury. I kept having tests and injections, one doctor put about 14 needles in me just to see if I could stand it. He injected all the way up one side of the stomach wall and there was blood everywhere. After the season one guy finally made me stand on one leg and x-rayed me and he could see my stomach drop three eighths of an inch and saw what the problem was.'

The fact that Nelson could capably fill McNab's position, just as John Roberts had filled in for Peter Simpson early in the season, bore testament to the quality of the players coming through the Arsenal support system. Nelson's Northern Ireland full-back partner Pat Rice had, of course, stepped up successfully after Peter Storey was moved into midfield, while Kennedy had grabbed a similar opportunity following Charlie George's injury and Kelly was also established in the first team squad.

Steve Burtenshaw, responsible for preparing those players for first team duties in his role as reserve team coach, remembers how Arsenal strove to make it an easy transition. 'We played the same system as the first team. We would alter it every now and again just so the younger players could get the opportunity to play in a different formation. But basically all the teams at the club played the same way so that everybody, from the most junior side upwards, could step up without worrying about whether they could slot in.

'Peter Storey ended up moving from right-back because of injuries, but if he had stayed in defence and had played badly, Pat would have been in. People like Pat and Sammy were so consistent in the reserves and there were often teams wanting to buy them. I remember Leicester coming in for Sammy and I said we would be silly to sell him because he was a super deputy for Bob McNab and could hold his own in there. I was quite certain Sammy would hold down the job very well, as he eventually did for several years.

'The nice thing about Bertie and Don was that they really listened to what you told them about the reserve team and when they asked you about moving a player up you would really be telling them what they already knew. We had meetings after the reserve games where I would put in a written report to Bertie. It was not just filed and forgotten; Bertie would actually go through it with me. I would always put down anything appertaining to how a player was doing and Bertie took a great interest.'

When a regular first team player was given a spell in the reserves because of form or injuries, Burtenshaw made his top priority the assurance that the player was prepared for his eventual return to the senior side. 'When I used to have senior players in the side, I would give them extra sessions of physical work because I knew they would have to huff and puff to stay with it when they got back into the first team. It's a lot harder physically in the first team if you have had a length of time out of the side. The kids had additional afternoon work for other reasons so they were more or less ready from a fitness point of view when they went in, but I felt the senior players needed topping up. It meant that anyone in the reserves was ready to play if called upon and Bertie and Don didn't have to take unnecessary chances with the first-teamers.

'Of course, if you are a young player in the reserves you never know when the call is going to come and you can never be 100 per cent ready. There will always be something extra required. But we tried to break down any pressure they might feel because of never having played there before. I used to tell them, "Keep your chin up and you will get your chance. Concentrate and work hard because it could come this week or next week and it's no use saying you weren't quite ready or you needed half a dozen games to get yourself up for it."'

Wilson, who also played in the reserves under Burtenshaw, says, 'Steve was a bit of an amateur psychologist. He realised that reserve football can produce stresses of its own and that all his charges needed handling in different ways.'

Burtenshaw's reserve team, including several of the players who had taken the FA Youth Cup to Highbury in 1966 and 1967, lifted the Football Combination Cup in 1968. The following season they were champions of the Football Combination itself, a competition contested by the reserve teams of clubs in the southern part of the country. McNab recalls the hunger and organisation of the reserve team players. 'Steve was doing a fantastic job sending the lads through. I hated playing the reserves, I couldn't get a kick. Our team, like every other great side, had a great development programme and these were well-schooled kids.'

Nelson explains, 'If you get the basics right and do those well then everything should follow. People said we were boring but it meant that for people like myself, coming in for the odd game, it was easy. You knew what your role was going to be. There was no real pressure on you, you just didn't want to let yourself and your team down, be made to look a mug.'

In modern football, McNab's injury would probably allow Nelson an extended run in the team, but the mentality of the early '70s, with smaller first team squads, was to play at all costs. McLintock says, 'If you got kicked you just got up, you wouldn't let the players know you were hurt, then wait for the chance to get him back again. That's why we played the season with so few players. You played with headache pills, painkillers, injections, because you didn't want to be out of the side.'

Graham adds, 'There is a saying in football that you are never 100 per cent fit. You carried knocks but as soon as the game started the adrenaline started flowing. There were games when you would feel a bit stiff beforehand – the majority of players today would not play. It was expected of you to play for the team. Whether that's right or wrong, that's the way we were. A lot of us played when we weren't fit.'

But there were some injuries that could not be repaired with needles and pills. So when Jon Sammels' broken foot necessitated Storey's move from right-back into midfield, it was one of Burtenshaw's students who graduated to play in all but one game in his first full season in the senior side. Pat Rice had been waiting for a regular run in the team ever since starting two games and making four appearances as a substitute during the 1967–68 season. Not many had expected him to get that far after he signed as an apprentice late in 1964, by which time he was already a familiar face to some of the established Arsenal players. 'I can remember Pat asking for my autograph as a schoolboy,' says Sammels. 'He used to live down the road and his brother, Alf, used to have a hairdresser's at the bottom of Avenell Road where a lot of the lads used to get their hair cut. He was always outside the ground kicking a football around.'

Peter Simpson remembers. 'He didn't have much ability when he first came to the club. He also had a stutter as a young lad and we didn't think he would come through because he didn't have enough confidence. But he has the greatest respect from me for what he has done because it takes a lot of nerve and he has bundles of it.'

Rice described himself as a 'little fat'n, not good enough to model myself on any player' and became a familiar sight at the training ground in the afternoons, working on his game after everyone else had departed. 'I'll never forget that first day at Highbury as an apprentice. I have never been so tired in my life. I lost six pounds in weight.'

Eddie Kelly states, 'Pat was the hardest-working pro I have ever seen. I never thought he was good enough when he was young. I used to live behind the East Stand and we could see on to the pitch. About four afternoons a week Pat would come back and do sprints around the red ash track, backward sprints and forward sprints. He got himself to such a great level of fitness.'

Burtenshaw devised special training sessions designed to address the weakness in Rice's game. 'Pat sometimes found it difficult to split his legs and slide tackle. He needed to be able to slide in on the odd occasion, so many, many afternoons I would be running up with the ball and working on that with him, making sure those things could be put into practice when needed. Many times it would just be shadow play, how to bend your runs. That's not natural to kids so you put on sessions so they can understand it. You have to give them as much time as they need to be able to understand things like that.

'I was also concerned about his long passing. I remember standing on the centre circle and he was on the penalty spot. We would take ten balls and I would tell him that if I had to take one stride from the kick-off spot that was okay, but not two strides. He had to kick eight out of ten balls to me accurately with his right foot and seven with his left. There are very few people who can do that, but Pat managed it and it is indicative of the amount of work he put in.'

By 1968, Rice, whose family had moved from Belfast when he was 11, had made it into the Northern Ireland team, where reserve team colleague Nelson was his travelling room-mate and partner on the field. 'We knew each other's style inside out,' says Nelson. 'He was very, very enthusiastic and that was what took him to the top. He wanted to succeed so much that he was prepared to give up all of his afternoons to do extra training sessions to improve his left side, right side, heading, speed or whatever.'

McNab adds, 'When people say Pat was a lucky man, he wasn't. It was hard work and he was a credit. He may not have been the sharpest knife in the drawer but he learned his stuff and became a good full-back. He dealt very well with being a young lad in that team.'

Rice's work-rate and dedication were undiminished by his elevation to regular first team status. 'I still had it in the back of my mind that Peter was the regular right-back, especially at first,' he says. 'I think that was a good thing because it stopped me being complacent.'

Unbeaten in 14 League games since their drubbing at Stoke, it was a buoyant Arsenal team that made the journey to Huddersfield. While the Gunners had been beating West Ham, an unexpected boost to their title hopes was being delivered by Tottenham, who won 2–1 at Leeds through a pair of goals by Martin Chivers. It meant Arsenal took the field against the Yorkshire side only one point behind their great rivals with a game in hand.

For Frank McLintock in particular, the day proved to be a painful experience. Only three minutes had elapsed before the Gunners' captain was caught by a flying elbow and left with a broken nose that would require straightening in surgery the following day. But that was nothing compared to McLintock's agony when referee Dennis Corbett ruled that he had handled the ball in the area while clearing from Steve Smith 16 minutes from time. 'It hit me outside the box,' argues McLintock with a passion that suggests the incident was only yesterday. 'It was on the telly that night and it was a clear travesty of justice. I was two yards outside the box. It was the only penalty I ever gave away playing centre-half.'

With the game level at 1–1, Frank Worthington stuck away a spot-kick that would win the contest for the home side. Earlier, Les Chapman had rounded off a good opening half-hour for Huddersfield by firing past Wilson from outside the box and Arsenal had equalised after 52 minutes when Kennedy diverted Graham's free-kick into the net.

A rare midweek without a game was enlivened by McLintock's recall to the Scotland squad for the upcoming game against Belgium. Then the Gunners were on their way to Anfield, where Liverpool manager Bill Shankly was up to his old tricks. 'Arsenal aren't as good as they were,' he said. 'My spies have told me they have gone off.'

Such mental warfare was typical of a man who, like his great rival Matt Busby, was the product of a Scottish mining village, Glenbuck in Ayrshire. One of 49 young men from the village who became professional footballers, he turned out a few times for Carlisle United before finding success as an enthusiastic right-half at Preston North End. He earned seven Scotland caps before the Second World War robbed him of a huge part of his playing career – although the hostilities did give him the opportunity to play some games in an Arsenal jersey. His early years in management consisted of unspectacular spells at Carlisle, Grimsby and Workington, but a four-year stint at Huddersfield, where he introduced a young Denis Law to League football, earned him the attention of Liverpool's directors.

The club that welcomed Shankly in 1959 was plodding along in Division Two, but within six years Liverpool had won two League Championships, in 1964 and '66, with an FA Cup triumph in the intervening season. Worshipped by the fans on the Kop, Shankly, with his gruff voice and sergeant major's crop, made up in the power of his personality what he lacked in physical stature. While Don Revie let his players do the intimidating on the pitch, Shankly would attempt to undermine the psyche of the opposition before the game, inducing self-doubt and a dread of trips to Anfield. Comments like those with which he taunted Arsenal were his standard weapons in the psychological campaign he waged so vigorously.

Tommy Smith, captain in 1970–71 in succession to Anfield giant Ron Yeats, recalls, 'He would always be looking for whatever it was that would give us the edge. In those days reputation was a big thing. If you could win a game before you went out, win it. That could mean winning it in the papers by saying certain things. He would do all that stuff, rubbishing the opposition, and he always met them when they arrived and watched them all get off their team bus. He would go into the opposition dressing-room half an hour before kick-off to wish them all the best and he would be taking everything in. He would only be in there for a minute or two and then he would be back in with us saying things like, "The right-back's got his right ankle strapped up, the winger's got a bandage on his elbow," – just little weaknesses they might have that would give you a little something as you ran out onto the pitch.'

Former England winger Peter Thompson, a survivor of Shankly's first Championship-winning team, adds, 'I remember a team talk he gave us before we played Manchester United when they were in their prime. Shanks started going through their team, saying, "Alex Stepney is in goal and they should call him Dracula he hates crosses so much. I have seen cement turn faster than the centre-half. Nobby Stiles is a blind man." He went through most of the players and then stopped. Somebody said, "What about Best, Charlton and Law?" Shanks replied, "Well, if you cannae beat three men there's something wrong with you." He was a great motivator and made all of his players feel like they were the best in the world.'

Thompson admits, however, that Shankly was no genius when it came to the technical side of the game. 'To be honest, as a tactician he was crap. We would have some team talks where he would go through formations and we would end up with 14 players and the opposition would have eight. There was a time before we played Everton when he came in and said, "Right, I have got a secret plan. We will have four at the back and keep it tight. We'll play four in midfield and tackle anything that moves. Then we'll play four up front to put pressure on their defence." Someone pointed out that it meant we would have 13 players, so he turned to Bob Paisley, his assistant, and said, "Christ, Bob. What's my plan?"'

Within four minutes of the kick-off against Arsenal, there appeared to be a grain of truth in Shankly's pre-game bluster as the home team took an early lead. Yeats, back in the side at left-back for the fourth of the eleven games he would start during the season, was the launch pad for a move that ended with Toshack converting following a Heighway cross.

Radford managed a couple of attempts on goal but for the most part he and Kennedy had little change out of Smith and Larry Lloyd, and, but for another fine display by Wilson, Liverpool could have won by a clear margin. Smith fired in the second goal early after half-time from a free-kick outside the box and Toshack was denied another by a breathtaking show of agility by Wilson. Leeds had followed their loss to Spurs by winning at West Ham and Manchester City, opening up a five-point lead over the north Londoners. 'It's still wide open,' insisted a defiant Mee. 'I still think Arsenal will be there at the finish.'

12

CHARLIE

BETWEEN THE LEAGUE DEFEATS AT HUDDERSFIELD AND LIVERPOOL, ARSENAL continued their FA Cup campaign at Portsmouth. Cup winners in 1939 and League champions in 1949 and 1950, the Fratton Park side now found themselves in the wrong half of the Second Division table, but they packed in a 40,000 crowd for the visit of Arsenal, generating club record gate receipts of £18,002.

Heavy rain produced yet another bog-like playing surface, but the running power of Jon Sammels helped him turn in an outstanding first-half performance. John Radford was denied by a post and then all hell broke loose after another effort by the big Yorkshireman was ruled to have been turned away by the fingertips of keeper John Milkins after 35 minutes. Referee Johnson from Lowestoft was immediately surrounded by Arsenal players. As McLintock tried to turn the official around to face him, Portsmouth's Brian Bromley attempted to pull the Arsenal captain away. Undeterred, McLintock, and several others, were back in the referee's face, urging him to speak to his linesman. Johnson scurried over to the left touchline and turned back with his finger pointing to the spot after being informed that full-back George Ley had made the save on the line. Storey placed the ball on the spot, wiped his hands on his sodden shirt and placed his shot to the left of the diving Milkins.

Despite the home team's incessant second-half pressure and the loss of Pat Rice to an ankle injury, Arsenal's lead lasted until the final minute of the game. The Gunners defence cleared the ball out of the area to Radford, who opted to dribble back toward the penalty box and lost possession to full-back Fred Smith. His cross was met by a series of muddied bodies sliding around in an effort to make clean contact before the ball finally broke for Mike Trebilcock. A two-goal hero for Everton in the 1966 FA Cup final, Trebilcock thumped in a shot from close range before running off to perform a celebration somersault. 'I gave away their goal,' Radford admits. 'I was back defending and I got the ball and I beat a man, but I was taking it the wrong way!'

The replay had to wait until two days after Arsenal's disappointing League display at Liverpool because of a waterlogged Highbury pitch. The postponement came as a surprise to those who had been told about the club's state-of-the-art heating and drainage system, installed at the cost of £30,000. 'Nothing went wrong with the system,' said secretary Bob Wall. 'The rain was bucketing down so hard it was bouncing 2 ft off the pavement outside.'

Charlie George was back in the starting line-up for the first time since the opening day of the season, at the expense of Graham, but Arsenal began as they had left off at Anfield and were behind within six minutes when Norman Piper fired home following a corner. But after seven more minutes, the Highbury fans were given a taste of the ingredient their team had been missing all season. George collected the ball inside his own half and, long hair streaming behind him, raced towards the Portsmouth goal before unleashing an unstoppable low drive from 20 yards. Peter Simpson was the unlikely scorer of a second goal after 33 minutes, converting Armstrong's corner on the volley. But after Bob McNab, Simpson and Sammels all failed to make the most of opportunities to increase the lead, the Gunners were stunned by a 58th minute equaliser from Ley, his soft-looking effort deceiving Wilson. The contest became increasingly physical and with five minutes remaining referee Jim Finney ruled that defender Eoin Hand had brought down Radford inside the box. Once again, Storey stepped up to beat Milkins from the spot, but the drama was not yet over.

With time almost elapsed, Pat Rice became involved in a tussle with Ley. Several others joined in the unsightly pushing and shoving and when the players were pulled apart it was Pompey midfielder Bromley who was sent to the dressing-room. Portsmouth manager Ron Tindall said, 'I am absolutely disgusted. It completely ruined a great night for Pompey. It was ludicrous – the wrong man was sent off. Bromley went in as a peacemaker.'

Tindall went even further with his accusations in his programme notes for Portsmouth's next home game. He wrote, 'Although some of our tackling was clumsy and deserved the punishment it got, our players were subjected to so much fouling off the ball, which included two thrown punches, none of it punished by the referee. I am proud of the way the team reacted under such provocation and assure you that we will not bring the game into disrepute in that fashion. Throw punches, whether provoked or not? Never.'

A fifth round tie at Manchester City now awaited Arsenal, but first they needed to get their Championship challenge back on track as their forthcoming Cup opponents visited London. An Arsenal goal looked on the cards on several occasions in the first half, notably when Armstrong broke into the box and shot past keeper Joe Corrigan, only to see Arthur Mann somehow clip the ball off the line with the back of his boot. Corrigan had to get his huge frame down quickly to stop a Jon Sammels effort after McNab pulled the ball back from the left, and the keeper then managed to smother Kennedy's attempt at the far post after George, Armstrong, Radford and Rice linked skilfully to turn defence into attack.

George was pulling most of the Arsenal strings and in one second-half sequence he intercepted a Francis Lee pass intended for Colin Bell, exchanged passes with feet and head with Armstrong and Radford and eventually got in a shot that was blocked by a defender. As City failed to clear the danger, Storey's cross to the far post from the left was met by Kennedy's head and scrambled off the line by George Heslop.

Wilson became busier as the game progressed, Arsenal leaving more opportunities for City to attack as they went in search of a goal. Bell's toe-poked shot saw the Gunners' keeper pull off an acrobatic save to his left and the same City player was denied by Wilson pouncing at his feet as he worked his way into a shooting position. Even Wilson would have stood little chance had Bell been on target, as he should have been, when the ball fell to him six yards out after a corner.

Only five minutes remained when Peter Simpson stepped forward from the back four, ran with the ball deep into City territory and, with no one eager to challenge, hit the ball low at Corrigan with his left foot from 25 yards. The shot was spilled, Radford arrived first and Arsenal had their precious goal. It had been a long time coming and Bertie Mee, his satisfaction increased by news of Leeds' latest home defeat against Liverpool, enthused over his team's perseverance. 'We learned long ago from high-morale teams like Leeds and Liverpool that you make your own luck,' he declared. 'Peter Simpson must have been tired but he still had enough belief to run on and try his luck with a shot. And following up on other people's shots is what we demand of John Radford. To make what looks like a useless run in the last few minutes takes character.'

City manager Joe Mercer had a rather different view of the manner of Arsenal's winner. 'If we had swapped keepers we would have won 2–1,' he claimed. Simpson's memory of the goal, incidentally, is closer to Mercer's version of events. 'The ball hardly reached Corrigan,' he smiles. 'It was bad goalkeeping and he should have held it.'

City's defeat meant they had now gone four League games without a victory and, in fact, they would win only one more First Division game all season. By the second week of February, it was clear that the FA Cup was their only hope of maintaining a remarkable sequence of domestic success under one of football's most unlikely managerial partnerships, Mercer and his colourful lieutenant, Malcolm Allison.

Charismatic, boastful and often intolerant, Allison was a man who wore his emotions like an overcoat, an unlikely foil for the grandfatherly Mercer, warm and humorous, one of football's statesmen. Yet City's record under the pair proved their effectiveness. Mercer had for a long time served as a steadying influence on Allison, helping him to fulfil his coaching potential while keeping him on an emotional even keel.

Only weeks before City's meeting with Arsenal, the outspoken Allison had been warned by City to stifle his opinions about the ongoing boardroom struggle at the club. And before the season was finished, the FA would ban him from football for 12 months, with 10 months of the sentence suspended until the end of 1973. Already with a suspended sentence hanging over him, Allison had landed himself in further trouble with a half-time outburst at Bolton referee Bob Matthewson, a former professional player, during a game against Burnley in December. He accused Matthewson of favouring the home team, although he claimed in defence that 'the remarks were intended to be light-hearted'.

Mercer said of his right-hand man, 'You have got to understand Malcolm, and I do. There was a time we wouldn't have lasted five minutes in the same room without fighting. He's got this arrogance and there's this gambler in him. But it works for us because we believe in the same things. You can't lead him anywhere, you have to guide him, apply a bit of pressure when his enthusiasm looks like running away with him. Malcolm is in touch with the players. He is closer to them than I am. He has the ability to get the best out of them and make them believe in themselves. It becomes an effort to keep in touch with the game as you get older.'

Typical of Allison's bravado was his attitude when Manchester City entered the European Cup as League champions in 1968. He boasted that his team would terrorise clubs reliant on defensive football. 'We'll show the cowards of Europe,' he crowed. To Allison's embarrassment, City got no further than the first round, beaten away from home by Turkish side Fenerbahce after a goalless draw at Maine Road.

Mercer, however, was happy to live with Allison's moods and outbursts. He had found out long before that, for him at least, management was a two-man job. His playing days ended in 1954, when a broken leg finally forced the sun to set on the glorious Indian summer of his career. An influential wing-half, Mercer was virtually written off by Everton after the war because of a troublesome knee. But Arsenal manager Tom Whittaker took a chance on the man who had won five England caps and was rewarded by seeing him lead the club to two League Championships and two FA Cup finals.

Mercer had managerial spells at Sheffield United and Aston Villa, where he suffered from ill-health, before City installed him as manager in the summer of 1965. This time he insisted on his own form of health insurance in Allison, whom he appointed as team coach. Allison had developed his football philosophy during his time as a West Ham player. He and a group of teammates – future managers like Noel Cantwell, John Bond, Frank O'Farrell and Malcolm Musgrave, who collectively formed the West Ham Academy – would spend hours at a local Italian café after training, discussing strategy and mapping out moves with ketchup jars and salt-cellars.

Bob McNab says, 'I remember Don Howe saying that when he was at Lilleshall in the mid-60s Malcolm Allison was doing stuff we had never even dreamt about. He was innovative and creative, a great thinking man.'

In 1968, City swashbuckled their way to their first league title in 61 years when they gained 23 points in their final 15 games, eventually denying Manchester United the title when they won 4–3 at Newcastle on the last day of the campaign. The following season, with Allison watching from the stand after being banned from the touchline by the FA, City triumphed at Wembley in the FA Cup final, a blast from forward Neil Young giving them a 1–0 victory over Leicester. The 1969–70 season saw City back at Wembley to beat West Brom 2–1 after extra time in the final of the League Cup. Two months later, they wiped out the memory of the previous season's let-down in Europe when they lifted the Cup-Winners' Cup in Vienna. In front of a sparse 10,000 crowd in the bleak Prater Stadium, and with all of England watching the Chelsea–Leeds FA Cup replay, Young and Francis Lee earned a 2–1 win against Gornik Zabrze of Poland.

England midfielder Bell, the dynamic fair-haired engine of the team who earned the nickname 'Nijinsky' – after the 1970 Derby winner, not the ballet dancer – said of City's management team, 'Joe is the sort of person you can go to with any problem and in Malcolm we have the best coach in the country. A lot of people misunderstand him, but when it comes to the crunch he is the man to have on your side.'

Lee, City's barrel-chested striker, added, 'Mal says what he thinks. He does what he thinks is right whatever the consequences. The boss is quieter. He thinks about what he is going to say. He is steeped in football, a man who pours oil on troubled waters. But the big thing about this pair is that they never disagree or contradict each other. Well, certainly not in public. They never do anything that could embarrass the other.'

Like Brian Clough, Allison was the kind of adversary who made opponents want to shove his words back down his throat. On a foggy, rainy night in Manchester, four days after Arsenal had yet another scheduled cup date fall foul of the weather, it was George who would delight in making Allison choke on his pre-game comments. John Radford explains, 'Frank McLintock pulled a great trick and goaded Charlie into winning the game for us. Frank went to Charlie and told him that Malcolm Allison had been in the papers saying that he was just an upstart, that he wasn't as good as everyone said he was. Well that was it for Charlie, he went out and had a blinder.'

Arsenal had the upper hand from the start, with the running of Radford, Kennedy and Armstrong causing concern in the City defence. After 17 minutes the Gunners won a free-kick two yards outside the penalty area and as City's players lined up their defensive wall, George and Sammels huddled over the ball. Without a word to his teammate, George spotted a space between the sky blue shirts, took a few quick strides and thrashed a low shot past a stunned Corrigan's left hand. 'After Charlie scored he was running along the touchline signalling at Allison,' Radford remembers happily.

City responded with vigour, Wilson being knocked to the ground in a goalmouth scramble, but it was from a City attack early in the second half that Arsenal sprung into attack to score their second goal. The home team surged forward and Booth's long ball eventually fell to Young in the box. The striker found himself outnumbered and McNab was able to bring the ball out and feed Radford on the left touchline. George held up his run so as to remain in his own half, and therefore onside, as the ball was clipped beyond the final line of defenders. City's appeals for offside were ignored as George raced for goal, cutting in from the left toward the area with Alan Oakes and Tommy Booth trailing hopelessly behind. As he entered the penalty area, he struck a low right-foot shot past the keeper and lay down in the mud with arms held above his head. Game over, and the first airing of what was to become a famous celebration. George came close to scoring a third with a low header and Bell's left-footed goal five minutes from time was not enough to spoil a great night for Arsenal's avenging hero.

George recalls, 'Frank told me what Malcolm had said and I suppose, at the time, it does wind you up – although if you need winding up for a big game like that there is something wrong with you. After the game, you do say, "Fuck you." I didn't like people saying personal things. I played well and I scored the goals. I preferred to play in the heavier conditions – I didn't like playing in the hot sunshine. I had a knack of scoring winning goals in the FA Cup games and in important League games. I was full of confidence and I suppose I had a bit of luck going with me. However important the game was, I felt I was capable of doing something. I could make something happen out of nothing.'

George's performance underlined his re-emergence after months on the sidelines. Although he can recall the disappointment of his early-season injury at Everton, George insists he never fretted about regaining his place in the team, even with Kennedy forming such an effective partnership alongside Radford. 'I was absolutely flying in pre-season. To get injured early was unfortunate, but football is a game where you get injured. The ball came in and Gordon West, the Everton goalkeeper, came for it with his feet. He was a sizeable bloke and he fell on my ankle. I was disappointed, but Ray came into the side and it was great to see another young lad come in and do well. I was an Arsenal fan so I was delighted to see them doing so well. I was disappointed not to be playing but I never worried about my place. I had a lot of confidence in my own ability and I felt I would get back in the side somewhere. As much as you miss being involved, it was great for the lads.'

The lads clearly thought it was great to have George back in the side and playing the way he had at Maine Road. McNab recalls the confidence he had in George when he bore down on City's area for the second goal. 'It was a heavy night and I won the ball and gave it to Raddy and he stuck Charlie in. He went one-on-one from wide out on the halfway line and I started walking back thinking, "We'll be kicking off in a minute." Charlie was like Jimmy Greaves when it came to one-on-ones. Charlie and Greavsie always hit it early, one stride earlier than you expect, when the goalie was still in forward motion with one leg in front of the other. You can't dive sideways unless you are planted. They passed the ball past the keeper.

'Charlie had so much confidence. It was like when he took penalties. Even at 20 when he took one in the Fairs Cup semi-final against Ajax. He said, "All right give it here, son." He used to call me "son" and I was in the England team! He was as gifted as anyone I have ever seen. His power was nothing short of extraordinary. If we had a free-kick we just used to tell him to hit it at the goalie as hard as he possibly could. Some people hit a sweet ball like Peter Lorimer and it would stay on line, but Charlie would hit you a crossfield ball and first you'd be going to trap it, then you were going to chest it and then you were going to head it. It moved around so much. Charlie could side-foot the ball for a penalty harder than I could kick it. I have seen Charlie stand on the halfway line at Highbury and kick it over the bar without a run-up, then do the same going the other way with his left foot. It would have been a driver and a wedge for me.'

Born into a family of Arsenal fans – 'his Mum and Dad had red and white curtains,' says McNab – George was soon taking his place on the North Bank, although he named Manchester United's Denis Law as his footballing idol. All through his schooldays at Holloway, which ended prematurely when he was expelled and sent to a different school, there was only ever one career goal in mind: to play professional football.

From the age of 13, George was training at Highbury and Bob Wilson was the first of George's future teammates to see evidence of an extraordinary young player in the making. Wilson and Spurs centre-half Mike England were watching a game at Holloway School, where they both worked as part-time teachers, when their attention was grabbed by one boy who could beat players on a whim, juggle the ball under pressure and toy with goalkeepers. 'Charlie was a free spirit,' remembers Wilson, who used to let the cantankerous teenager get away with chirping, 'How you doin', Bob?' whenever he ran into him at school. 'He was also on the books at Arsenal and I trained with him two nights a week. He was this precocious talent who could do anything. We had a time when we used to wellie balls up into the air and Charlie would wait for it and just kill it. Plonk.'

George duly signed as an apprentice at the club he adored, but there was never any danger of him being overawed by his surroundings. 'I wasn't really a shy person. I never felt out of place. As a kid I always played with older people so I never felt inferior. It's a cockiness from knowing what I could do when I played football. There wasn't anything I didn't think I could do with a ball.'

McNab remembers reporting to the club after his transfer from Huddersfield and being confronted by the young George. 'Charlie was the first person I saw when I walked through the door at Highbury. He had an overcoat on and a skinhead haircut. I was a big signing, although I didn't feel like it, and he was this young cocky teenage kid and he says, "Allo, Bob. You all right, mate?" He was only an apprentice but he was like a big star. I absolutely loved him. Frank and I used to tell him not to get involved in any fights, to let us take care of it. He wanted to fight people, but we said, "That's what we do, you just play. You can win the game. I can make sure we don't lose it, but I can't win it like you can."'

The older Arsenal players were soon fully aware of the budding star in their midst. Sammels explains, 'Everyone was raving about how good he was. We knew he was something special. He had all the attributes, deceptively quick, very strong lad, two good feet, could pass it short or long with imagination and score great goals. He didn't mind physical confrontation and always seemed to have a strong mental approach to the game. He was always sure of himself and I think that's what made him the player he was. If he hadn't done it on the field people would have said, "What's he got to shout about?" but he had that belief in himself and he could really play.'

A member of Steve Burtenshaw's successful reserve team, George made his full debut as an 18 year old against Everton on the first day of the 1969–70 season. He scored his first goal a week later against West Brom and by the end of the season was an important member of the Fairs Cup-winning side, scoring two goals in the 3–0 semi-final victory against Ajax.

Missing since the opening game of the current season, George's influence on the side had been obvious since his return to fitness. His performance against Manchester City was typical of the arrogance and dash he could give a team, elements that had been missing at times as Arsenal lost their early-season momentum. George was back in the Arsenal team ostensibly as a right-sided midfielder, but he dismisses the notion that he was asked to play a certain role on his recall. 'No one told me how to play. Don would maybe say there were certain things he wanted me to do when we didn't have the ball, but he knew I could play and let me get on with it. By the time I came back after the injury I was like a new player because I had been out so long. People think Don preached to players all the time, and maybe sometimes he would shout at me to do something when we didn't have the ball, but there was a lot of mutual respect there and he knew I could play football. I could play either up front or midfield. It didn't matter, I always felt football was easy. If you gave me the ball I would do the work. I only wanted the ball, then I would do whatever you wanted me to do with it.'

Howe reveals, however, that there was more to George than the self-assured kid from the terraces who was ready to take on the world and says he suffered the same doubts that inflict every professional footballer at times. 'If you meet Charlie he comes across as cocky and has this aura of confidence, not a fear in the world. But that's just his style. He had just as many doubts as everyone else and was just as nervous on the big occasions as the rest of us. He was a nice bloke and I could see that. He needed a bit of a talk before games and he was very responsive.'

George's habit of being sick before games has grown into legend down the years, but he insists it was not simply a case of nerves. 'I couldn't eat before a game because I used to burn up a lot of acid in my body. Once I was out there I was okay. I've never felt in awe of anybody, never ever in my life. There was nothing that any footballer could do that I felt I couldn't do.'

McLintock agrees with George's self-assessment. 'Charlie was a law unto himself, more talented than anyone else on the team. He was a real genius. John and Ray were brilliant but they were quite straightforward. You might not be able to stop them, but you could read them. Charlie could just drop the shoulder here or there, get in a bit of acceleration and fire in a shot with either foot. He was good with his head as well, could hit the ball with the outside of his foot like Franz Beckenbauer and spread it across the field 40 yards like it was a table tennis ball.

'Probably his biggest fault was that he was a bit of a renegade. You were always privileged if Charlie liked you. He loved Dave Mackay, Frannie Lee and people like that. Certain people he really takes to, but he hasn't got time for those he sees as fools on the field. Whether it was "bottler" or "wanker", he always had a word for them. He got a lot of injuries and was a little inconsistent and sometimes got left out of the side, but the talent was enormous. You should have seen him in training. He would volley it over his right shoulder and then his left shoulder into the back of the net. You'd think: How can he do that?'

According to Wilson, one of George's strengths was his ability to focus on the positive parts of his game. 'Charlie could have had a really poor first half and you'd say "Come on, Charlie," and he'd answer back, "What about that ball I hit in the sixth minute?" He would always have made one 35-yard defence-splitting pass and that would be all he remembered. He didn't remember the bad things he did. The game up at City was one of Charlie's great hours.'

Indicative of his prodigious talent is his teammates' disappointment that there were not more moments like that in George's Arsenal career once the Double season had passed. In fact, dogged by injury, inconsistency and the whim of management, he never played more than two-thirds of Arsenal's League games in any season and in the summer of 1975 was signed for a bargain £90,000 by one his favourite football figures, Derby manager Dave Mackay.

George won his only international cap in 1976, by which time Don Revie had left Leeds to manage the England team. Says McNab, 'I remember Charlie getting into the England team years later and I thought, "He won't last past half-time." And he didn't.' For the record, McNab's memory lets him down a little as George, asked to play wide on the left, made it to 60 minutes of his debut against the Republic of Ireland in a Wembley friendly before Revie took him out of the action. George made his dissatisfaction known and was never selected again.

'Charlie was an arrogant sort of person,' says Peter Simpson. 'He had lots of ability but didn't make full use of it. He didn't give his lot on every occasion; he went missing sometimes. But you wonder if he had worked harder whether he would have been the same player.'

McLintock ventures, 'Maybe Charlie didn't get the best out of himself. He should have done better with his career. We maybe should have accommodated him a bit more, not expected him to run and tackle like we used to expect of people like him and Tony Currie and Frank Worthington in those days. We may have got a little bit more out of him. He did well, but he could have had a lot of international caps, he was good enough for that.'

Through to the last eight of the FA Cup and the Fairs Cup, but stumbling in their attempts to catch Leeds at the top of the First Division, Bertie Mee chose the days after the George-inspired victory at Manchester City to remind his team what could be achieved. 'I told the players we could expect two games a week for the rest of the season. I told them, "This is the time to be really ambitious and to aim for the success which may never be possible for you as players again in your lifetimes." The point was expressed that all three trophies should be aimed for.'

Radford recalls that the manager's message struck home. 'Bert told us we could still win it. I think we were maybe just getting to the point where we were thinking we would just coast along, second in the League and go for the cups. We needed that lift. Bertie made sure that our ambition matched his.'

If Arsenal's players were guilty of perceiving the FA Cup as the most realistic of their three targets, a valid excuse lay in the extraordinary fifth-round game at Colchester United's Layer Road ground, an event which took Leeds out of that particular equation. The Fourth Division side thrilled an all-ticket crowd of 16,000 and stunned a nation of football fans by pulling off a 3–2 victory. Colchester's entire team cost only £20,000, one eighth of the fee Leeds paid for Allan Clarke. Their manager, Dick Graham, said before the game, 'Leeds have got the same fears and failings as the rest of us. There is no point in thinking about defending. We shall have to attack them. It's no use adopting a cautious attitude.'

Former England striker Ray Crawford headed Colchester in front after Gary Sprake's tentative attempt to cut out a free-kick and then hooked in the second goal from a prone position. Former Arsenal reserve player David Simmons scored a third after Sprake and his defence failed to cut out a long ball downfield and even though Leeds rallied to pull back two goals, they could not prevent one of the biggest FA Cup upsets for years. 'Gary Sprake had one of those days when everything went wrong for him,' recalls Leeds striker Peter Lorimer. 'There were balls going in and he was missing balls and it created mayhem.'

With their great rivals out of the FA Cup, Arsenal's focus returned to the gathering of League points against Ipswich at Highbury. George, denied by a good save from Laurie Sivell, highlighted another outstanding first-half performance by finding the net with a near-post header from Armstrong's cross after 22 minutes. Radford, also denied by the bravery of Sivell, hooked in a second goal after 33 minutes when he capitalised on some good approach work by Kennedy. Five minutes later, McLintock moved forward to score from an Armstrong corner and after George struck the post with a powerful shot the Gunners went in at half-time with a comfortable three-goal lead. The second half was a different story altogether. Former Highbury winger Jimmy Robertson drilled in a corner that flew into the net off McNab and five minutes from time he scored again from close range. Robertson had also beaten Wilson with a free-kick, only to see the effort ruled out because of pushing in the box. The Scot had been booked for throwing a punch at Storey and been on the end of a foul that in turn earned Storey a caution. As well as a couple of worrying injuries – Kennedy having burst a blood vessel in his ankle and George having twisted his knee and taken a knock in the back – the second 45 minutes had thrown up troubling signs of Arsenal's growing inconsistency. A week later they faced another serious threat to their title aspirations at Derby County.

The home team's midfield took a firm grip on the game and Mackay did another outstanding job of organising at the back in one of his last games before agreeing an end-of-season move to Swindon. It added up to a quiet, untroubled day for Colin Todd in his first game following his £170,000 transfer from Sunderland as Arsenal were reduced to momentary glimpses of inspiration from George. Armstrong forced a save from Colin Boulton after 15 minutes, but the Gunners, described in one report as 'inaccurately programmed automatons', fell behind after 31 minutes when Kevin Hector helped on a free-kick for Roy McFarland to head past Wilson. Five minutes after the interval it was 2–0 as Hector received the ball from John O'Hare, beat two defenders and shot past Wilson with an angled drive from 20 yards. Kennedy's drive after 70 minutes, tipped over by Boulton, was Arsenal's only genuine response.

Seven points behind Leeds after three away defeats and two less than convincing home wins in their previous five games, the Gunners found themselves being written off by the Fleet Street headline writers. Their two games in hand over Leeds were considered to be insignificant, especially as the first of them was another away game at high-flying Wolves. If ever the Gunners needed a good start to lift their confidence, it was now at Molineux. And they got it.

With less than two minutes played, Wolves defender John Holsgrove went airborne to head Rice's effort round the post and Armstrong sent over a corner that Kennedy headed into the net. Arsenal's play possessed the drive and urgency that had been missing at Derby three days earlier and after 30 minutes they went further ahead. Holsgrove tried to deal with a McLintock clearance but allowed the ball to run to Radford, who pushed ahead and shot past the advancing Phil Parkes.

Arsenal's confidence was running so high that it prompted an incident late in the first half that McNab remembers clearly. 'We were 2–0 up and were playing unbelievably. It was just one of those games where we ran them off the park. Five minutes before half-time the ball comes to Pat Rice on the edge of the box. He is trying to look composed and he's done a drag back on the edge of the box and lost it. Peter Storey races over to Ricey, and me and Bob Wilson have to pull Peter off him. I had run over there to strangle Pat as well but I had to be a mediator. I thought Peter was going to kill him and the blood ran out of Ricey's face. He never did that again in all his career.

'Bertie comes in at half-time and says, "Well done, boys. We are doing very well, but let's not get magnanimous." All of a sudden down the other end of the changing-room, Raddy pipes up, "What the fuck's magnanimous mean?" That was Raddy. He didn't say a lot, but when he did he said a lot. Bertie said, "Well, let's not give anything away. We've got another half to play. We have won the wrong half."'

But it was soon apparent that Arsenal's superiority would extend through the rest of the game. Radford's header grazed the crossbar before Kennedy's second goal killed the game after 55 minutes. George set it up by beating three defenders and flicking the ball forward to Kennedy, who scored with a low right-foot shot. George came close to adding a fourth when he hit the bar 20 minutes from time.

'This result showed the character of the side,' said Mee. 'They came back to give one of their best performances of the season. It was absolutely wonderful. The title doesn't belong to Leeds yet. There are 12 games to go and if we keep playing like this we must be in with a fine chance.'

In the FA Cup, Arsenal had been given their fourth consecutive away draw, an awkward tie against a Leicester team on their way to winning the Second Division title. Beaten in the final by Manchester City two seasons earlier, Leicester clearly had the scent of Wembley in their nostrils again and tore into the Gunners on a freezing afternoon. Using the high wind to help them bombard the Arsenal box with long balls, they kept the Gunners on the back foot throughout the first half, even though they failed to call Wilson into serious action. Arsenal's only first-half attempt was from Sammels, who hit the ball straight at Shilton. With the wind at their backs, Arsenal ventured out a little more in the second half but, like the home team, could create only half chances.

Wilson made the most important save of the game after 70 minutes when he anticipated the direction of a shot from Rodney Fern, the Marty Feldman lookalike striker, and turned the ball away at full stretch. Winger Len Glover came within inches of converting a cross from Willie Carlin in the closing moments, but the resilient Gunners held on for a replay they could have done without but would gratefully accept.

For their 47th competitive game of the season, Arsenal welcomed the resumption of their European Fairs Cup defence. FC Cologne took an experienced team to Highbury for the first leg of their quarter-final, including midfielder Wolfgang Overath, a veteran of two World Cups, and Hannes Lohr, another member of West Germany's victorious team against England in Mexico. Most of the pre-match talk among the crowd, however, centred not on the game but discussion of the previous night's events in New York. In Madison Square Garden, Muhammad Ali had been beaten for the first time in his career and had his jaw broken by Joe Frazier in their showdown for the undisputed world heavyweight title.

Looking for the goals that would give them a safe cushion to take to Germany, Arsenal piled forward and McLintock secured an early opening goal, knocking in a rebound after Kennedy had forced a save from goalkeeper Manglitz following Radford's long throw. But Radford and Kennedy struggled for space up front and by half-time the scores were level. Cologne scored their important away goal after Wilson was left unsighted at a crowded far post and full-back Thielen's corner ricocheted in off the woodwork.

Mee withdrew Sammels to bring on Graham for the second half, but there was to be only one more goal against the physical German defence, even though Arsenal won 15 corners. Storey scored 20 minutes from time with a low shot through a crowded penalty area after good work by Radford, but the Gunners fans feared the worst when the final whistle blew.

The Cologne coach Ernst Ocwirk warned, 'We will win 1–0 in Cologne. Arsenal played as well as I expected but they did not make the most of their chances.'

The relentless pace of the games continued as Arsenal travelled across London to Crystal Palace. It was the unique claret and sky-blue pin-striped shirts of the home side that went quickly into attack and came close to scoring when Steve Kember drilled the ball against the bar from the right of the penalty area, Jimmy Scott firing the rebound wide of the post. Graham had kept his place in the Arsenal team, his first start for six weeks, and it was he who scored a trademark goal after 20 minutes when he rose to meet McLintock's long diagonal ball with a ramrod header. 'Frank says it was one of the best passes he ever hit in his life,' Graham laughs. 'It was a clearance! I just got up with a great header.'

Armstrong cut inside from the left wing to force a low save from John Jackson, and McNab should have scored after the break when he shot into the side netting after substitute Sammels, on for George, put him through on goal. But typical persistence by Armstrong helped set up the second goal, snaffling the ball away from full-back John Sewell by the corner flag and feeding Graham. His high ball was headed back across goal by McLintock and Sammels bounced a shot into the net off the leg of a defender. Sammels' muted response to his goal perhaps gave an indication that he knew the turn his career was about to take.

13

ODD MAN OUT

IT IS FOOTBALL'S VERSION OF THE OLD MOVIE LINE, 'YOU'RE GOING OUT there an understudy and coming back a star.' The substitute enters the game, scores an important goal and turns up for training the next day secure in the knowledge that he will be in the starting line-up for the next match. But this was Highbury, not Hollywood, and for Jon Sammels the story was not to have a happy ending.

The games coming up in the week following the win at Crystal Palace were back at Arsenal, against Leicester in the replayed sixth round FA Cup tie and Blackpool in the League. Sammels, despite his contribution at Selhurst Park, was informed he would not even be on the bench, a decision that signalled victory for those in the Highbury crowd who, over the years, had been quick to target him with their spite. It had become a familiar pattern: when things weren't going well and the crowd needed someone to blame, Sammels, one of the club's biggest fans, was their man. Now, with the Gunners having lost important League games since Christmas and the defence of the Fairs Cup hanging by a thread, it had begun again. An announcement of Sammels' name over the Highbury loud speakers would prompt a mixed response from the North Bank; the first signs of the game not going exactly to plan brought calls for him to be substituted.

In the face of such hostility, even Sammels admits that he could no longer be trusted to perform capably. The low point had been the home leg of the European quarter-final against Cologne. 'I was in a terrible mental state,' he admits. 'You start thinking, "I'll show you," and you try to do silly things that you wouldn't usually dream of doing. I was awful. I remember Don

Howe saying to me at half-time, "Come on, it's not your night." I was substituted and I could understand it.'

The man whose Highbury goal less than a year earlier had clinched the club's first trophy in a generation would never again set foot on Arsenal's turf. There would be a couple more assignments as a substitute away from home, but it was effectively the end of his season, and ultimately the end of a ten-year career at Arsenal.

He says, 'Bertie Mee made the decision to leave me out, and I would have done the same thing,' the passing of time having brought a melancholy acceptance that he will always be remembered as that season's odd man out. 'At that time, you couldn't afford to have somebody out there playing in the home games who, for whatever reason, was going to do something that would affect the team.'

Only weeks earlier Mee had been hailing Sammels' return to form and fitness by saying after the FA Cup game at Portsmouth, 'It was certainly Jon's best game back after injury and Arsenal will give him every encouragement to get to the very top in football.'

For as long as Sammels could remember, his idea of reaching that summit had been to pull on the red and white of Arsenal. Born in Ipswich and a leading light in the Suffolk Schoolboys team, Sammels still counts his blessings that he signed for the team of his dreams. 'I remember the day I signed. Thursday, 5 January 1961,' he says without pause. 'I was 15. I just loved the whole place, the history of it. You think of all the great players who have been there and you see all the players you think a lot of, Jimmy Bloomfield, Tommy Docherty, David Herd. I used to get excited going to the ground to train and watch the games. I was a little country boy from Suffolk and I never thought I would get the opportunity to play for Arsenal. I thought that didn't happen to boys where I came from.'

Evidence of his lasting love for the club that made his dreams come true and eventually broke his heart is all around as he sits in the study of his home in the Leicestershire countryside, where he has spent his post-football days as a driving instructor. Framed action sequences, team pictures and reunion mementos decorate the walls, while their owner sits within touching distance of a glass-fronted trophy cabinet that tells the story of his rise through the Arsenal ranks and ultimate disappointment. Youth team honours occupy the rear spaces on the shelves, giving way to League Cup, Fairs Cup and League Championship medals in positions of prominence. There is, however, no reminder of the 1971 FA Cup final.

Having collected his trophies with the youth team, Sammels was introduced to the first team within months of several other members of the future Double squad, John Radford, Peter Simpson, Peter Storey and George Armstrong. It was part of a decision by manager Billy Wright to place the future of the club in the hands of its younger players. 'I feel a bit sorry for Billy Wright because he didn't get a lot of thanks for what his work led to in the future,' Sammels explains. 'Many of the Double squad were home-grown lads who Billy helped bring through. Before coming to Arsenal, he had been in charge of the England Under-23s and he maybe felt more comfortable working with younger players. He felt he wanted to get his own lads in. He left out Joe Baker and George Eastham, who were hero-worshipped by the fans, and brought in two youngsters, me and John Radford, to replace them. It was a brave decision. John and I felt under pressure from that decision.'

Radford adds, 'We were replacing popular players so it wasn't very enjoyable to play as kids. Even when we ran out there and were kicking in before the game, we were getting stick. It came from frustration because the club had not won anything for so long and I can understand it a little bit because we were replacing two superstars. But they were superstars who had never won anything for the team. It was very upsetting as players when we got stick that we didn't deserve. It takes a few years to straighten out a club when it has been in decline and I don't think people realise the harm they can do to young players.'

By the mid-60s, Sammels had become established at the heart of Arsenal's midfield. With his dark and fashionably-styled hair, passing ability and eye for a spectacular goal, he was a neat complement to the bustling, ball-winning style of his partner, Frank McLintock. England Under-23 honours came his way, along with recommendations from many members of the media that a full England cap should follow. These days Sammels speaks with nothing but great affection of his beloved Arsenal and the club's fans, although at the time the relationship with a small number of those on the terraces was not always as smooth as he would have liked.

Radford observes, 'For me, it changed when I scored a hat-trick in a game against Wolves and the crowd turned. But it never really happened like that for Jon. Even up to the day he left he was getting stick and it was a great shame because he loves the club. It was upsetting because he was a smashing lad and it hit him hard.'

As early as the 1967–68 season, Sammels considered a future away from Highbury after feeling that the fans were quick to use him as a scapegoat for poor performances, while newspaper reports of an approach to the management for increased wages also cast him in a less than complimentary light. 'I remember going to Bertie a couple of years before the Double season and saying that we had a lot of young lads there who were the nucleus of the side and were going to be the nucleus of the side for a long time. I said, "I don't think you are looking after us very well." Players coming in had been given signing-on fees that were quite a lot of money in those days and I asked if the club could do something to bring Simmo, Geordie, Johnny Radford, Peter Storey and myself into line. I didn't go in thinking I was going to sort it all out for the lads, I just went in for selfish reasons. I got quite a lot of bad publicity out of that and it looked like I was trying to be bigger than the club, but that wasn't the case. I eventually signed and I got a bit more on my basic wage, plus a loyalty bonus. The papers said I was getting about £220 a week – it was nowhere near that. I didn't come out of that very well and it looked like I was money grabbing.'

By the summer of 1970, however, all of that was in the past and Sammels had scored the goal that gave the Gunners their 4–3 aggregate advantage over Anderlecht in the final of the Fairs Cup. 'You never really feel secure at a big club like Arsenal,' he says, 'but it had been a good year. My first daughter had been born, I had played pretty well and scored quite a few goals, and I was really looking forward to the new season.'

But disappointment – in hindsight, maybe even disaster – was around the corner. During a pre-season game in Denmark, Sammels received an injury that was to cost him his place in the team. 'To get injured then was my biggest disappointment because I sensed something special was going to happen. I had felt really good that summer and I knew I had to be in there from the start. As soon as it happened, I knew my ankle had gone. I got a little ball rolled to me and I could tell this big Dane was going to clatter me. I was planted there and I couldn't get out of the way. I got this whack and it all swelled up that night. When we got back they were still talking about me playing against Everton in the first game of the season, but I was thinking there was no way I could make it. It turned out I had broken a bone and I ended up in plaster. It really hit me at the first home game, a really hot day against Manchester United. I remember the Fairs Cup being paraded before the game and I thought how much I would love to be out there.'

As the weeks went by, all Sammels could do was doggedly go through his rehabilitation work with Charlie George, who suffered a similar injury in the first game of the season, and watch enviously as his teammates racked up the wins. 'Once you were out of the team then it was very difficult to get back in. I can remember watching us beating teams 4–0 and I am sat there with this pot on my foot thinking, "Leave a bit for me." If you are honest, you know the only way you are going to get back is if they go off the boil a little bit or someone gets injured. In those days there was no squad system, you just wanted to be in there playing all the time.'

Sammels' growing insecurity was compounded by the stories of a bid for another midfield player, West Bromwich Albion's Bobby Hope. 'Obviously I was hoping they didn't sign him. It was going to be hard enough getting back in the team, without them buying another creative player.'

Even after the bid failed, the success of Ray Kennedy up front meant the prospect of a midfield place eventually being the accommodation for George's return from injury. 'Charlie and me were up in the gym doing a lot of weights, press-ups, anything to keep ourselves ticking over because we were in plaster and couldn't do any running. It helped having each other to work with and the club made us feel involved by having us in the dressing-room before kick-off, along with the 12 lads playing in the game.'

But the feeling of being an outsider continued to grow, especially when the fit players returned with battle stories from the infamous street fight in Rome. Sammels explains, 'I felt I missed out on something by not being part of the Lazio thing. I missed out on that togetherness that the lads had through that brawl. You just don't feel part of the team when you are watching games, even if you've played a thousand before. You are not taking the knocks so you don't feel like part of it.'

Sammels was finally back in the side for the game at Ipswich, more than three months into the season and with the team having posted a run of seven League games unbeaten. 'When I came back I felt under more pressure. I thought there must be people saying, "What have they brought him back for? Why not keep it as it was?"'

The first five games with Sammels back in the line-up were won, but as Arsenal stumbled in the early months of 1971, the fans turned on their favourite fall guy. Sensitive to the criticism, Sammels' insecurity turned into unhappiness. 'I was at Arsenal for ten and a half years and for ten I felt really happy, felt as one with the supporters most of the time. You can't please everyone and there had been little bits of criticism in the past, but that is part of football. But this time I felt like it was always me they picked on first.'

Sammels is honest enough to accept a large part of the blame for the escalation of the situation. 'If I am honest, I was too emotionally involved with the club. It was my club and I was unprofessional for letting it affect me. I didn't play very well through it all. I don't think I was imagining the situation, but I was a bit too sensitive. I remember sitting at Southampton later in the season when I was out of the team and there was a bloke sitting in front of me, one of our so-called celebrity fans. He was saying, "I hope they don't bring Sammels on," and he was going on about me, and it really got to me. He didn't even know enough to realise I wasn't even in the squad. It was so silly and it really got into my head.

'You know, the next season I remember hearing that George Armstrong was getting it and thinking, "How can they do that to George?" But I am not knocking the Arsenal supporters. Looking back I wasn't very professional. But it was missing all those games and being desperate to get back in there and catch up, and worrying I was not going to be involved in something special.'

Sammels goes to great pains not to come across as bitter about his treatment by some of the Highbury fans, preferring to count his blessings for the good times. Teammate Bob McNab, however, is not so forgiving. 'I cannot say enough about Jon. He was a great lad and he got slaughtered by our fans. I don't bother with the fans much because I saw what happened and I remember the bad as well as the good. The season after the Double, we ran around with the trophies before the first game next season and I found it embarrassing. Twenty minutes into the game we are getting slow hand-clapped, and at half-time we got booed off. We had just won the Double! Talk about, "what have you done for us lately?"

'In 1968–69 I was playing out of my brains. The fans voted for the Player of the Year award and Frank McLintock won it. Nightmare. I was the first Arsenal player to play for England for however many years and even Ian Ure beat me for second. These people don't know what we do for a living.'

McLintock believes that Sammels might have received the assistance he needed to combat the critics if he had played in the modern era. 'Jon was very giving and kind, a lovely boy. He should have been a great player. He had great talent and it wasn't for the want of trying. He just needed a bit more self-confidence. He could have done with a psychologist working with him like they do today, telling him how good he was.

'He could run forever, do cross-countries and come in whistling, and he had a fantastic shot. He was a great passer and he would look up sometimes and think about passing it and change his mind and dither on it. Not a lot, just occasionally, and he would get robbed sometimes. If he'd had a wee bit of the Jim Baxter confidence and the Paul Gascoigne confidence he would have been unbelievable. He came from Ipswich and maybe he always felt the fact that he was at a big club like Arsenal. A bit more arrogance and he would have been unbelievable. The fans liked him, they just got frustrated at him sometimes. And Jon was an Arsenal fanatic, which was one of his downfalls. He was dying to do so well and he took it to heart.'

Peter Storey remembers, 'Among all of us, he was the one who we thought would be the star player. I used to live with him in the early days and even then he used to take it to heart if he had a few bad games. Instead of going out and forgetting about it he used to come home and stay indoors and let it get to him. He was quiet and sensitive, not like some people who couldn't give a monkey's. He then tried too hard. Instead of getting the ball and giving short passes so the crowd wouldn't get on to him, he would try another long crossfield ball and if it went astray the crowd would be after him. Sometimes you can't do any wrong and other days everything goes wrong. When that happens you should just do the easy thing until your confidence comes back.'

Peter Simpson suggests, 'He sometimes went backwards instead of forwards, which is why he got some stick from some of the supporters. The trouble with Sammy was that he had a glass of lager and went home. I wanted him to come out and get drunk but he went home and worried over what had happened in the game instead of forgetting it until Monday. He'd think about it and make it worse. I was disappointed for him because he should have been there at the end.'

Eddie Kelly was one of the players who would help to keep Sammels out of the team as the season reached its climax, but he admits, 'It was a terrible shame. Every club always seems to have a culprit. I think it was because Sammy was so gifted and people expected more of him. He was a great passer of the ball and could shoot long range from 30 or 40 yards and they were expecting it all the time. But there are some games where you just can't do it. He was hurt by the situation, but he wasn't a person who would stir up trouble. He was very good to me when I was a young player. I would often get advice from him, he was just a gentleman. Maybe he was too gentle sometimes and you'd think, "Fucking hell, Sammy, just get on with it." He was too nice a man to play football sometimes.'

As the season neared its end, Sammels would realise the only solution to his problem lay away from Highbury and he ended up accepting a transfer to Leicester in the days following the FA Cup final. 'I wanted to get back and enjoy my football again. I thought I would have to move on, but then part of you thinks you are running away, you are quitting. But anyone who knows me knows I wasn't a quitter. I just knew the only way I was going to get back to enjoying football was to move, as much as it hurt me.

'But I still look back at my career at Highbury with happy memories. I am not the first person it has happened to and I won't be the last. At the time it was the end of the world, but you get to know what is really important. My wife and my family, they were everything to me. And they meant even more after something like that. My wife, Angela, went though it with me and my mum and dad knew how much it meant to me to be in the Arsenal team. Now I just feel so grateful that I was able to be there and play for Arsenal and win things and experience good times and bad times.'

Sammels, along with a Highbury crowd of more than 57,000, waited to see if Arsenal could take their place in an FA Cup semi-final line-up that would pair Merseyside rivals Everton and Liverpool at Old Trafford, with Stoke poised to play the Highbury victors at Hillsborough. Everton had clinched their place by ending Colchester's heroics with an emphatic 5–0 thumping at Goodison Park, Howard Kendall grabbing a couple of goals. Liverpool's berth would be secured a day after the Arsenal replay when Steve Heighway scored the only goal in two games against Tottenham. John Ritchie's two goals had seen Stoke home 3–2 in an exciting quarter-final at Hull City, managed by former Arsenal skipper Terry Neill.

The Gunners appeared to have gone behind after 13 minutes when Rodney Fern headed home from a John Farrington cross, but referee Jim Finney reprieved the home side when he decided the Leicester forward had shoved his way past Pat Rice. 'Fern climbed on my shoulders and held me down,' said Rice later. 'The ball was going straight for my head and I would have cleared it otherwise.'

On the stroke of half-time, Armstrong was sent away down the left flank by Graham, panicking the Leicester defence into conceding a corner. The winger's inswinging delivery was met at the near post by the late-arriving George, who beat the challenge of Peter Shilton to head down into goal.

Leicester began and finished the second half brightly, forcing Wilson to save from Alistair Brown early in the half and having a series of shots blocked as the last few seconds ebbed away. In between there had been some nasty fouls, with George and Brown having their names taken. But there were no more goals and Arsenal were one victory away from their fourth final appearance in successive seasons.

One of the teams destined to exchange places with Leicester at the end of the season, Blackpool, were expected to offer little resistance when Arsenal returned to League action. But for the second time during the season, the Gunners made heavy weather of the struggling Seasiders and Wilson had to be on top of his game once again, notably in turning a close-range header by John Craven over the bar after only eight minutes. Wilson went on to deny Micky Burns, Craven twice more and Tony Green, prompting Bob Stokoe, the Blackpool manager, to describe the keeper as football's most improved player over the previous 12 months. 'Wilson has made remarkable progress when you consider he was not a kid when he turned professional. There was a time when he looked and played like an amateur, now he is the picture of professionalism.'

Neil Ramsbottom in the Blackpool goal was no less busy, making good saves from Radford, Graham and George. But it was his mistake seven minutes after half-time that handed Arsenal the game's only goal. He should have dealt easily with Graham's cross but allowed the ball to wriggle out of his grasp for Peter Storey to nod in, the first senior goal he had ever scored with his head. Storey was pleased to be attracting attention for something other than the hammering he had received two weeks running from Jimmy Hill on *The Big Match*. Hill had criticised his tackling and his temperament, saying he was quick to dish out tough tackles but unhappy when similar challenges were aimed at him or his teammates. 'I'm surprised, that's all,' was Storey's response to Hill's comments. Vindication of his methods was on its way.

14

'BANKSIE BOTTLED IT'

AN IMPORTANT WEEK OF CUP ACTION BEGAN WITH ARSENAL FLYING OUT
to West Germany to resume their European Fairs Cup quarter-final tie
against FC Cologne. Three days later would come the FA Cup semi-final
against Stoke. Comments made to journalists at the airport by Bertie Mee
and chairman Denis Hill-Wood hinted at the financial rewards for which
the team was playing. With Arsenal's salaries structured to reward success
and loyalty instead of offering huge amounts up front, estimates of a
£15,000 jackpot if Arsenal won three trophies were confirmed by the club.
'No players in the country have ever been better rewarded than ours,' said
Mee. 'Even if we were to win one competition their rewards would be
tremendous.' Hill-Wood added, 'Let's just say that if we achieve all we are
aiming for, the players are going to be facing a problem with super tax.'

Knowing that a 1–0 victory by the home side would, by virtue of their
away goal at Highbury, end Arsenal's defence of their European crown, the
last thing Mee's team needed was to run into a referee who seemed
determined to make himself the centre of attention in the Mungersdorf
Stadium. Only four minutes had been played when Bob McNab attempted
to return Bob Wilson's mis-hit clearance to the goalkeeper, only to find
Kapellman lurking. As McNab chased back and Wilson raced out, the three
players collapsed in a heap and Romanian official Konstantin Petres ruled
that McNab had been the guilty party. The forward's tumble had seemed
suspiciously premeditated, but Werner Biskup gratefully fired past Wilson
and the home side were level 2–2 on aggregate, effectively ahead in the tie.

The penalty award proved to be only the first act in a refereeing
performance that angered and frustrated the Gunners. Coach Don Howe

was seen running up and down the touchline more often than winger George Armstrong as he protested the Romanian's decisions. Pat Rice was cautioned for a challenge that would not have raised a murmur in a First Division game and Charlie George suffered the same fate for pretending to throw the ball at the referee in frustration. Ray Kennedy was pulled down from behind and was the one to receive a caution when he brushed aside the hand of apology from his assailant.

The normally calm Mee would say later, 'It was the worst display of refereeing Arsenal have ever met during their Fairs Cup history. He killed the game and even penalised our lads because they called to teammates for the ball. I left my touchline seat and approached officials in the stand. I asked them to appeal to the FIFA observer to visit the referee at half-time. I asked for the referee to be told that when a player calls for the ball it does not constitute an offence. Now I hope the European football union will take steps to remedy the situation.'

Arsenal's mood was not helped, either, by the sight of Cologne players making a meal of every tackle, writhing on the floor while trainers huddled around with blankets and medical bags. Yet the German team were not devoid of ability. Their forward line was quick and penetrative and asked serious questions of the Gunners defence and keeper Wilson.

Arsenal created their own chances, with George not far off target and John Radford and Ray Kennedy having attempts blocked by defenders at close range. In the final minute George Graham, who had also come close earlier in the game, saw his shot thump off the post into the hands of keeper Manglitz. The final whistle sounded the end of a night of bitter disappointment and George was so angry that he had to be hauled off towards the dressing-room by Eddie Kelly before he could get to the referee. Mee's anger was not confined to the referee. 'The childish histrionics of some of the West Germans is bringing the game into disrepute. We saw this in the 1966 World Cup and now we have seen it again. My players have never known such frustration, but they kept their self-control.'

So the Fairs Cup was history and, after arriving back in England, Arsenal's party had little more than 48 hours to turn their attention to Stoke City. 'One day in May, I think we will look back at last night's episode and see it as a good thing,' said Mee. 'It has cleared our minds for what we have to do against Stoke.'

The second-oldest Football League club, who had never reached a major final in their 108-year history, stood between Arsenal and their first FA Cup final appearance for 19 years. The Gunners had seen more than enough evidence of Stoke's potential back in October, although an FA Cup path through Millwall, Huddersfield, Ipswich and Hull had yet to pitch them against a team approaching Arsenal's calibre.

Arsenal needed no reminding of what had happened the last time they had run into Stoke. 'We probably went into that match with the wrong attitude. We were a bit complacent and we paid for it,' said Peter Storey of the 5–0 defeat at the Victoria Ground. But he promised, 'We will be mentally prepared for them this time. We will be treating them just like Leeds.' And with a hint of foresight, he added, 'I've got five penalties so far this season. Nothing would give me greater pleasure than to stick one past Gordon Banks in the semi-final. That would really be something.'

On a bright afternoon at Sheffield Wednesday's Hillsborough ground, wearing yellow and blue against the all-white strip of their opponents, Arsenal had the greater share of possession in the first 20 minutes. Wilson, though, was forced to concede a corner when he pushed a dangerous cross from Jimmy Greenhoff behind the goal. In front of the Stoke fans in the 55,000 crowd, the left-footed Harry Burrows swung the ball in low from the right. The danger appeared to have been averted as Storey shaped to clear, but relief turned to horror as the ball pinballed back off Stoke centre-half Denis Smith into the Arsenal goal. Stoke were quickly back on the attack and Conroy and Mahoney combined well before the former fired narrowly wide of the target.

Looking for an equaliser, McNab played the ball forward to Kennedy, who controlled and turned in one swift movement and forced Gordon Banks into an excellent low save to his left. What happened next, however, displayed what Arsenal's players believe to be the England goalkeeper's extreme nerves on the day. Choosing to roll the ball in front of him so as to avoid taking more than four steps in possession, Banks unwittingly proffered it to Kennedy. He was saved greater embarrassment by the intervention of a teammate and the referee's ruling that he had been fouled as he groped to regain possession. Somewhat sheepishly, Banks rubbed his neck, although it appeared as though it was his composure that had suffered the biggest injury. He took the free-kick himself and, like a golf-course hacker using a driver for the first time, shanked his effort straight at Radford on the edge of the penalty area. It was Banks himself who booted the ball away from the Arsenal man, but the Gunners worked their way back into the danger area, where Storey's left-foot shot was blocked by full-back Mike Pejic and Kennedy's follow-up effort was spectacularly turned aside by Banks. This time, the Stoke keeper masked his relief by berating referee Pat Partridge.

After 29 minutes, disaster struck Arsenal again. Pejic's pass forward for

Burrows was knocked away by Simpson to George. Facing his own goal, the young maestro chose to play the ball back to Wilson, only for striker John Ritchie to intervene and nudge past the Arsenal keeper before scoring into an empty net. Trailing 2–0 at the break, it was time for the famous Arsenal spirit to reveal itself in the tightest corner in which the Gunners had yet found themselves. 'We had this fire about us,' says McLintock. 'It was a matter of, "Come on, let's get back in it. We shouldn't be two–nothing down against this lot. We are better than them."'

Howe decided against major changes, although he attempted to get George more involved in the game. 'If someone looked like he was not doing it, we would try something. Charlie was not playing very well so we tried to switch him about, make it harder for them to surround him, and pushed people forward.'

Yet it was Stoke who had an opportunity to kill the game shortly after the interval when Greenhoff caught the Arsenal defence square by slipping the ball through for Mahoney. The Welsh midfielder's attempt to poke a shot underneath Wilson was foiled, but McNab recalls that the lucky escape was symptomatic of the tactical change Arsenal had decided upon before the game. 'What we tried to do was compensate for the way they had beaten us 5–0 in the League earlier in the season,' the full-back explains. 'Me and Ricey pushed forward on their wide men, Burrows and Conroy, and squeezed them, stood on them. We wanted to stop them coming forward, but what happened was that Frank and Peter got a bit isolated and were run ragged. Neither one of them had real pace so it was one-on-one for them against Ritchie and Greenhoff. Ritchie was a big lad for Frank. It would have helped if they had done a better job of catching them offside a couple of times but we were always chasing the game.'

Arsenal, relieved at Mahoney's miss, swept downfield and won a throw. Armstrong fed Kennedy and he hooked over his shoulder into the heart of the penalty area, where Radford and Graham jumped for the ball. It broke to the edge of the penalty area and Storey reacted quickest, connecting powerfully with his right foot and seeing his shot go past Banks' outstretched right arm. 'It just fell for me and I hit it,' said Storey. 'I didn't see it go in but I think it took a deflection off someone's shoulder.'

With 40 minutes still to play, the Double was back within reach, yet Greenhoff continued to tie up the Arsenal defence, making them wary of conceding a third goal rather than being able to press ahead for an equaliser. The former Leeds striker should have restored Stoke's two-goal cushion when he turned deftly on the halfway line and raced away from the defence, but he shot hopelessly high with only Wilson to beat.

Referee Partridge added two minutes of injury time, maybe the most important 120 seconds of Arsenal's season, and the Gunners won a free-kick. Armstrong clipped the ball forward into the penalty area, Banks failed to hold it as Graham challenged and substitute Sammels had his shot charged down, prompting Radford to throw up his arms in search of a penalty. The loose ball broke towards McLintock, but the attention of Banks sent it spinning out for a corner. While Radford continued his appeal for a spot-kick, an enraged Banks was back in the face of the referee to claim he had been impeded in the mêlée.

Armstrong's corner drifted over the group of players at the near post and fell for McLintock to head towards the keeper's right-hand post. Banks, one of eight Stoke players in the six-yard box, was well beaten but Mahoney dived to push the ball away with his hand. Arsenal's players jumped around and hugged each other in celebration at the award of a penalty, while Stoke's crestfallen players pointed accusing fingers at each other. For Storey, of course, the job was just beginning. ITV's excitable commentator Brian Moore spoke of the midfielder's 'terrible responsibility' and Wilson knelt in prayer as the ball was placed on the spot. Storey stood calmly with hands on hips as Banks returned slowly to his line and crouched in readiness. As the Arsenal player approached, Banks flexed his knees several times but remained rooted to the spot, his only movement being a slight lean to his right, as a less than perfect penalty slid no more than a yard past his left foot. 'Peter must have lost half a stone taking that penalty,' says Graham. 'He was very quiet, but he was just sweating without saying anything. He was soaked.'

The Gunners had survived and Banks was furious. 'I had the ball knocked out of my hands,' he argued. 'It should have been a free-kick to us, not a penalty to them.' Stoke manager Tony Waddington backed up his keeper by saying, 'It had to be a bad one. I have never seen Gordon hang his head before.' It was a desperate end to a traumatic day for the man who less than a year earlier had cemented his reputation as the world's best goalkeeper with his miraculous save from Pelé in the World Cup. Peter Simpson puts it bluntly: 'Banksie bottled it.'

McNab expands on that view. 'Banksie had a nightmare. He was throwing the ball to us. Gordon was still the best goalie at that time for England but not in the First Division. He was a pretty nervous guy. I was his room-mate once and he was shitting himself. He lost his cool, he lost everything.'

On the morning of the game, Banks himself had spoken about how difficult he had found it to maintain a detached calm since taking over as team captain after Peter Dobing broke his leg earlier in the season. 'I found I got too wrapped up in the action,' he admitted. 'When a referee gave a questionable decision I found myself haring up the field to see him. I volunteered to hand over the captaincy but Mr Waddington told me that if I could keep calm then it would be an example to the rest of the side.'

Radford suggests, 'I think Banksie thought we had the sign over him. I remember him throwing the ball up to kick it away and I turned my back and he kicked it against me. When we got the penalty, I remember everybody punching the air and celebrating and I was thinking, "Hang on, Peter has still got to score this." But Banksie just leaned to his right and it went in. The following year we had another penalty against them in the semi-final and Charlie took it. Charlie said to Banksie, "Same way as last year." Gordon went the wrong way again, went down on one knee to his right, and Charlie put his to his left. I think Banksie did bottle it.'

Storey had refused to be distracted by Banks's antics on the line. 'He kept moving about a lot, which was probably to put me off, but I didn't let it. I hit it to his left but not as far as I meant to. It was meant to be more in the corner. When you see the ball in the back of the net you feel the tension go out of you. It's not something you're conscious of before. It's just a job up until then. I didn't ever think about missing it.'

Arsenal's players felt that Stoke had been given their chance to cause an upset and blown it. McLintock claims, 'As we were walking back after the penalty John Ritchie just nutted me on the nose. Bosh! It was like he didn't want me to play in the next game, but I just took it. When you are up against a team that is not quite as good as you and they are magnificent on the day, they usually have only one chance.'

Arsenal's only fitness worry for the replay at Villa Park four days later was George, but the ankle injury that had seen him go off with 15 minutes remaining at Hillsborough did not prevent him taking his place in an unchanged starting line-up. Of equal concern was George's mental state following the error that handed Stoke their second goal and an unconvincing all-round performance. Howe told reporters that George had 'found the occasion a bit big for him', while Stoke midfielder Mike Bernard commented, 'My job was to mark Charlie and I was surprised how easily I got on top of him.'

As if to prove a point, George's first touch in the replay was a long-range backpass to Wilson. 'I was very conscious of what had happened in the previous game and I did it just to prove to myself that everything was going to be all right.'

Arsenal took control from the start, with none of the defensive frailties they had displayed at Hillsborough. 'We changed tactically for the second game to the way we usually played,' says McNab. 'I dropped back and we kept the back four at home and kept our shape. We didn't invite the ball over the top. Technically we killed them, it was no contest.'

Banks, the centre of so much of Saturday's drama, was quickly into action again to deal with a McNab cross and it took only 13 minutes for the arrival of an Arsenal goal. Armstrong delivered a corner from the right and Graham's powerful header from 15 yards eluded Banks and Pejic on the line. 'It was a good goal,' says Graham. 'It all comes from movement in the box. If you are clever and you have five or six players moving in the box it is very hard to mark them. That was one of my strengths. If I took a chance and got ahead of my marker and was in the right place, I always fancied myself to score.'

Graham almost had a second when Banks needed two attempts to keep out his shot and then came close again with a header early in the opening moments of the second half. Two minutes after half-time, Radford charged down the left, trundled a low cross into the box and Kennedy turned home his first goal in seven games. Unlike Arsenal a few days earlier, Stoke had nothing with which to respond to a two-goal deficit. Wembley, and Liverpool, awaited.

For the first time, the Arsenal players allowed themselves to talk about the proximity of the Double. 'We are going to show we can win the League and FA Cup,' said McLintock. 'This will be my fifth time at Wembley and after being on the losing side in four finals the law of averages says I must have a great chance. The way we are playing we can certainly do it.'

Comparisons with a Tottenham side that had become only the third team in history, and the first in the 20th century, to win the League and FA Cup in the same season would now become more frequent. Derby's Dave Mackay, a member of that triumphant Spurs side, explained why the Gunners found themselves in a much tougher situation than the 1961 Double winners: 'We were top of the table with points in hand. We were under some pressure because of the final and all that it means to those who have a chance to play in it. But we were ten points clear at Christmas and there was never any real danger that anyone could make it up. Arsenal have to make up points on Leeds and they have a problem with rearranged fixtures.'

Spurs manager Bill Nicholson warned, 'Once you get through to the final there are all sorts of pressures put on the players. They are in demand for a variety of reasons and it is not always easy for them to concentrate.

There are countless examples of teams going to pieces while waiting to play at Wembley. We were lucky because we had the Championship in hand.'

One of those distractions described by Nicholson was a new phenomenon, the FA Cup final record. Inspired by the success of the England World Cup squad's number one hit, 'Back Home', and urged by Jimmy Hill on *The Big Match* to come up with an Arsenal anthem to rival the Kop's 'You'll Never Walk Alone', the Gunners players would soon be in the recording studios. In the end it was Hill himself who was the unlikely lyric writer for 'Good Old Arsenal', changing the words of 'Rule Britannia' to, 'Good old Arsenal, we're proud to say that name. While we sing this song, we'll win the game.' Many, including Arsenal's own fans, cringed at such corn, yet the song was released as a single by Pye Records, cracked the top 10 and was still echoing around Highbury 30 years later.

While Mee and his players had been sipping their FA Cup champagne at Villa Park, news came through that their quest for the League title had also taken a turn for the better. Leeds had lost at Chelsea, leaving Arsenal six points adrift with three games in hand. Ironically, Chelsea posed the next test for the Gunners in front of a 62,087 crowd, Highbury's best of the season, and it was the visitors who asked the first questions. Midfielder Alan Hudson was knocked to the ground by Storey and John Hollins picked out Peter Osgood with a clever free-kick. The centre-forward's nudge squeezed under Wilson but as the players looked to the linesman for a ruling on whether Simpson had managed to get the ball away before it crossed the line, they noticed the referee awarding offside against Osgood.

At the other end, Simpson robbed Baldwin and fed Kennedy, who helped the ball on to George. He headed into the path of Graham and his long-range effort flashed outside the post. Arsenal came even closer after Kennedy made a typically unselfish run into a wide position and set up Graham to deliver an awkward bouncing ball into the area. Storey made glancing contact with his head but saw his effort denied by the post. Chelsea did get the ball into the Clock End goal before half-time but Irish centre-half John Dempsey had been climbing over a red shirt in the act of creating a chance for Baldwin.

Half-time discussions revolved around how Arsenal would wear down Chelsea's resistance and the news that the Grand National favourite and previous year's winner, Gay Trip, had fallen at the first fence of a race won by the nine-year-old outsider Specify. The smart money among the North Bank fans would have been on George being the man who held the key to breaking the deadlock. So it proved, within two minutes of the restart. Armstrong turned Ron Harris this way and that before crossing from the left and George bamboozled the Chelsea defence by stepping over the ball. The dummy afforded Kennedy the time and space to thump his shot past the Welshman John Phillips in the Chelsea goal.

Radford headed over from a Rice cross and with 15 minutes remaining the creative genius of George was responsible for generating a second goal after he seized on possession following the breakdown of a Chelsea attack. George probed down the right with a powerful run, cut inside as he played a one-two with Radford and clipped a perfect ball to Kennedy on the left edge of the box. As Chelsea appealed for offside, Kennedy chested the ball forward and drove in low with his left foot.

There was time for a scare for the Gunners when McLintock and Osgood battled for the ball and the Arsenal skipper ended on the ground writhing in agony. It transpired that his left elbow, which he feared had been broken, had merely suffered a trapped nerve. The incident attracted the kind of attention Osgood could have done without in only his third game back from an eight-week suspension, but McLintock argued the Chelsea man's innocence, saying, 'You are bound to have the odd bump with the man you are marking. I just fell badly.'

Kennedy's third goal in two games after a seven-match scoring drought followed Arsenal's decision to allow him to resume normal eating after an attempt at making him drop below his fighting weight of more than 13 stone. 'The club put me on a strict diet to try to quicken me up. I lost half a stone and felt as weak as a kitten. So Don Howe ordered me to start eating again. The result has been that I am much happier with my game. I need that weight in the penalty box.'

While the Gunners were winning at home, Allan Clarke scored all four goals in Leeds' defeat of Burnley and then warned, 'The pressure is on Arsenal. They've got to catch us.' Jack Charlton, meanwhile, betrayed signs of Leeds' nerves when he said, 'The situation is very tense. It is difficult not to keep looking over your shoulder for a peep at the Gunners.'

Arsenal set about clearing their backlog of games in hand with the visit of Coventry, which proved to be a more difficult task than expected. A couple of hurried efforts from Kennedy were all they had to show for their first-half labours and Peter Simpson twice had to clear off the line, from Billy Rafferty and Ernie Hunt, before Arsenal sprung from defence after 52 minutes. Graham and Armstrong launched the attack and Kennedy's sure first touch saw off the attention of two defenders. He controlled with his chest and shot cleverly over Bill Glazier for his 25th goal of the campaign. Coventry came back at the home side and Hunt should have done better from close range with the goal at his mercy. Wilson saved from Brian Joicey, Simpson blocked Willie Carr's effort and referee David Smith eventually blew the whistle to a sigh of relief from the home crowd.

15

ALF AND THE ASSASSIN

ON 7 APRIL, PETER STOREY RECEIVED A PHONE CALL THAT, FOR TWO YEARS
at least, would change his footballing life. 'We had just played Coventry the
day before and Jeff Powell of the *Daily Mail* rang me up and said, "What do
you think?" I said, "I don't really know. What do you mean?" I couldn't
believe it when he told me I had been selected for England. It had never
even crossed my mind.'

Storey's surprise was justified, not a case of false modesty. Despite his
consistent displays in Arsenal's midfield, his name was not among those
being touted for a place in the forthcoming European Championship
qualifier against Greece at Wembley. Nor had the Arsenal team had much
recent success in sending players to the England party. Storey would
become only the third member of the Arsenal squad to be awarded a full
cap.

Bob McNab, called up for the Greece game along with Storey but not
used, had played four times for England during the 1968–69 season, while
John Radford had earned a cap during the same year in a Wembley friendly
against Romania, a game that ended in a 1–1 draw. Both have somewhat
bitter memories of their England experience under Sir Alf Ramsey. 'I
remember asking Raddy what he thought of Alf Ramsey and he just said,
"Don't like the fella,"' recalls Bob Wilson.

Radford's international debut had been a while in arriving, for reasons
that still leave him mystified. 'I was feeling good and confident at that stage
of my career but it was a funny time and Alf Ramsey was a funny bloke,' he
says. 'I went with the squad two or three times, but he said he wouldn't play
me until Alan Ball was fit. Why not, I don't know. He just felt he wanted

Ballie in the side before he would pick me. I thought it would have been just the same with anyone else – Bobby Charlton could have given me the ball. But it wasn't until the Romania game that I was in.

'The game seems a bit of a blur now. I played wider on the right in the number 7 shirt that night and I played with Roger Hunt and Geoff Hurst. I was disappointed with them. It was just a routine game for them and I felt they were just going through the motions, whereas for me it was a big game. Alf said nothing to me after the game. They had won the World Cup and Alf was trying to change things gradually but I don't think he really knew what he wanted at that time.'

Radford felt uncomfortable with Ramsey's manner and was conscious of trying to infiltrate a dressing-room that still included most of the 1966 heroes. 'I found Alf a very strange bloke. He would remember little things in the game that didn't really mean anything. He'd say to you, "Do you remember that incident in the 60th minute at Tottenham when you did . . ." whatever? You felt like saying, "What about the 80th minute when I got up and headed the winner?" That never got a mention. There were lots of little things like that. The team talks used to go on for hours and we would watch games on film. It seemed like the 1966 team was a family and I remember watching one game on film and someone like Bobby Moore actually fell asleep. Alf had to go up and shake him and say, "Would you mind?" It was, "Right. Sorry, Alf," and we'd carry on.'

It would be another three years until Ramsey selected Radford again, giving him an appearance as substitute in a 3–2 win against Switzerland.

McNab's memories of his England career are no more favourable than his fellow Yorkshireman's. Picked four times during the 1968–69 season, he was also included in the final 28 for the Mexico World Cup after Leeds full-back Paul Reaney broke his leg late in the season. McNab, however, was one of the six players sent home after the reduction of the squad to 22. A keen tactician, McNab found his involvement in the England squad a somewhat primitive experience. 'It was not very enjoyable. I didn't like the way they played. As a full-back you were always dropping off, whereas at Arsenal we used to squeeze up on teams. Bobby Moore *was* the England team at that time and he liked to drop off players because he was frightened of pace, so he would drop like a sweeper. I was used to doing two jobs at Arsenal. If we kept the game condensed, I could cover midfield if we were short.

'We were very tactical under Don Howe and that is what frustrated me with England. The training was Mickey Mouse. We went to Mexico and South America for several weeks in the summer of 1969 and it was the biggest waste of time in my life. I had never seen such amateurish training since I was at Huddersfield. It was like a pub trip. Not that we were drinking, but we never trained properly. The other players didn't notice it because they were part of it. They would be leaning on the post and talking. "Yeh, that's a great record," or talking about where they went the night before. It was a joke. The game was changing and becoming more technical. In the old days, if you were the better team you won. When you had the ball you played and when they had the ball they played. There was no pressuring. Arsenal were pressuring, hustling, knocking people down all over the field like ice hockey.'

McNab contends that the absence of full international recognition for the likes of Peter Simpson and George Armstrong stemmed from Alf Ramsey's attitude towards Arsenal. 'Alf didn't like Arsenal and he didn't like me. He would give me stick all the time. I was on my own as well, although Bobby Moore was great with me because all the other lads had club teammates and I had no one. It wasn't really a comfortable experience. Alf Ramsey never made me feel comfortable and he needed to because I could have played in his team, although Terry Cooper suited it better because he could beat people. I never understood why I was not in the final World Cup squad. I got in the 28 because of an injury to Paul Reaney and I did the business out there in the warm-ups.'

For Storey, however, it was to be a different tale. Born and raised in Surrey, he joined Arsenal from school as a 15 year old after representing England Schoolboys at centre-half in a team that also included Everton's Howard Kendall and Manchester City's Glyn Pardoe. 'I played for England Schoolboys and there were scouts at the game, but I knew about a year before that I was going to Arsenal. There was a scout who was in contact with my dad all the time and that was my favourite team. When I left school at Easter in 1961 I went straight there and George Male signed me.'

Storey, dubbed 'Snouty' by his teammates, was pleased to discover a club policy that flew in the face of tradition at other clubs and kept the apprentices away from boot-cleaning and floor-scrubbing duties. 'When you sign on with the Arsenal the only worry you have is out there on the field,' he said at the time. 'Your one worry is how good you can be as a player. Right from when I was a young player all my other problems were looked after. They deduct money when you are a youngster so that you end up with money in the bank. When you become a senior, advice is on hand about what to do with your savings.'

After only a handful of reserve games, Storey was picked to face Leicester in October 1965 and for the next two seasons was established as the club's first choice left-back. He eventually switched with McNab and was settled in the number 2 shirt until the eve of the 1970–71 season. 'I was still playing at right-back in the build-up to the season but when we got injuries they put me in midfield. I had never played there before.'

Storey's dark, wavy hair is now cut short and mostly grey, and he laughs a lot behind his glass of red wine as he discusses the old days. Yet in the dark features, and, of course, the smile that still retains some of the half-sneer that seemed to permanently adorn his face when he wore the Arsenal colours, it is easy to catch glimpses of one of football's most renowned destroyers. As a converted defender with a reputation for making life difficult for even the most gifted ball-players, Storey was always the obvious choice when there was a man-to-man marking job to be done.

McNab recalls, 'Peter was a nightmare for players when he man-to-man marked them. It was great having Peter to do that because it meant we weren't having to pull someone out of the back four. You can keep your balance. And when the front men split, one behind the other, Peter could drop and pick up the deeper man and you could retain your four at the back. It forced the forward back into the centre-half. If one of their players was having a good session, Peter would mark him for a few minutes. He didn't like doing it, he would be swearing under his breath and snarling. He hated it that much it made it worse for the poor bastard he was marking. I think we played Johan Cruyff six times and marked him man-for-man five times. The one time we didn't was in a testimonial against Barcelona for Geordie Armstrong. We thought, "We can't mark him man-for-man when he has come here for an exhibition game." Well, we were 3–0 down at half-time, so the call went out, "Peter! Mark him." They didn't score again.'

Storey agrees with McNab's memories. 'I enjoyed playing midfield because it gave you more of an opportunity to express yourself. I didn't actually like doing the marking job. I think I was good at it, but I would rather go out and play. If they told me to do a marking job and make sure someone didn't play, I would do it, but I didn't get a lot of enjoyment out of it. You are doing a good job for the team but it is very negative, soul destroying really. I liked getting the ball and giving it to someone who could use it. I believed in going hard for the ball, but I didn't believe in the tackle from behind or tackling through a man to get the ball.'

McLintock recalls, 'If you put him on someone he was like an assassin. He would focus on that player and wouldn't give him a kick of the ball. I remember when he played against Eusebio of Benfica. You could see Eusebio's eyes getting bigger and bigger all the time and he would be jumping when he passed the ball. Snouty used to make lots of noises, he would grunt and growl and snarl as he was playing.'

And it was not only the opposition who would be on the receiving end, according to McLintock. 'I remember a time when Bob Wilson had done his knee. Bob was very dramatic, a grammar school boy, and he was down saying, "My knee, my knee," and I was on one side of him saying, "Get up and get back in goal." Peter comes up the other side and says, "Get up, you cunt," and spat on him! He was a headcase, a loony. But you wanted him in your side.

'When he got the ball, he wasn't a 40-yard passer but he could knock shorter passes and rarely gave the ball away. He was tactically very aware. If a fellow was jockeying he would keep stopping and starting with him; he wouldn't get tired. He would get his tackle in and if he missed his tackle he would make sure his studs were into him. A nasty bugger, but a very, very good player.'

The first part of that description tended to disguise the second – to all except his teammates. McNab says, 'People never realise what a good footballer Peter was. He could whack you and kick you but he was also a very skilful tackler. Actually, if you wanted someone sorted out there was more chance of me doing it because I was sneaky and Peter's reputation preceded him. But Peter would pressure people, he had a great instinct for closing people down and protecting the team. You have to have people protecting your back four, you can't let people get into your defence straight away. Peter did that. He was a very good passer, not ambitious. He would win the ball and give it to someone in a better position than him as early as possible. That's great football. You know, Bobby Moore once said that Peter Storey was one of the best three players he ever played with.'

Sammels, a former flatmate of Storey's in their early days at Arsenal, argues, 'Peter was a hard player but never dirty. He would never deliberately go over the top on someone. He was a hard man and wouldn't pull out of any tackles or take any nonsense from anybody. We needed those players to combat teams like Leeds. People like Billy Bremner knew they would not get their own way. If you didn't combat them, they would walk all over you. As a right-back I can never remember anyone giving him the runaround.

'Peter would play the same whatever the situation. I can remember playing against Peter at Leicester when he was marking me. I had been in digs with him and we were great mates but he wasn't going to give me any quarter or take it easy. Good tackler, good at closing people down and stopping them playing, but very underrated when he got the ball. He could pass it very accurately.'

Storey, with his quiet manner, was never going to cajole teammates in the style of a McLintock or McNab, but Kelly recalls him leading by example.

'He worked very hard at his game. He might have been limited but he was a great professional. He really worked hard to do well in a midfield role, covering the back four and allowing players like George Graham and Charlie George a bit of freedom. He wasn't one of these talkers, he would come in and do his training or even a bit extra, and everything he did was spot on. He was never one to piss about in training, even in the five-a-sides he took it all very seriously.'

Storey enjoyed several clashes with George Best, the results of which are a subject of debate. Sammels claims, 'Against Manchester United we always used to put Snouty on George Best and he used to keep him quiet.' But in his book *The Good, the Bad and the Bubbly*, Best says of Storey, 'Goodness knows why he was ever selected to play for his country.' The United star claims Storey threatened to break his leg every time they faced each other and reported that his preferred counter-attack against the Arsenal man and his like was to 'run straight at them and slip the ball through their legs' at the first opportunity.

Meanwhile, McNab laughs when he remembers the time Denis Law became involved in a Storey–Best battle. 'When Bestie started going all over the forward line for United instead of playing on the wing, we assigned Peter to mark him. In one game there was bedlam going on and it ended with Denis Law hitting Peter. Denis went up to him to shake his hand and he head butted him. Denis Law was a god, even to us players, so Peter was really excited when he thought he was going to shake his hand!'

A feature of his game that would have surprised Best and the rest of the anti-Storey brigade during Arsenal's quest for the Double was his success at taking Arsenal's penalties following the injury to Charlie George. As well as the game-saver against Stoke under the most intense pressure possible, he had also scored late to win the fourth-round replay against Portsmouth.

'Actually, I had always taken penalties,' he explains. 'Even when Billy Wright was manager, I had taken a few. Charlie was definitely the better penalty taker but I hadn't missed, so when he got back in the team I carried on taking them. I used to practise them. You have to, I think it is rubbish to say you don't. You have to establish your own style. I never made my mind up until I was running up to the ball. I used to practise running up to the ball the same way and at the last moment putting it one way or another by positioning my foot. Sometimes you can see someone move, but I tried not to make up my mind until the last second. I always just tried to stay calm and not rush it, but it was hard against Stoke in the semi-final. The lads were all jumping around and thinking that we had done it. You are pleased you have got the penalty, but you are thinking, "Fucking hell, I have still got to score it."'

Storey's composed demeanour on the field in moments of high tension reflected the quiet, impenetrable, personality that his teammates found difficult to understand away from the game. 'Peter was very cool, but he was a real sweater,' McLintock reveals. 'He would hold a paper and it would disintegrate, his hands were sweating so much. Peter had a side to him that was quite shy when he was sober, but when he was drunk all you could see were his tonsils. You could introduce him to people and he would just grunt. But the birds loved him. He was a good-looking guy in a quiet, broody way.'

Radford says, 'Peter was a hard lad but he was so quiet off the pitch, he wouldn't say boo to a goose. But it was like Jekyll and Hyde when he crossed the line on to the pitch.'

Simpson adds, 'You can't get anything out of Peter. He is one of these deep people. I have known him since he was a young lad at the club and I never got inside of him. Don't know how his brain works at all. But I liked him. Peter had a lot more ability than people thought he had. I didn't think he was hard, just awkward going into tackles. He didn't look classy, he went in with his arse or his elbow, so he got a bad reputation. He could pass a ball, cross a ball, volley a ball and I thought he was underrated, despite playing those games for England.'

Storey was still taking in the news of his England call-up when he and fellow England selection McNab were called to the manager's office for an extraordinary meeting. He explains, 'We were due to play a home game against Burnley the night before the England match. Bertie called us in and said, "I want you two to drop out of the England squad because we have got a game." We looked at Bertie and Don Howe said to him, "You can't say that. You can't ask them to drop out of the England side." If Don hadn't spoken up, I might have had to pull out and I don't think I would ever have got picked again if I had done that.'

Mee continued to voice concerns about the timing of his players' selection and admitted he had spoken to Ramsey on the subject. 'You can't say I asked for their release but we have discussed the whole situation,' he said. 'Sir Alf was adamant. He has called up 22 players and he insists on 22 turning up. It is out of my hands now.'

Storey was drafted into an England team that had won both games since returning from Mexico, earning varied reviews from the critics as 18 different players featured in the two starting line-ups. The November friendly against East Germany marked the beginning of a new era. Gone were the Charlton brothers, never to return. Gone, for one game at least, was Gordon Banks, a first cap being awarded to Leicester's Peter Shilton. In front of a 93,000 crowd at Wembley, England had played with confidence and flair in an entertaining game, winning 3–1 through goals from Francis Lee, Martin Peters and Allan Clarke.

The serious business of the European Championship had begun in February with a game on a sandpit of a pitch in Valletta, Malta. The home team, along with Switzerland and Greece, were England's qualifying group opponents in their bid for a place in the quarter-finals of what had previously been called the European Nations Cup. None were expected to place a serious obstacle in the way of England's progress. Two players who might otherwise have expected to be in the squad for the Maltese game were left behind as the consequence of disciplinary issues. Two weeks before the game, Chelsea striker Peter Osgood was suspended for eight weeks by the FA after a series of bookings, while skipper Bobby Moore was in the middle of his five-week absence from the West Ham first team after the events in Blackpool. The Manchester City pair of Francis Lee and Colin Bell were injured, as were Clarke and Terry Cooper of Leeds. Derby's Roy McFarland was given a first cap, along with Tottenham centre-forward Martin Chivers and Everton teammates Colin Harvey and Joe Royle. Spurs' Alan Mullery was given the task of leading the team.

The team's luggage was lost, the players were forced to train in the dark at the Gezira Stadium and the game itself was not much more successful. Martin Peters capped the most impressive individual performance of the game by scoring the only goal. Ramsey admitted, 'I was a little disappointed with the team. I thought they would overcome the conditions. I believe the England team did their best but next time their best must be better.'

The next time was the game against Greece, a match that saw Moore back in the fold. His exile from a struggling Hammers team had eventually ended when he made an appearance as substitute in a home game against Derby. By that time banners were appearing at Upton Park calling for manager Ron Greenwood's head. One placard read, 'Moore sub! The final sick joke.'

Having heard of his teammate's experiences as rookie England players, Storey was tentative when he arrived at the Bank of England ground in Roehampton, Surrey. Unlike McNab and Radford, however, he has only fond memories of his international career and the England manager. 'I was a bit worried about it because I had never been there with the England squad, but it was great. I loved it. Alf Ramsey comes across as a bit of a loner but all the players loved him. Bobby Moore, all of them, thought the world of him. When you were with him he was very warm, a lovely man, which didn't come across otherwise. He looked so cold and as though he didn't have much personality.'

Ramsey clearly had a lot of time for Storey, a man he would reward with 19 caps over the next two years. The first came against Greece. 'It was the day before the game and Alf hadn't announced the team,' Storey remembers. 'We were at training and Alf came and sat down next to me. I think someone had been injured at full-back and he said, "How do you fancy playing right-back?" I said, "Yeh, I don't mind."'

Ramsey's philosophy was that with Greece likely to sit back, he might as well play full-backs who could get forward. On the left flank of the defence was Liverpool's Emlyn Hughes, another player who had spent the season in midfield. It was a disappointing Wembley crowd of 55,000 that saw Storey make his debut in this England team: Banks, Storey, Hughes, Mullery, McFarland, Moore, Lee, Ball, Chivers, Hurst, Peters.

Until 70 minutes had been played, the fans had been given only one England goal to cheer, a first international strike for Chivers. But Geoff Hurst headed a second and Storey contributed towards a third, delivering an accurate cross for Francis Lee. Storey almost scored a debut goal of his own with his head.

Storey would miss the 5–0 home victory against Malta in May through injury before returning to play in midfield in victories against Northern Ireland and Scotland in the end-of-season Home International Championship. He retained his place in a squad that would go on to finish on top of its European Championship qualifying group and earn a two-legged quarter-final tie against West Germany at the end of the following season. Storey was left out of the first leg as Ramsey opted for a midfield of Ball, Bell and Peters in a 4–3–3 formation and saw the brilliant blond-haired Gunther Netzer trample all over England in a 3–1 victory at Wembley. Strangely, with the need now for all-out attack in the hope of making up the deficit, Ramsey selected Storey and Norman Hunter in midfield for the return game in Berlin and was rewarded by seeing his team grind out a rain-sodden 0–0 draw.

That was the beginning of a run of 15 consecutive England appearances by the Arsenal man, including a 2–0 defeat by Poland in a crunch World Cup game in Chorzow a year later. Storey was a helpless onlooker on the night the nation's qualification hopes ended at Wembley in a 1–1 draw against the same opposition. And there would be no more caps once Ramsey was removed from his position as England manager.

A rueful Storey says, 'I was in every England squad for two or three years but it was a transitional period and some of the results weren't so good. We were getting a bit of stick in the newspapers. I wish we had done better and qualified for the 1974 World Cup. It would have been nice to be involved in a situation where you get a run and play several games. You would play one game and then not see everyone for two months and it was hard to get into a rhythm. When you just turn up every few months you are not playing as a team, you are trying to do well as individuals.'

16

CLOSING IN

ONE DATE IN ARSENAL'S DIARY FOR APRIL 1971 WAS CIRCLED IN THICK red marker pen. On the final Monday of the month, the Gunners would visit Elland Road to take on their great Championship rivals. But before heading to Leeds, there was the small matter of five games in fifteen days. All were against teams they could reasonably expect to beat – Southampton, Nottingham Forest, Newcastle, Burnley and West Brom – and with no one predicting that Leeds would falter, five wins clearly had to be the target.

As far as the Gunners management was concerned there was to be no easing up on the players in the face of quick-fire fixtures. 'Bertie and Don were great ones for pushing, pushing, pushing all the time,' says George Graham. 'They were very consistent in what they demanded of the players, they just wanted them to get the best out of their potential.'

That comment is supported by Bertie Mee's statement late in the season. 'You must expect to win every game if you want to end up winning anything. It came home to me two years ago when I started my pep talk by saying something like, "Look, lads, this is an important game." I just stopped because it didn't mean a thing. We no longer talk in that way or about the pressures on players we hear so much about. These two philosophies have no part in the thinking of any club that wants to be among the top few. You accept the need to win every game.'

First up was an Easter Saturday trip to The Dell, where Southampton were unbeaten in their previous 11 Division One games and were pressing for a place in Europe. Arsenal's first goal after 34 minutes was, therefore, most welcome – as was the identity of the scorer. Bob McNab took possession away from Saints skipper Terry Paine and fed the ball on to

George Armstrong, whose cross found John Radford getting in ahead of full-back Denis Hollywood to convert his first goal in 11 games.

Southampton could count themselves unfortunate to be behind after having the better of the first half-hour and they took only two minutes to cancel out Arsenal's goal. Peter Simpson and Bob Wilson appeared slow to react in the box, allowing Paine to score with a header. The parity lasted only until ten minutes into the second half when Radford lined up one of his long throws, Graham headed on and Frank McLintock scored with his right foot after beating defender Jimmy Gabriel to the ball. Goalkeeper Eric Martin, hero of the Saints' Boxing Day draw at Highbury, made a diving stop from Graham and the spirited home side mounted a late challenge. Wilson saved bravely from Ron Davies and denied Mick Channon before Southampton unsuccessfully claimed a penalty when Simpson prevented Davies getting in a header. With six wins in a row, Arsenal were now only three points behind Leeds with two games in hand following Don Revie's team's failure to get more than a point at Newcastle.

Nottingham Forest had seen an improvement in their fortunes since being hammered at Highbury in October. Five wins in six games meant they were high on confidence, but so were Arsenal after hearing that Leeds had only drawn at Huddersfield the night before the game at the City Ground, the fourth time in six matches the League leaders had failed to take maximum points. Wilson needed treatment from trainer George Wright after making the first save of the game, a typically gallant effort at the feet of Neil Martin, who had been signed for £66,000 since scoring against Arsenal for Coventry. After 17 minutes, McLintock put himself on the scoresheet for the second consecutive game, although it appeared at first as though Ray Kennedy might have been the one to scramble the ball over the line following the skipper's header. There was no doubt about Arsenal's second shortly before half-time, Kennedy applying the finishing touch after Graham had helped on Radford's long throw. By the time George added a third goal five minutes from time, set up by McNab, the points were already in the bag.

And so to Saturday, 17 April. Over the course of a nine-month First Division season there are many days that can be said to have had a crucial, even decisive, bearing on its outcome. This was to be one such afternoon.

While Leeds were facing West Bromwich Albion at Elland Road, the Arsenal fans were enduring a dour struggle against a stubborn Newcastle United team who had not conceded a goal on their three most recent visits to Highbury. Centre-backs John McNamee and Bobby Moncur were intent on extending that run and dealt capably with the aerial threat posed by the home side. When Arsenal kept the ball on the ground, they were frustrated by a bumpy pitch and the swarming hoards of black and white shirts. Tempers became worn as the game drifted towards a scoreless conclusion, Kennedy clashing with full-back John Craggs and George picking up a booking for retaliating after being fouled by Keith Dyson.

Graham, pushing further forward as Arsenal chased a winner, brought a tumbling, groping save from McFaul with a shot from 18 yards. With 19 minutes to play there was still no sign of a goal. It was time for Charlie George to step forward. Simpson launched a free-kick from the halfway line into the Newcastle box, where the visiting captain Moncur rose to head clear. George picked up possession 25 yards out and after attempting to knock the ball forward found it rebounding back to him off opposing winger Alan Foggon. Needing no further invitation, George took two strides and lashed an unstoppable shot inside the right hand post from the edge of the box. 'We hadn't played well but we needed the win,' recalls George. 'At the same time as being pleased, I was drained.'

At Leeds, meanwhile, incredible events were unfolding that would have lasting repercussions. It was bad enough for the First Division leaders when Tony Brown put West Brom ahead in the first half, but worse was to come with 20 minutes remaining in the game. There was no doubt that Albion's Colin Suggett was standing yards offside when Brown intercepted a pass from Norman Hunter and saw the ball rebound forward across the halfway line in the direction of his teammate. Linesman Bill Troupe raised his flag but Boston referee Ray Tinkler, deciding Suggett was not interfering with play, allowed Brown to chase after the ball and bear down on goal. With only Gary Sprake to beat, Brown slipped the ball to his left to set up an easy finish for Jeff Astle, who may himself have been in an offside position. 'Leeds will go mad!' screamed *Match of the Day* commentator Barry Davies. 'And they have every right to go mad.'

Billy Bremner, Terry Cooper, Jack Charlton and Allan Clarke were the first players to confront Tinkler with their rage, actions which some newspapers later claimed incited a number of Leeds supporters to mount their own protest. Suddenly there were fans all over the pitch, with policemen and players dragging them away. Revie was out there too, an incongruous, somewhat comical sight with the blanket under which he had been sitting still draped over his arm. He succeeded in ushering the linesman, Troupe, to the middle of the field to speak with Tinkler. Meanwhile, second linesman Colin Cartlich, who had played no part in the controversy, fell to the ground after being struck by an object thrown from the stands. Tinkler's discussion with his colleague brought no change of mind and Revie marched back to the sideline, shaking his head and casting a rueful look to the heavens. Discussing Tinkler's decision some years later, Bremner said, 'When everybody started running about I turned to the gaffer and said, "This fellow's going to have a heart attack if we don't watch it." There were so many people hustling and bustling him, and a lot of people have never forgiven him.'

Despite a late goal by Clarke, West Brom registered their first away victory for 16 months, which meant that Arsenal were top of the First Division on goal average. Unaware, in the immediate aftermath of their own game, quite how the Elland Road incident would overshadow their achievement, Gunners' coach Don Howe took the opportunity to throw down a challenge to Leeds. 'For eight months we have been chasing them, but now they have to catch us. We must be favourites, but we will not be celebrating any championships tonight. To be sure of the title we need seven points from our five remaining games. Six would probably be enough, but we can't let up.'

By the time Howe's words found their way into print the next day, the pitch invasion at Leeds was reverberating round the country. It was revealed that the final tally of arrests stood at 23, while reports emerged that a plate glass window had been smashed at Elland Road during the mayhem. There was no condemnation of the fans from the Leeds management, with Revie defending their actions. 'I have never been so sick in all my life. How can you blame the fans when the man to blame was the referee?' he said. 'To let the goal stand was the worst decision I have ever seen. The referee caused the riot and people could have lost their lives out there. It is unbelievable.'

So, some might say, was the endorsement of the fans' action by Revie, who promised that Leeds would be making an official complaint about Tinkler's handling of the game and called for the introduction of full-time referees. That proposal would be quickly shot down by Football League president Len Shipman, who said, 'Referees are human and they make mistakes from time to time. But I still believe we have the best referees in the world. We have never given serous consideration to introducing professional referees and there is no likelihood that we shall.'

Interviewed the day after the game, Tinkler said, 'It was obvious to me at the time and even more obvious when I saw the television re-run that my decision was correct. Leeds should stop blaming others for their own mistakes.' For further vindication, Tinkler could have pointed to an editorial a few weeks earlier in the *Football League Review*, which had criticised referees for restricting goalscoring by applying the offside rule too rigidly and penalising players who were not interfering with play.

Recalling the reaction of the Arsenal players when they saw the incident for themselves, Bob Wilson can understand the anger Leeds felt but believes they were unprofessional in standing by and waiting for the offside decision to be given. 'We thought Leeds were silly. We weren't looking at it as a bad decision – we were totally blinkered. Leeds shouldn't have stopped playing. After that it was just panic and anger. People don't quite understand the anger of footballers in the heat of the moment and they get all prim and proper and say, "What a disgusting way to act." There are times when you are not pleased with yourself when you look back, but in the heat of the moment the gap between legality and everything else is very narrow and you just want to win.'

In 1971, despite the Elland Road incident, the days of the orchestrated pitch invasion were still a few years away. Even after this one, no one suggested they would ever witness scenes like those at St James' Park and Old Trafford in the mid-70s, when fans of Newcastle and Manchester United stormed the playing field with the express purpose of forcing the abandonment of games in which their teams were losing. There was, however, concern at the increasing number of incidents of violence surrounding football matches, even though the instances of fans wrecking trains and staging pitched battles inside and outside grounds had not yet reached the epidemic proportions of later in the decade.

The nature of football fans had certainly changed during the '60s. They had become more organised in their chanting and wearing of team colours, while better transport made them more mobile and allowed greater numbers to travel to away games. The violence that was to dog football first revealed itself in the habit of away fans trying to invade the home supporters' favourite end, charging at them in large numbers and driving them from their prized territory behind the goal. The punches and kicks exchanged in such action were mostly insignificant, although as such warfare spread to the streets surrounding grounds and sometimes the pitch itself, the damage done, both to the fans and the game's image, would become more serious.

At the start of the 1970–71 season, Football League secretary Alan Hardaker had demanded that the civil authorities take increased action against those found guilty of committing acts of violence at football matches, warning, 'Somebody is going to get killed before long.' Only a month later, however, the Football League had withdrawn its backing of a sponsored scheme called the John White Awards that was aimed at reducing hooliganism. The reason Hardaker gave was 'extreme administration difficulties'.

Ironically, Leeds had been at the forefront of efforts to eradicate misbehaviour among fans. At the beginning of the season they had become the first club to install a police station on their own premises. But the Football Association was not about to tolerate the kind of scenes witnessed in the West Brom game. Leeds would be fined £750 and ordered to play their first four home games of the 1971–72 season on neutral grounds. Traipsing from Hull to Huddersfield to Hillsborough, Leeds would drop two points in those 'home' games and end up losing the First Division title by one point, thereby ensuring that Ray Tinkler is remembered by Leeds fans as the man who cost them two League titles. The FA took similar sanctions against Manchester United following another missile-throwing incident at Old Trafford, where Manchester City goalkeeper Joe Corrigan and Arsenal's Bob Wilson had already been targets. In late February, a penknife had been thrown at Newcastle keeper Iam McFaul and United were informed that their first two home games of the next season would have to be played at neutral venues.

There are no reports of any Arsenal games being affected by serious crowd disturbances during the Double season, nor can any of the players remember such an occasion. Media interest in Arsenal's fans towards the end of the 1970–71 campaign centred on the simple numbers travelling to watch the team away from Highbury. For the semi-final game at Hillsborough, the club had been unable to sell its full quota of tickets and been forced to return 5,000 for re-sale to Stoke fans. After the game was drawn, Arsenal received 25,000 tickets for the Villa Park replay, but this time sent back 10,000, along with complaints about the amount of travelling their fans were being expected to undertake.

'We had so many replays that year in both cups and also we had a few European away games,' says McNab. 'Then you have to remember that we never had a home draw in the FA Cup – nor did we the following year when we got to the final again. I think it is fair to say that 30 years ago people were expected to work longer hours and did not have quite the disposable income of later years. Plus, the type of fans have changed, moving away from the working class more to middle class. Maybe that could explain why we did not receive quite the full support you might have expected. But I don't think the players ever felt that we were not supported well by the fans.'

Three days after taking over at the top of the League, Arsenal were without their England players, Storey and McNab, as they defended their new-found status as leaders against Burnley, which meant Highbury recalls for

Eddie Kelly and John Roberts. Storey's absence was noted in the 26th minute when a penalty was awarded after Eric Probert used his hand to keep Kennedy's header out of goal. But the confident George, Arsenal's best player on the night, grabbed the ball and buried his eighth goal since his return from injury. George had three second-half attempts but there were no more goals to ease the Arsenal fans' nerves. Neither were there too many anxious moments against a Burnley team destined to join Blackpool in dropping to Division Two. A ninth successive League win was duly confirmed, only one goal having been conceded in that time.

The quality of Arsenal's defence was by this stage of the season beyond debate and there was considerable satisfaction around Highbury when the same football writers who had earlier in the year knocked the Gunners' perceived defensive leanings now named McLintock as their Footballer of the Year. He was the first Arsenal player to receive the honour since Joe Mercer in 1950 and had won as much for his leadership as his defensive fortitude.

'He was one of the great captains for Arsenal and also in football,' says Graham. 'He was a leader on the pitch and the players would follow him. He could gee up everybody on the pitch before games, so he and Bertie and Don made the perfect combination. He laid into me many times and called me a lazy sod but we loved him. We had the highest respect for him, and still do with all the work he does for the lads who have not done so well financially. He will go down as one of the great Arsenal players.'

McLintock's first game as Footballer of the Year saw Arsenal's run of victories and their proud defensive record come to an end at West Bromwich Albion. Asa Hartford created and scored an opening goal for the home team after 37 minutes, running at the Gunners' defence and playing a one-two off the head of Astle before executing a calm finish. The lead lasted only four minutes as Armstrong's right-wing corner was flapped at unconvincingly by goalkeeper John Osborne and George banged in a shot from the edge of the area. The ball struck one defender and was blocked on the line, but McLintock was on hand to knock in an easy rebound.

Reorganising at half-time after the loss of the injured Rice, who had damaged his ankle in a tackle with Suggett, Arsenal took the lead nine minutes after half-time. George scooped the ball forward on the slippery surface for Storey surging into the penalty area. Hartford was too quick for his opponent, but in attempting to play the ball back to Osborne he succeeded only in running it into his own goal. A week after beating Leeds, it appeared as though the Midlands side had done the Gunners another huge favour, but they retrieved a point with only four minutes remaining through a fierce finish by Brown. Playing a part in the build-up was Astle, who had been in the news a month earlier when he was fined £100 by his club and stripped of the captaincy after it was revealed he had made £200 by selling FA Cup final tickets.

With 61 points from 39 matches, Arsenal were in a position to win the Championship if they could pull off a victory at Leeds, who had 60 points from 40 games. One of the men destined to play a leading role in the game was referee Norman Burtenshaw, who discovered his involvement in the biggest match of the season at only a day's notice. Burtenshaw, one of the country's leading referees, was sitting at home in Great Yarmouth on Sunday afternoon, contemplating his appointment at the Colchester versus Barrow game the following day, when he received a call informing him that Jim Finney had been involved in a car crash. Even then it was not until ten o'clock on the morning of the game that he was given instructions to take to the M1 and head for Leeds.

The game had originally been scheduled for the Tuesday night but was brought forward to allow Leeds to play Liverpool in the second leg of their European Fairs Cup semi-final two days later. Although Leeds were slight favourites, by virtue of home advantage, their season was taking on a disturbingly similar pattern to the previous year, when important League and European games piled up and they finished with nothing. McLintock told reporters, 'I am sure Leeds would happily swap places with us.'

Arsenal's players were summoned to Highbury on the day before the game, expecting a work-out from coach Don Howe but instead found themselves taking part in an FA Cup final photoshoot with wives, girlfriends and children. John Radford was excused as a precaution against a cold, while Rice stayed on for heat treatment and stretching on his injured ankle and declared himself ready to take his place in an unchanged team. Unlike 12 months earlier, when Don Revie had eventually conceded the League and sent out a virtual reserve team for some First Division games, Leeds named a near full-strength side to face Arsenal: Sprake, Reaney, Cooper, Bremner, Charlton, Hunter, Bates, Clarke, Jones, Giles, Gray, Sub: Madeley. The only notable absentee was the injured Peter Lorimer.

The battle lines were drawn once more and Graham remembers, 'We knew we could match them mentally and they knew it. But they always thought they were better technically, and they were right. Leeds would go out to make sure they won the physical battle and then play nice football, so we said, "Right, we are not having that. We are going to stand up to you." You either wilt against a team like that or you stand up to be counted.'

Once again, concern was voiced at the small number of travelling

Arsenal fans, estimated at only 1,000. The supporters' clubs reported they were running no coaches to Leeds, while British Rail was putting on only one special train which would hold 450 fans. Attempts to get the game screened live in London on closed-circuit television had failed. League regulations ruled out such a screening within 35 miles of a live game and, with Chelsea playing Burnley at Stamford Bridge and Orient at home to Portsmouth on the same night, the Gunners fans were out of luck. Jarvis Astaire of Viewsport, whose company had screened the Ali–Frazier fight in London cinemas in March and Henry Cooper's controversial loss to Joe Bugner a week later, said, 'We had to wait 20 years for floodlights and 20 years for substitutes. It seems we will have to wait just as long for another breakthrough. The Leeds–Arsenal match was the perfect opportunity for closed-circuit presentation. It would have satisfied the needs of a large section of the public who keep the game alive.'

Police estimated that 20,000 people were left outside when Elland Road closed its gates on a crowd of 48,350. Those who made it inside created a deafening level of noise but saw both teams make a tentative start, with few openings fashioned in the first half. Terry Cooper was booked for a foul on Graham, who was himself cautioned for thumping into the back of Bremner. But for a Leeds–Arsenal game of that era, there were relatively few serious misdemeanours, although Burtenshaw would have to whistle for 43 fouls during the 90 minutes.

Arsenal played with patience and for most of the opening period their well-organised defence never let the home side threaten. Wilson had little more to do than deal with a series of crosses, although Mick Jones did rise above Simpson to send a header flying over the bar from a Johnny Giles cross and Norman Hunter shot into the wide open spaces behind the Elland Road goal from long range. Arsenal, for their part, could not find the attacking options to match their defensive solidarity. 'We were respectful almost to the point of being fearful of them,' says Wilson. 'We knew that to win up there, to take the title, would have been quite an extraordinary feat, but we played brilliantly. They tried everything, right from the first whistle. They had the first 20 minutes, as you would expect, and had us pinned in our own half but we survived, and deserved to. Our defensive play was brilliant and eventually we looked as if we might score.'

Radford's shot on the turn from the edge of the box brought a diving save from Gary Sprake, and the same Arsenal forward headed over the bar, but for much of the game a draw continued to look the likely result. That would have suited the Gunners nicely, leaving them needing to beat Stoke at home to secure the Championship in front of their own fans on the last Saturday of the season. In an effort to prevent that happening, Leeds' attacks became more frantic and Bremner and Giles began to command the middle of the field.

The game had advanced into injury time when substitute Paul Madeley put Bremner in position to deliver into the box from the right wing. The Leeds captain pulled his cross back and Simpson knocked it away from the toe of Clarke to Giles, whose half-hit shot was blocked by Storey. The ball fell at the feet of Clarke, who pushed it forward to Charlton, looking suspiciously offside on the edge of the six-yard box. Charlton needed two attempts at goal, hitting the post with the first and holding off the attention of McNab to bundle the ball over the line with the second. The referee pointed to the centre and began to run back for the kick-off. Leeds were in front, and Arsenal's players were outraged.

The scenes were reminiscent of those at the same ground nine days earlier. Police were back on the pitch to keep fans at a safe distance, although this time the deliriously happy home supporters were celebrating rather than demonstrating. And on this occasion it was Wilson and McLintock who led the pack of players hounding Burtenshaw. 'I have never seen players so incensed by one decision,' the referee said later. The linesman who had refused to flag for offside was treated to a volley of abuse and Burtenshaw was considering whether he might have to book everyone to quell the storm when George broke the tension by booting the ball into the stand. That gave Burtenshaw an obvious subject for a caution and the emergence of the notebook seemed to persuade Arsenal's players to call off their protest.

Five minutes had elapsed by the time the game restarted but once Graham had headed over the Leeds bar and the final whistle had blown, the arguing continued. Wilson made his feelings known to the referee as they left the field, and Howe complained, 'The goal was well offside and should not have been allowed.' Mee, ever the diplomat, confined his comments to lamenting Arsenal's bad luck, saying, 'Never was a defeat less deserved.'

The game had been covered by a television news camera only, so there was no opportunity to dissect the incident from all angles later in the evening. But as Arsenal sat disconsolately on the team bus, a picture of what had happened began to emerge. McLintock explains, 'We felt Jackie Charlton's goal was offside and we were absolutely fuming about it. We were all saying, "Lucky bastards", when Bob McNab said very quietly, "I think I played him on. I was right on the touchline and I couldn't get up in time." I said to Bob I wish he hadn't told us that, because I felt we all needed a cause to go for.'

Closer examination of the news footage later in the week would indicate that Burtenshaw's judgement had been correct. McNab, who had been stuck close to the byline after attempting to block the original cross by Bremner, had indeed been the man to play Charlton onside. But he was angry at McLintock's reaction to his admission of culpability. 'I got blamed for playing them onside,' he says, 'and then Frank opened his mouth again and didn't think. I was on the byline stopping a near-post cross and he pulled it back 20 yards. I'd been on the corner of the box near the line and Bremner has shown me the near post and cut it back. Which way do you go? Do you run out when they are shooting at goal? What do you do when Jack Charlton is shooting from the edge of the six-yard box? I run towards the ball, don't I, because I am stuck. Frank said I should have run out. But that's Frank's emotions again.'

For Burtenshaw, approval of his decision was a particular relief in view of his appointment as referee for the FA Cup final. The day after the Elland Road game he received the first of several phone calls from irate Arsenal fans. 'They were going to get me. I wouldn't reach Wembley alive,' he said. In their search for a sensational story, reporters looked for Mee to request a change of Wembley referee. They should have known better. The Arsenal manager's response was, 'I never even considered such a move. He was admirable in handling a game that would have been extremely difficult for any referee. Mr Burtenshaw has been in charge of two other Arsenal games this season and on each occasion I went to compliment him upon his handling of those games.'

One unexpected outcome of the Elland Road contest was Arsenal's discovery that winning the title would make them millionaires – in Green Shield Stamps. Graham explains, 'We went back to the hotel and we were all a bit down and this guy came up to me while I was sitting in a corner. His name was Biff Lewis and he said, "I am a big, big fan and I am the boss of Green Shield Stamps. I will give you half a million stamps if you win the League, and if you win the FA Cup as well I will make it a million." We all got the brochure out to see what we could get for a million stamps. We could have got a car between us, but after we shared it all out I ended up getting a Hoover!'

17

HAPPY RETURNS

A FEW HOURS AFTER ARRIVING BACK FROM A DISAPPOINTING TRIP TO LEEDS, the Arsenal players found themselves, dressed in their Sunday best, at Islington Town Hall. The club was awarded the freedom of the London Borough of Islington in a ceremony that would have had more point to it had they returned with the League Championship. Four days later, back in their work clothes, they struggled for the freedom of their own Highbury pitch against a Stoke City team that contained the Arsenal men with the vigour of over-zealous prison wardens. The visitors' approach made rather a mockery of manager Tony Waddington's pre-game promise that 'we will be going all out for a positive result at Highbury'.

Stoke bore visibly the bitterness of their FA Cup failure against Bertie Mee's side and seemed intent on consoling themselves with the role of spoilers in Arsenal's final push for the Double. Any ambitions they had beyond the gaining of one point dissipated when Jimmy Greenhoff turned out to be their only healthy first team striker. Consequently, Stoke packed their midfield with five players and dared Arsenal to break them down. With Leeds finishing their League programme with a home game against Nottingham Forest, no one at Highbury was expecting any favours from elsewhere. 'We had not lost at home all season so Stoke put nine men behind the ball,' Bob Wilson remembers. 'We knew we had to go out and win the game and take our chances, like Charlie had against Newcastle.'

George Graham and Charlie George, Arsenal's most inventive players, were stifled and there was no obvious scoring opportunity for the home side until 42 minutes had elapsed, when George's pass sprung John Radford. But as the centre-forward checked to see if he was onside and then pondered how to beat Gordon Banks, centre-half Denis Smith took the opportunity to make an important block. Stoke created their own opening when defender Stuart Jump's header hit the post from a John Marsh free-kick. As the Metropolitan Police band undertook their half-time lap of the pitch, home fans didn't need to refer to the letter-coded fixture list in the programme and watch for the numbers going up on the half-time scoreboards in the two corners of the ground to know that things were not going their way. Fed by numerous transistor radios, the terraces brought darkly murmured reports of goals by Billy Bremner and Peter Lorimer. Leeds, unsurprisingly, were on their way to victory in a game that would remain 2–0 at full-time.

Highbury's mood hardly improved early in the second half when Storey limped off with an ankle injury that was to have a deep impact on the final few days of the season. Eddie Kelly took his place and had been on the field only 12 minutes when he made a telling contribution. George Armstrong launched the ball into the area, Graham flicked it on and Radford found Kelly, who had made ground from midfield to get into the kind of threatening position that Storey arguably would not have been looking for. Kelly made contact with a powerful shot and Banks was beaten. 'The lads weren't playing particularly well that day,' Kelly says. 'I think it was because of the pressure. It was really a bit of a blessing in disguise that Peter got injured – it gave me the chance to go on. I didn't score many goals but that was certainly an important one.'

Even with 25 minutes still to play, Arsenal could not get a second. In fact, it required a clearance on the line by Radford following a John Mahoney drive to preserve a victory that left the Gunners needing to win or draw 0–0 at Tottenham two days later to lift the title. Relieved to have scrambled to the prized acquisition of two points, Arsenal found Waddington blaming them for their failure to make the game a greater spectacle. 'That's no way to play football,' he said. 'You've got to show some enterprise. We played all the football and it certainly wasn't our fault that it wasn't entertaining. Sure we played defensively. We had to. They were our last 12 fit men.'

The early prognosis from the dressing-room was that Storey had little chance of being fit to play at White Hart Lane. So, just a few days after believing that he was destined to be merely an extra in the final scenes of Arsenal's season, Kelly was thrust back into the spotlight. It would be the biggest week of a Highbury career that was almost ended before it began – by a three-piece suite.

Kelly had arrived from Glasgow as a 15 year old in 1966, shortly before the end of Billy Wright's reign as manager, the latest recruit from the

Possilpark YMCA team. 'It was almost a nursery team for Arsenal because about 10 or 12 lads must have gone down from there,' he explains. 'Kenny Dalglish was in that team as well, and Ian Ross, who went to Liverpool. I wanted to play professional football but in Glasgow it was a bit rough and ready. I had been approached by Celtic, Aberdeen and Hibernian, but Arsenal told me from an early age that they wanted me. With my mum and dad, I decided that was where I wanted to go, especially after I went down there and saw the stadium as a 14 year old. They looked after us so well. I remember the first person I bumped into was Frank McLintock. I was only a kid but he made us welcome just by saying hello, and I really appreciated it. Then outside I saw Ian Ure running round the track. I think he'd just been sent off against Denis Law. We spoke to him too.

'It was nice and cosy, and there was quite a Scottish contingent down there. It was hard leaving home to start with and you miss your family, but it was OK. I was in digs with some of the Glasgow boys, which made it easy to settle in. It was the first time I'd had upstairs and downstairs lavatories. We still had outside toilets in Glasgow! It was like moving into a massive castle as far as I was concerned.

'The first day I reported to the club, Alf Fields, who sorted out all the kit, sat me down and asked what size boot I wore, so I told him size seven. Then he said, "What stud?" I didn't even know what a stud was, so I said, "I'm sorry, Alf. I don't know what you mean." He said, "You know, studded boots." All I had ever played on was black ash in Glasgow, wearing rubber boots. He explained, "You're playing on grass now in England." I felt embarrassed.'

It was not as harrowing, however, as the meeting Kelly had with manager Bertie Mee two years later. 'I was 17 when I signed professional. I saw Frank and I told him they wanted me to sign pro and asked for a wee bit of advice. He asked what I needed and I said, "To be honest, what I'd really like is to get a three-piece suite for my mum and dad to thank them for everything." So Frank said to me, "Well, if the club want you they will sort something out."

'They had just introduced this new thing where you got a £250 signing-on fee, so I went to see Bertie and I sat down with him and he said, "Eddie, we want to sign you as a professional and you know you also get £250 to help you out. Are you going to sign?" I said to him, "Well, I want to sign but I'd like to get my mum and dad something to show my appreciation for what they've done for me growing up." Bertie asked what I was talking about so I said, "Is there any chance of the club getting them a three-piece suite or something?"

'Bertie blew his top. He said, "Get up and get out of this office. Arsenal don't do things like that. Come back in the morning and your plane ticket will be ready for you to go back to Glasgow." So there I was walking down the stairs to the Marble Hall and I was almost in tears. I had to go and see George Male, the old Arsenal full-back who looked after the young kids and fixed up their accommodation. He said, "Yes, the manager's told me what has happened and you are going home." Next day I came back and Bertie had changed his mind. He said they'd sort something out for my mum and dad and in the end they did get their three-piece suite. I think that was the start of me losing my hair. I just couldn't believe it.'

The initial reaction to his request had been even more shocking to Kelly after two years of experiencing the care with which Arsenal nurtured their young players. 'The first guy who took care of me was Ernie Whalley and he was a brilliant coach for the likes of me and Charlie George. He was great with the kids and I really appreciate what he did for me more than anybody. He was fair and he gave everybody a crack. Steve Burtenshaw was great as well with the reserve team. Arsenal had coaches who could understand the concerns of young players. If anything came up they looked after you. We were even sent home for a weekend every six weeks to stop us getting homesick.

'The first year I was there I didn't play many games because you couldn't really play until you were 16. They explained why I couldn't play, but it made it difficult to get into a routine and I felt a little bit out of it. I really missed that part of it. I did play in some friendly games, and a couple of games where they put me in under a dodgy name – maybe I shouldn't say that. But I never got the bonuses. They went to the lads whose name I was in under.'

Having reached an age where he was able to step out of the shadows, Kelly's progress was steady enough to take him to the fringe of the team by late 1969. After giving him his debut at Sheffield Wednesday just before Christmas, Mee decided it was time to see what Kelly could really do. 'Bert told me, "You have got a run of 10 or 15 games to show what you can do." I think he more or less decided he was going to bring in one or two players and give guys like myself and Charlie a run. He said, "If you prove yourself to me, the places are there for you. Prove you are man enough."'

Kelly played in the majority of Arsenal's games in the latter stages of the season, including the final six matches of the triumphant Fairs Cup run, which he felt helped ease his way into first team football. 'Playing in Europe helped me a lot. I never thought it was as hard as playing against British teams. In midfield you got a bit more room and it wasn't as hard and physical. You had time on the ball. Winning the competition was fantastic, especially with it being my first season and the club not having won anything for so long. My mother was there the night we won it, which was big for me because she never used to come to games. She would have loved to have come more but I think she would have been too emotional. She came to the banquet afterwards, which was lovely for her.'

Throughout the first three months of the 1970–71 season, Kelly retained the number 4 jersey. 'I felt I was a good all-rounder. I knew I could tackle and pass, I could read the game and I was a good talker. I felt I could get the best out of the players around me.'

What sticks in the mind of Jon Sammels is the speed of Kelly's footballing brain, demonstrated by the goal he stole in the early-season Highbury victory against Derby after reading the intentions of the defence. 'Eddie was not the quickest in a sprint but was a very quick thinker. He knew what he was going to do before the ball came to him. He was very quick off the ball, he had a good first touch and quite often he would have his pass away before the defence could do anything about it. He was very consistent and had no weaknesses in his game.'

McLintock adds, 'Eddie was a bit like Bobby Murdoch, the Celtic and Scotland midfielder. He had all the talent and you couldn't believe how clever he was. He had great aplomb on the ball, great first touch, two good feet and a great shot. He was brilliant, even as a 19 year old.'

But when Sammels, one of Kelly's greatest admirers, was deemed fit enough to fight for a place in the team after his pre-season ankle injury, the Scot's position was under threat. The first to make way for Highbury stalwart Sammels was George Graham, but after the future Arsenal manager came off the bench to score his spectacular goal in the home victory against Liverpool in November, Bertie Mee had a change of mind. Graham was reinstated and Mee explained to the press that Kelly had been left out because he was 'thinking too much'.

Kelly admits, 'Playing every week caught up with me. It was very hard. Bertie said to me, "You look tired, Eddie," and he was right. You do get tired, not physically but mentally. I used to think about the game a lot. It was a demanding game. Bertie said, "You will get back in the side, but we are going to rest you for a month, play you in the reserves." I was satisfied with that in the beginning, but because we were so consistent I couldn't get back in. It was so frustrating.'

Even when Sammels lost his place in the side, it was the fit-again George, not Kelly, who returned to the line-up. Having started against Liverpool on the final Saturday of November, it was almost five months until Kelly started his next League game against Burnley, thanks to Storey's England call-up. In the meantime, Kelly had scored on his Scotland Under-23 debut against England, missed some reserve team games because of an ankle injury, and felt the sharp edge of coach Don Howe's tongue. 'I wasn't in the team and I was getting the hump. I wasn't training properly. Don asked to see me in the boot room. I didn't know what it was about and he proceeded to give me the biggest bollocking I have ever had. He said, "Eddie, you are a fucking disgrace. Look at the state of you. You are 20 years old and you are walking around being miserable because you are not in the side." I said that it was the way I felt. I thought I was good enough to be in the team. He said, "You are one of the best players we have here, but your attitude is one of the worst and until you get that sorted out you will be in the reserves."

'He almost got me by the throat. He said, "Peter Storey is not as good as you as a football player but as a competitor and in terms of attitude he is 100 per cent better. That's the way our team works. It is up to you to get yourself in the team and make sure you are not the one left out." I was a bad trainer. I knew my attitude was crap. I was strolling about and Don said I was not giving them a chance to put me back in the team because I was just sulking.'

Given another chance with a week left in the season, this time due to Storey's injury, Kelly would write himself a place in Arsenal history with vital contributions in the decisive games. But for the rest of his Arsenal career, Kelly remained an under-achiever. Only twice in the next five seasons would he manage to play thirty League games in a season and many observers wondered what had happened to the teenager with seemingly limitless potential. 'The last time I saw Bob McNab,' laughs Kelly, 'he said to me, "Eddie, you were the most talented 19 year old I have ever seen. What the fuck happened?"'

Several teammates have their own theories. McLintock argues, 'Eddie was a fool to himself. He liked a pint of lager and he would eat crisps and that sort of stuff – the wrong diet. He struggled to get up and down the pitch on a regular basis over the years. That was the only thing that stopped him being a superstar. Maybe modern-day football, with all the special diets, would have suited him more.'

McNab ventures, 'Eddie wasted the talent he had. He was like an old man on the field because of his great knowledge. You could tell him nothing. The only problem was that in the end he used that knowledge to cheat. In cross-country, he'd be a little bit smart, cutting across the course. People who do that don't realise they are cheating themselves. Eddie was an impact player, good shot, good awareness, but used it to cut corners in his game instead of building. But I liked the team with Eddie in it.'

Peter Simpson agrees. 'Eddie had all the ability. He had a fiery streak, which was not a bad thing, and he liked to get stuck in. He could have been the best player at the club. But I am not sure he took the game terribly seriously and he had a little bit of a weight problem.'

Graham contends that 'when the good times tailed off, Eddie tailed off because he needed to be in a well-organised machine' and Kelly himself does not dispute any of his colleagues' opinions. He does, however, believe Arsenal could have given him more guidance in controlling his diet and weight. Yet he cites another factor that played a big part in his unfulfilled promise. As he looked for fresh challenges in the wake of winning the game's biggest honours in his first two seasons of first team football, the international arena was suddenly closed to him. Unknown to those around him, and undisclosed in the press, Kelly had been prevented from playing for his country.

'I was in the Scotland Under-23 squad and after one of the games we had a bit of a party in one of the hotel rooms. Tommy Docherty, the Scotland manager, came up and came into the room. It was nothing different to what I had done at Arsenal after games. It was me and two other players. A little while later Bertie told me that Tommy had told him on the phone that I would not be picked for Scotland. I couldn't believe it. I have never told anyone until recently, but a lot of people keep asking me why I never played for Scotland. It was a big blow to me. I didn't see the reason why we should have been banned. I think that if I had played for Scotland I would have achieved even more in the game. In later years, Jock Wallace tried to do something about the situation while I was with him at Leicester, but nothing happened.'

There was one more honour to come at Highbury, when Kelly was made team captain at the beginning of the 1975–76 season in place of the transfer-seeking Alan Ball. In an unusual arrangement, the cheerful bald defender Terry Mancini had been appointed club captain with Kelly in charge on the field. But the captaincy signalled the beginning of the end of Kelly's Arsenal career. At the end of November, he went down with pneumonia and Ball was given back the captaincy, apparently on a temporary basis. But when Kelly returned for the home game against Burnley a week before Christmas, Ball remained in charge.

'The biggest thing for me, bigger than winning the Double, was being captain of Arsenal,' Kelly says. 'I was only captain for a short time but I loved it. My mother came to see me take the team out for the first time – she didn't even stay for the game! The only thing I was ever upset about at Arsenal was the way they took the captaincy away from me. I still don't know to this day why they did it. No one ever told me. That was me finished with Arsenal as far as I was concerned. I felt like I gave up after that.

'I'd not been able to play for about three weeks because of my illness, but when I recovered I was back in the team. Bertie called me into the office at about quarter to three to tell me I wasn't captain. I felt so deflated it wasn't true and from that day on I went downhill quick. I wasn't so much bothered about them giving the captaincy back to Ballie, it was the fact they didn't tell me. Bobby Campbell was coach by then and I said to him, "Couldn't you have told me two or three days beforehand? Didn't you think of my emotions?" It was the only thing I never agreed with Bertie about. I don't think I got over it until I finished playing. By that time I appreciated how great a club Arsenal are. Other clubs were good but not in the same class as Arsenal.'

The bitterness continued through to Kelly's departure for Queens Park Rangers in the summer of 1976, shortly after the arrival of former Gunners captain Terry Neill as Bertie Mee's successor as manager. 'When Terry arrived I said to him, "It is nothing to do with you, but I have got to get away from Arsenal." He said he didn't want me to leave, he wanted me in the team, so I ended up training with the first team again. I went on the pre-season tour, but I just wasn't with it. Frank McLintock tried to get me to join him at QPR and eventually I came home from the tour. What Terry said in the papers was that I wasn't good enough for his side, which was ridiculous. Fair enough if I wasn't, but the day before he'd said he was sending me home because I obviously didn't want to be at Arsenal and that they would tell the press I had a hamstring problem. I couldn't believe it when I read the papers.

'I was so low at the time and I was thinking of jacking it in. Dave Sexton had bid about £125,000 for me at QPR, but when I came back from the tour they sold me for about £50,000 just to get me out of the door. I was upset with the whole situation. It hurt me a lot leaving Arsenal like that. I would rather have left on a high note.'

18

CHAMPIONS

IT WAS ONE OF THOSE OUTRAGEOUSLY DRAMATIC, YET DELICIOUSLY uncontrived, moments that give sport the edge over the cinema or theatre. Forget the violin-backed emotion of Bogart and Bergman in *Casablanca*, the backs-to-the-wall heroism of Michael Caine in *Zulu* or the rousing last-minute triumph of the rebel forces in *Star Wars*. For raw – and unscripted – drama, there is no competing with Ali and Frazier beating each other to a standstill, Ian Botham defying 500–1 odds against the Aussies at Headingley, or Michael Thomas winning the League in injury-time at Anfield. For those with an appreciation of such things, how was this for the concluding scene to the 1970–71 First Division season? To win the Championship and achieve the first leg of the Double, Arsenal had to succeed at the home of their bitterest rivals, Tottenham Hotspur. Spurs just happened to be the only team so far in the 20th century to have won the League and FA Cup in the same year, an honour they were in no mood to share with the red half of north London. 'Arsenal won't get anything out of us,' warned their captain, Alan Mullery.

Bill Nicholson's Tottenham team was one of the best around, third in the First Division and winners of the League Cup, so the task facing Arsenal was going to be as tough as the mathematics involved in defining their exact requirements from the game. Victory would be enough to overhaul Leeds' tally of 64 points by a one-point margin. Things became more complicated, however, if the game ended in a draw. With 70 goals scored and 29 against, a goalless draw would retain Arsenal's superior goal average, the numbers of goals scored per goals conceded. Leeds' figures were 72 for and 30 against, which meant that any kind of score draw would reduce Arsenal's goal average below Leeds' figure of 2.4. The five-goal defeat at Stoke in October had a lot to answer for and the bookies made Leeds odd-on favourites to emerge as champions.

'The big question was how to approach a game when you can win or draw nothing–nothing and win the Championship, but you can't win with a score draw,' says Bob McNab. 'It was going to be strange game for me as an attacking full-back. Tactically, it was like defending a 1–0 lead in the last five minutes for the whole game. I was going to go forward if I had to, but it would have to be very safe. Don Howe's approach was not a lot different to any other game. We did everything the same.'

Arsenal's commitments had led the game to be scheduled for the Monday after the final Saturday of the League programme, having originally been on the calendar for the day of the FA Cup semi-finals. One day after beating Stoke in their last home game, the Arsenal team assembled for a light training session. It was clear that Peter Storey's ankle injury would not allow him to play. 'I had gone into a tackle against Stoke and it hurt. I couldn't play on and I was on crutches,' he remembers. 'They took me in on Monday and gave me an injection but I knew I wasn't playing against Tottenham.'

Eddie Kelly, therefore, prepared to play only his second full League game since November. 'The club tried to keep Peter's situation low key,' he explains. 'They didn't want to say he was out because he was the key man in the team in that midfield position. But the players knew he wouldn't make it and Bert had more or less told me I would be in the side. The way things were going there was no way they would have changed the set-up unless they got an injury. Sometimes you have got to be cruel to be kind to yourself and hope that people in your position get an injury, because it is the only way you can get back in.'

Across north London, meanwhile, the Tottenham camp was bristling at innuendoes from Don Revie that they might take it easy on their neighbours in order to see the League Championship come to London. Spurs centre-forward Martin Chivers confirms that such suggestions were ludicrous. 'The Double may be old hat now, but we were the only club that century to have done it and we obviously wanted to keep it that way. We heard Don Revie was around on the day of the game and was tempted to have a chat with us, but we didn't need any incentive to go out and try to beat Arsenal that night. We would never have given it to them. I suppose we had nothing to gain by winning other than stopping Arsenal taking the title, but Bill Nicholson always used to tell us that the two most important games of the season were those against Arsenal. I could feel how much we wanted to stop them and I was relatively new to the club. So for players like Alan Mullery and Alan Gilzean, who had been there a long time, there was an even greater determination to beat Arsenal.'

McNab adds, 'Don Revie said he had come to the game because he was afraid Tottenham would let us have it. Yeah, right! Mullery was running around like a chicken with his head cut off trying to kill everyone, and that was just in the kick-in. He was going potty he was so competitive. That is how we would have been. They were a smashing team.'

'We were a good side,' Chivers concurs. 'We had won the League Cup and were at the start of a sequence of four finals in four years. We were really starting to click. We had a very different style to Arsenal. When I was transferred from Southampton a few years earlier, there were rumours that Arsenal and Spurs were the two teams interested in signing me. But Spurs were the only team that really went out and tried to get me, so that is how I ended up there. Funnily enough, I could never imagine playing the Arsenal way. It was very successful for them but they did build on a strong defence, whereas we tended to play more attacking football, which as a striker is what you enjoy.'

Chivers was clearly the biggest threat to Arsenal after a season in which he had won over those who doubted his ability to succeed at a big club following a £125,000 transfer from Southampton. He had scored three goals in his first two games for Tottenham, but by September 1968 he was laid up in hospital with a severed knee ligament. When he returned for the following campaign, he looked lethargic and too worried about his knee to discomfort defenders. Nicholson tried to make him more aggressive by assigning centre-halves Mike England and Peter Collins to rattle him in practice games, and on one occasion Chivers even ended up trading blows with England.

Yet as quickly as Chivers' form and fire had disappeared, so it returned after a summer spent watching England lose their hold on the World Cup. By the mid-point of the 1970–71 season, he had scored 20 goals in all competitions and went on to finish with 21 in the League, plus eight in the League Cup, including the two late goals that beat Third Division Aston Villa in the final. 'The key was simply that I came back and scored some goals early on. It was all a matter of confidence. I found myself ready to take on defenders with my old assurance again.'

The sight of the toothless Chivers barging through the centre of defences and smashing the ball past helpless goalkeepers became a familiar one. It had been a particularly welcome one for Arsenal when he did it twice to beat Leeds at Elland Road. But now it was Arsenal's turn to stop the man goalkeeper Bob Wilson recalls as having the hardest shot in the game at the time.

Looking at the other end of the field, Arsenal coach Don Howe felt he had seen a pattern in Tottenham's play that could be exploited. 'If there is one thing I can always remember about matches it is the tactics,' he explains. 'We knew Bill Nicholson liked a bit of man-to-man marking, with a touch of zonal. He liked his centre-halves to mark the centre-forwards wherever they went. So we told John Radford, "Play wide on the left or right and Collins, the centre-back, will come out with you." John pulled him all over the place and Collins went with him.'

But Howe issued no instructions about whether to play for the 0–0 draw or to go all out for victory. 'Nobody ever knows how many goals you will score. You send your team out with tactical ideas and motivation. Sometimes you score three and sometimes you can't score at all, which is when, as a coach, you have to change things around. You just try to get the team right, every individual player right and the shape right – and then you send them out. From there it might surprise you.'

With tactics and team line-up decided, including Jon Sammels returning to the squad in the number 12 shirt, the Gunners met up at lunchtime on the day of the game at South Herts Golf Club in Totteridge. In the late afternoon, pre-game meal having been digested, the players boarded the team bus for what would prove to be an unforgettable journey. For every one of the 51,992 who would find their way into the White Hart Lane ground, someone, it seemed, was destined to be locked out. The game had not been designated as an all-ticket match and for those wanting to follow the action there was simply no alternative other than to be in the stadium, or at least outside listening to the roars. Not only was there no television coverage, not even late-night highlights, but these were the days when the Football League would only permit live radio commentary for 45 minutes on a Saturday afternoon. Like television, radio's midweek output was restricted to cup games and internationals. 'The amount of people on the roads after we left the golf club was incredible,' says Kelly. 'It took us an hour and a half to get to the ground. People were jumping on the roof of the bus and that's when it hit me how big this game was.'

McNab adds, 'I have never seen crowds like it. In Tottenham High Road, if you had dropped a pin off a helicopter it would not have hit the ground. They could have put up a big screen at Highbury to show the game and sold it out three times. People were giving up their Cup final tickets to get tickets for the Spurs game because they knew they could see the Cup final on telly. We dragged Frank McLintock's wife on the bus at one point because she was being crushed outside in the crowd. The handbrake was on the bus and we were still moving, being pushed by the crowd.'

Peter Simpson recalls, 'The crowds were so vast I was worrying about whether we would get in the ground. I remember Geordie Armstrong's father trying to get on the coach after Geordie spotted him in the crowd. We tried to get him on but we couldn't stop the coach because once it had stopped that was it. I felt sorry for Geordie because he was worried about his dad.'

There were only about 30 minutes to go before kick-off when the Arsenal players, having eventually abandoned the coach and walked the last few yards, made it to the changing-room. Bob Wilson believes the hazardous journey may have calmed Arsenal's nerves. 'We were stuck in the queues of traffic and that helped in some way, because by the time we got there we just had to go in and play the game. We just got changed and got on with it.'

John Radford explains that it was a relaxed squad in any case. 'I felt there was more pressure before the Stoke game than before we played Spurs. We knew we needed a result against Stoke but we didn't know what it would mean because Leeds were playing as well and we didn't know what was happening in that game. Once the Spurs game came around we knew exactly what we needed to do, so the situation was easier.'

Tottenham's pre-game worries about Mullery, who had been rested for the game against Manchester City two days earlier because of lumbago, were eased when he declared himself fit to play, allowing Nicholson to send out this team: Jennings, Kinnear, Knowles, Mullery, Collins, Beal, Gilzean, Perryman, Chivers, Peters, Neighbour. Sub: Pearce. 'The atmosphere when we got on the pitch was unbelievable,' says Kelly. 'Every touch either team had was cheered or booed, because they hated us and we hated them.'

The Arsenal contingent was the first to cheer as George launched into a volley after three minutes, forcing Pat Jennings to throw up his giant hands to prevent an early goal. McNab says, 'I remember we started off and Charlie hit a great shot that screamed just over the bar and I thought, "Charlie is buzzing." That was a good sign.' It was George who then sent Kelly away with an instinctive pass, giving his teammate the opportunity to shoot into the side netting, before Wilson passed his first test, grasping a cross under pressure from Gilzean. Mullery launched into a challenge on George, who turned intent on retaliation and was restrained by Kelly and referee Kevin Howley, who was taking charge of his final game before retirement. The official was soon having to whistle for more fouls as Rice brought down Jimmy Neighbour and Simpson caught Chivers with an ugly lunge.

The questions about Arsenal's approach to the game had been quickly answered. There was no doubting their desire to win, and their gaining of seven corners in the first half compared to Tottenham's one was proof of that. It was Spurs, however, who came closest to scoring before half-time when Peters hit a 25-yard volley on to the roof of the net after build-up work by Cyril Knowles and Chivers. Shortly before the break, Mullery and Gilzean combined to set up another shot for Peters and Wilson had to dive low to make the save.

Arsenal had the greater possession after half-time, but remained aware of the ever-present threat of Chivers. And with an hour played they were relieved when Gilzean narrowly failed to make contact with a low cross after Mullery, Neighbour and Knowles has constructed one of the best moves of the night. Kennedy shot wide from long range with his left foot and Graham headed an Armstrong corner over the bar. Rice cleared off the line from a Peters header and Knowles almost turned the ball into his own goal. Still the Gunners resisted the temptation to sit back and defend as the minutes ticked towards the 0–0 result that would have secured the Championship. 'We were out for a win,' says McLintock. 'With about 15 minutes to go I was about to shoot from 12 yards and I ran into the referee and knocked him over and loosened his teeth a little bit. I was fuming.'

Tottenham brought on Jimmy Pearce for Alan Gilzean and with four minutes remaining there appeared little danger when a long Arsenal pass ended at the feet of Neighbour, back on the right side of his defence. Yet the winger made the mistake of trying to poke the ball across the edge of his own area with his right foot and succeeded only in creating pressure for Knowles, who lost possession to the bustling George. A low cross was met untidily by a combination of Radford and full-back Joe Kinnear, racing back to cover, and as the ball bounced towards goal Jennings stretched to his right to turn it away. Armstrong gained control on the left as the players jostled to reposition themselves in the penalty area. Spotting that Kennedy had dropped back outside the six-yard box, Armstrong floated a left-footed cross over the heads of several Spurs defenders to Kennedy ten yards out and his header flew triumphantly above Knowles on the line and under the crossbar for a goal.

The Championship, however, was still far from won as referee Howley extended play by four additional minutes. 'The worst thing we did was actually score a goal,' Simpson suggests. 'It was nice to win the game but I felt if it had stayed 0–0 it wouldn't have been a problem. Once we scored we got nervous because they were 1–0 down and were going to come at us. It was no disgrace for them having a 0–0 draw but to lose on their home ground? Alan Mullery must have hated it!'

Wilson adds, 'For the eight minutes after the goal, all hell broke loose. They came piling back and the atmosphere was extraordinary. I remember Martin Peters clattering into me and somehow I hung on to the ball. The lads were all round him as one, saying, "You dirty so-and-so." I got kicked in the head by Alan Mullery, but it didn't matter. We would just take the win whatever way it came.'

And, at last, it came, as Neighbour jockeyed for a position to cross from the left. Before he could deliver the ball for one final Spurs attack, three sharp whistles somehow rose above the din of the crowd and, in scenes reminiscent of the European triumph a year earlier, Arsenal's players disappeared under a human tide of celebration. The new champions emerging after differing intervals and in various stages of dishevelment and undress. When McLintock finally surfaced he did so with a white and blue scarf draped around his neck. 'Doing it at Tottenham was incredible,' he sighs. 'That night in the Fairs Cup at Highbury and winning the Championship at Tottenham were the two greatest nights of my life. The Championship was the hardest thing of all to win. The emotion that night and the feeling I got were everything I had always dreamed of.'

Wilson remembers, 'When the final whistle went it was extraordinary. I went looking for whoever I could find to celebrate with and ended up hugging the referee, I was so excited. Yes, the Fairs Cup meant we had won something, but now we had won the League Championship and that is the be all and end all of football in any country.'

The facts of Arsenal's season were that 29 wins and seven draws had brought them a total of 65 points. There could be no claims about Leeds having lost the title; Arsenal had won it the hard way. No First Division team had ever recorded the Yorkshire side's total of 64 points without finishing on top of the table. Leeds had lost one game fewer than the Gunners, but posted two fewer victories. The manner of Arsenal's final

League win of the season was typical of many of their performances, especially away from Highbury. Six of their final nine victories, including the last four, were by one goal to nil. The critics made much of the fact that Tottenham's Double-winning team of 1961 had scored 115 League goals, while Arsenal had managed only 71, which was 15 fewer than relegated Newcastle had netted 10 years earlier. The average of 2.36 goals per game had been the First Division's lowest since the Second World War. The Football League's publication, *Viewpoint*, commented, 'The man on the terrace, enjoying a better standard of living than ever before, is becoming more selective about what he watches. There must be a return to the so-called "old fashioned ideas" when scoring was the fundamental object of the game.'

Graham admits, 'People said we were like a machine. Well, when you get a successful team you are like a machine. Everybody knows your style of play but they can't beat it.'

Luck, as always, had played its part. Not only in the bounce of the ball and the decisions of certain referees, but in the way that Mee and Howe had shaped the team. Injuries had led to the emergence of Kennedy as one of the country's best young strikers and Storey as an effective force in midfield. Of course, it helped that one of the brightest minds in football was there to implement changes in personnel and playing systems, including the influential introduction of new defensive methods. 'We did a lot of converting,' says Howe. 'We converted two midfield players into centre-backs, turned George Graham and Peter Storey into midfield players. We changed to a zonal back four and players got used to it and enjoyed it. I didn't know exactly how it would go.'

Howe believes that the quality of the players themselves should not be overlooked when discussing playing systems, but he does point out a similarity between the team he coached in 1971 and the next three Arsenal teams to win the Championship, in 1989, 1991 and 1998. 'When Arsenal have had successful periods, it is always the same tactics that have brought it about – a zonal back four, a withdrawn outside right and an attacking outside left. George Graham had the same in his two Championship teams and Arsene Wenger also the same. We always had our outside right, either Eddie or Charlie, tucked in and we had a terrific attacking outside left in Geordie Armstrong. George's team had Brian Marwood and then Anders Limpar on the left with someone withdrawn on the right, while Arsene had Ray Parlour tucked in on the right and Marc Overmars attacking on the left.'

For Mee's tired and triumphant team, one final commitment remained in an exhausting season: the FA Cup final. It was the game that would determine whether Arsenal would end the season simply as the latest champions of the Football League or as makers of history, the winners of the most gruelling Double in more than 100 years of organised football.

19

DOUBLE

WITH THE CHAMPIONSHIP WON, ARSENAL'S PLAYERS HAD 24 HOURS TO enjoy the moment before getting down to the business of beginning their preparations to face Liverpool at Wembley. Victory would see the Gunners follow Preston, in 1889, Aston Villa, in 1897, and Tottenham, in 1961, as the only teams in football history to achieve the Double. The achievement that had seemed intangible a few weeks earlier was now only 90 minutes from their grasp.

The first item on the agenda after the victory at Spurs was to get back to the White Hart public house in Southgate. 'Don Howe said that as we had won the most important thing it was all right to have a drink,' George Graham remembers. 'We had a right few that night.'

Bob Wilson adds, 'We did celebrate a bit and even Bertie let his hair down a little. They said, "If you want a drink, have a drink, but be sensible." There was a bit of champagne around when I got home and then we got the day off and reported back on Wednesday.'

Such had been the tension around the battle for the First Division title, no one had spoken about, or even given much thought to, the FA Cup since winning the semi-final replay. Except Mee, that is. Typical of the manager's foresight and attention to detail was the field that awaited the team at their London Colney training ground when they reported back to work. 'They had prepared a pitch that was very much like Wembley, very wide, long grass and everything,' says Wilson. 'We trained very lightly on it, just very gentle five-a-sides.'

Arsenal's team selection depended on the condition of Peter Storey's ankle. Having sat out the climax to the League season, the hero of the semi-final did not want to be an onlooker once more. 'Although I played 40 League games, when you don't play the last game you feel out of it,' he explains. 'I was sitting on the bench at Spurs watching everyone jumping around after the game and I felt a bit left out. You shouldn't feel like that but you do.'

The early signs did not bode well for Storey. 'I could hardly walk most of the week. We had a meeting about tickets on the Wednesday and Bertie came in and said, "You will be sitting with us," pointing at me. Don Howe said to him, "You can't say that, he might be fit." It wasn't until the Friday it suddenly felt better and I had a fitness test. Bertie really made me run, made it ache in fact. When they said, "Are you fit?" I said yes. But by half-time it was really killing me.'

Waiting more anxiously than anyone for the medical bulletin was Eddie Kelly, the man who would step aside if his teammate was passed fit. 'Peter more or less knew on Friday that he was going to play, but I knew he wasn't going to last the whole game. The way I looked at it was that I had got the chance to play against Tottenham, and I would rather have played in that game than the Cup final. It had given me the chance to get right back into the scene and be there at the end. And I knew I would get on at Wembley at some point.'

Wilson remembers a confident Arsenal team, relaxed after achieving their primary objective of winning the League. He says, 'We thought what Bill Shankly feared: that eight out of ten times we would beat Liverpool, one time we would draw and one time they would win. They had so many new players and were a team in transition.'

Kelly's recollection that 'we feared Bill Shankly more than Liverpool' is a reflection of the exceptional job the Anfield manager had done during a season that had been one of rebuilding and reshaping. The team that had won a pair of League Championships and an FA Cup during the first half of the '60s had been dismantled and in its place was the foundation of a team that would go on to dominate the '70s. Young players like goalkeeper Ray Clemence, centre-back Larry Lloyd and university graduates Steve Heighway and Brian Hall were cementing their places as members of the Anfield first team. In addition, Shankly had been forced to endure a series of injuries early in the season. It was some achievement, therefore, to have reached the semi-finals of the European Fairs Cup, where they had gone out by a single goal over two legs to Leeds, and made it to Wembley. It appeared to many as though Shankly had hauled the team there himself by the sheer force of his management style.

Liverpool, like Arsenal, had attracted criticism for their style of play, particularly after injuries robbed them of winger Ian Callaghan and strikers Alun Evans and Bobby Graham before Christmas. 'I had a whole forward line out with injuries,' was Shankly's typically prickly response. 'You tell me any other team that would have played differently under the circumstances. We had to be defensive. You must play to the strengths of your players and try to disguise your weaknesses.' It was a philosophy not far removed from that of Don Howe and Arsenal, leaving some observers fearful about what image of English football would be shown to the 400 million anticipated television viewers in 45 countries.

To bolster his ailing strike force, Shankly had spent £110,000 in November on Cardiff's John Toshack. In Cup final week, Shankly completed the transfer of the player with whom the Welshman was to form such a famous partnership. In fact, Kevin Keegan's first Liverpool experience after signing from Scunthorpe United was to accompany his new teammates to London. Toshack had totalled only five goals in 21 First Division games, while the 3–2 victory over Everton in his second appearance was the last time during the season Liverpool would score more than twice in a match. There were, however, 22 clean sheets in 42 League games.

Anchoring an inexperienced yet stubborn defence was battle-worn skipper Tommy Smith, whose contribution had been so immense that Shankly claimed late in the season, 'If he isn't Footballer of the Year then the award should be stopped. We've gotten to Wembley virtually with a team of boys. No one has done more for us than Tommy. He has held our team together. Many people think of him as just a big strong lad who got into trouble with the referees. But all that is over. He is still a powerful boy but he has grown up. He's a born leader with unflinching determination and natural ability.'

Alongside Smith was Lloyd, the imposing dark-haired successor to Ron Yeats. Lloyd, who earned an England Under-23 cap only a few games after being signed for £50,000 from Bristol Rovers, was strong on his left side and powerful in the air. In goal, Clemence had won inclusion in the first England squad of the season, despite playing only a handful of First Division games following his £20,000 transfer from Scunthorpe three seasons earlier. His chances had been limited by the presence of the stocky Scot Tommy Lawrence, but he staked an impressive claim for inclusion by conceding only 45 goals in 84 reserve games.

One of the revelations of the season had been Dublin-born Heighway, a leggy, mustachioed 23 year old who wore number 9 but played out wide. He had come within one game of Wembley a year earlier, when his

Skelmersdale team lost in the semi-finals of the FA Amateur Cup, and had proved his professional pedigree with consistent performances throughout the season. Considered one of the keys to opening Arsenal's defence, Heighway warned, 'We've beaten them once and we can do it again. The immense size of the pitch will suit my style.'

Liverpool, whose 1965 triumph was their only previous success in the FA Cup, had progressed to Wembley in six games, having been drawn at home in every round. That was in stark contrast to Arsenal, who had been taken to three replays and faced nothing but away ties. Victories over Aldershot and Swansea, the latter game most notable for the last Liverpool goal scored by Ian St John, were followed by a fifth-round win against Southampton, courtesy of a goal by Chris Lawler, one of the most free-scoring full-backs in the game. Liverpool were held 0–0 at home by Tottenham in the last eight and Spurs, already through to one Wembley final, were the favourites for the replay. But Heighway grabbed a goal and the defence made it five FA Cup games without conceding a goal. At Old Trafford, an all-Merseyside semi-final pitched the artistry of Everton against the organisation of Shankly's team. Everton were in command early on and led through Alan Ball. But as well as losing centre-back Brian Labone shortly after half-time, Everton relinquished their grip on the midfield and were beaten by goals from Evans and Hall.

As Liverpool prepared for Wembley, their opponents were preoccupied with their Championship challenge. Typically, Shankly chose the minutes immediately after Arsenal's victory at Tottenham to begin his mental jousting. Through the din of the celebrations in the Gunners' changing-room at White Hart Lane, someone realised the telephone was ringing and heard Shankly demanding that Bertie Mee be put on the line. 'A tremendous performance, Bertie,' said the Liverpool boss. 'You may even give us a game on Saturday.'

Liverpool were wary of the fact that Arsenal already had the League Championship to show for their season's efforts. Former England winger Peter Thompson explains, 'On the night Arsenal played Spurs, I don't think we were really hoping for a particular result, but we knew that if Arsenal lost to Spurs it might make them a bit more desperate at Wembley, a bit of panic might have set in. Maybe winning would make them more relaxed and able to play better. And football teams are greedy and ambitious. The more you win the more you want to win so we knew they would still be giving it 100 per cent.'

Thompson, a veteran of 400 games and a member of the 1966 World Cup squad, was at the centre of the biggest decision facing Shankly before the final. Having recovered from a cartilage operation, Thompson had played well in a handful of comeback games and the final place in the starting 11 rested between him and the young striker Evans, who had become the first £100,000 teenager when Shankly signed him from Wolves two seasons earlier.

'The local paper in Liverpool even ran a poll and asked readers to vote on who they thought should play,' says Thompson. 'I can't remember who the readers voted for but Shanks called us both into his office in the middle of the week and told us he didn't like it, and that Alun would play at Wembley. It was only when I told a friend about it that I realised I had forgotten to ask if I would be substitute. I went back and Shanks told me I would be on the bench.'

Arsenal picked up some more silverware on the Wednesday of Cup final week with victory against Cardiff in the FA Youth Cup final. Meanwhile, tickets for the senior side's big day were becoming a hot item on the black market. The *Daily Mail* celebrated its first edition as a tabloid newspaper with a back page lead story that tickets had been on sale in a Highbury pub at five times the face value before any had even been available to the public. They were said to have come from a club official. Terrace tickets with a face value of 75 pence were reported to be changing hands for £20 and the best seats were going for £60, although by the day of the game fans would be able to pick up a last-minute ticket for £16.

Arsenal's preparations included spending the night before the game at the Grosvenor House Hotel in London, while Liverpool travelled south on the Thursday. There was something of a stink kicked up, however, by the arrangements to take the Merseyside fans to Wembley. Train drivers in Liverpool voted to boycott the 12 scheduled 'Cup final specials' after they were given the chance to man only three of them. 'Liverpool fans should be taken by Liverpool drivers,' was the sentiment as drivers were brought in from neighbouring depots to man the trains. The usual Wembley crowd of 100,000, generating record receipts of £187,000, consisted of 20,000 fans of each team. The ticket allocation for the competing clubs had been increased by 4,000 compared to the previous year, but it was still not enough to accommodate even half the average attendance at Highbury or Anfield.

The day of the final found London bathed in sunshine and while the sweaty fans shuffled along Wembley Way, the television audience settled down for the traditional build-up to the action on two channels. For those in their living rooms, this was the highlight of the football season – the only domestic club game broadcast live all year, with the most famous trophy in the world up for grabs. Regulars on the North Bank may have been willing to trade Wembley tickets to get into White Hart Lane earlier in the week, but for millions around the country this game was a bigger occasion than a League title decider that had not even been televised. Some of the day's other sporting events need hardly have bothered opening their gates. Only 121 spectators paid to see Essex play Glamorgan in cricket's County Championship at Chelmsford; takings for the day amounting to a princely sum of £30.

The BBC kicked-off *Grandstand* at 11.45 a.m. and included in its line-up of features the perennial favourite, *It's a Cup Final Knockout*, contested by the supporters' clubs of the two teams. ITV went on the air at 11.30 with a schedule of Cup final items that was interrupted only when Kent Walton welcomed his 'grapple fans' to a lunchtime serving of professional wrestling from some obscure town hall or other.

Despite their status as League champions, Arsenal were regarded as slight underdogs in the eyes of many of the experts whose opinions had been solicited by the media. Stoke manager Tony Waddington picked Liverpool because of the strain Arsenal had been under and Manchester United's Matt Busby felt Liverpool had more variety, although Brian Clough felt Arsenal were 'just about certainties'.

On television, the BBC's panel of experts, which was due to have included Wilson until he became otherwise engaged, were unanimous in their verdict. Don Revie tipped Liverpool in extra time 'because of that defence', while Bobby Charlton voted for 'Bill Shankly's infectious enthusiasm' and match commentator Kenneth Wolstenholme predicted that 'Shanks will get what he deserves.' ITV's Brian Moore forecast a Liverpool success, but his colleague, Jimmy Hill, was in the Gunners' camp, saying, 'Arsenal have a slight advantage in midfield. Their players have a greater ability to score than Liverpool's. I take Arsenal to sneak home by 2–1.'

Radford comments, 'I couldn't believe so many people made Liverpool favourites. I don't think it was because of Liverpool, it was because of Wembley. We had lost there in our last two finals, the League Cups, and people were saying that we were jinxed and we couldn't win at Wembley. Also, Liverpool had been able to take it easy for a few weeks since getting to the final while we were playing important games.'

The Wembley crowd waited impatiently through a pre-game entertainment package that amounted to virtually an entire military tattoo. A 45-minute performance by the Combined Bands of the Grenadier and Scots Guards was followed by a 20-minute display by the Royal Air Force police-dog team. Then, to the accompaniment of the Band of the Coldstream Guards, came the community singing, a long-standing – some would say outdated – Wembley tradition in which fans whose musical tastes probably ranged from the Rolling Stones to T. Rex, were expected to sing along lustily to 'Roll out the Barrel'.

Liverpool were the first team into the Wembley tunnel, Shankly having performed his usual verbal destruction of the opposition. 'He didn't really give Arsenal any credit,' Thompson explains. 'He said, "They're nothing to beat, these Cockneys from London." He didn't like any of the London teams, not just Arsenal. He called them all Cockneys.'

But it wasn't just Shankly who could play games. Arsenal waited until the match officials knocked on the door for the third time before leaving the sanctuary of their changing-room, Mee having decided to let Liverpool stew in the heat of the tunnel. Those Arsenal fans who were nervous about such matters were disturbed by the first sight of Arsenal's choice of Cup final colours. Having lost the toss for the right to wear their home kit, the Gunners had abandoned the plain yellow shirts that had served them so well throughout the season and gone for a version with blue collars and cuffs. The last time they had worn them they had lost 5–0 at Stoke.

Once the players had made their sun-bathed, gladiatorial walk to the playing field and completed the pre-match formalities, Arsenal made a nervous start. Storey, Rice, McLintock and Simpson all conceded free-kicks around the penalty area in the first three minutes, with Storey's challenge on Heighway being typically cold-hearted. After three errant deliveries, Liverpool finally managed to get the ball into the danger area, but McLintock hooked clear. The ball was worked forward again and Hall was unable to get it untangled from under his feet following Callaghan's low cross from the right. From there, Arsenal sprang forward, crossing the halfway line for the first time, and Kennedy shot weakly across Clemence and beyond the goal. As Liverpool attacked again, Hughes spun away from an Arsenal shirt to scuff a weak shot at Wilson.

With the game still in its early stages, there were visible signs of tension in Callaghan's wild swing of the leg at McNab and Radford's gesture of tossing the ball away in front of referee Burtenshaw after being penalised. A somewhat half-hearted chant of 'We are the champions' from the Arsenal end reflected the tentative nature of the opening stages. As Smith snapped at the heels of Radford, the ball broke on the edge of the Liverpool box to Hall. His attempt to work it back to Clemence was almost seized upon by Kennedy, who could only push it away from the goalkeeper and out of play. At this point it was still all probing, George having played one exquisite pass from right to left but seeing two attempts at raking through balls miss their target.

'It was such a hot day,' says Simpson. 'I can remember all my mistakes, and there were a few. I gave away some free-kicks and passed the ball to them half the time. I was absolutely knackered after about 15 minutes. The build-up and the Wembley pitch takes a lot out of you. It was hot and hazy. I didn't feel terribly good up against Toshack, who was very good in the air.'

The confident, upright figure of Graham was the one player who appeared to be revelling in the occasion and conditions. In the kind of heat for which his languid style could have been made, he knocked the ball away from opponents and slipped lazily perfect passes to teammates. He could almost have been playing in slippers, so comfortable did he look. And he had even won a couple of tackles. After 25 minutes, it was his turn on the halfway line followed by a scooped pass that forced Clemence to come bounding out of goal to knock the ball away.

The early panic attack suffered by the Gunners' defence had subsided. Simpson was calmly marshalling his territory, while McLintock searched for opportunities to push forward into midfield. Radford earned a lecture from Liverpool skipper Smith and referee Burtenshaw after illegally blocking Clemence's clearance, and there was more anger two minutes later when the Liverpool keeper went up to claim the ball and, with possession already his, found Storey clattering into him with his shoulder. Smith and Lloyd left Storey in no doubt about their feelings. It was an ugly moment. As Clemence recovered his wind, Storey scurried off unrepentant.

Graham made his first slip after dispossessing Hughes, who already had his socks round his ankles with less than half an hour played. The ball was given away to Heighway, who was felled by a combination of Graham's boot and Storey's arm. It was fascinating stuff, if a little grim, and one weak shot per team was all there was to show for 30 minutes of sweat. When Graham linked with Kennedy after more fancy footwork and George's optimistic effort was blocked almost as soon as it left his foot, it hardly counted as an additional attempt on goal.

Storey leaned too far back on a shot from the edge of the box, sending the ball harmlessly over the bar, and minutes later the Arsenal midfielder was penalised yet again for clipping Heighway's heels. From the free-kick, Lawler plopped a weak header into Wilson's arms. With half-time getting closer Arsenal were still struggling to find their front men under the close attention of Lloyd and Smith and they looked far more threatening when they built through Graham, George and Storey in midfield. On the wing George Armstrong was little more than a spectator.

Five minutes before the break, Simpson won a header, Graham laid the ball off and George, 40 yards out, lashed a rising shot that was too close to the bar for Liverpool's comfort. It was the first time the fans and viewers had been up out of their seats. Moments later Radford, dropping deep in search of the ball, clipped a pass into the box and Armstrong arrived late between Smith and Lawler to make connection with a firm header, forcing Clemence into an outstanding reflex save. Liverpool quickly won a free-kick outside the box, Callaghan rolled the ball to his left and the beak-nosed full-back Alec Lindsay forced Wilson to dive left to push away a powerful low shot. Lawler's attempt to turn the loose ball back across goal was thwarted by Wilson's quick recovery. It was the last action of a half that had seen more goalmouth incidents in the final five minutes than the whole of the first 40.

Six minutes into the second half, Arsenal carved out their clearest opening after McNab knocked forward a hopeful pass. Radford lifted the ball over Smith and poked it across the six-yard box, where Kennedy, only needing to make clean contact to score, made a hash of the chance. After 57 minutes, Liverpool found Toshack in the air in the penalty area for the first time, beating Simpson to Heighway's cross and forcing a covering clearance from Rice. George, who had fired powerfully but harmlessly wide a few minutes earlier with his right foot, was equally unsuccessful with his left and, with 63 minutes played, the Gunners decided it was time for a change.

Storey crossed the width of the field to leave the game as Kelly, crossing himself and putting his hands together in a quick prayer, entered the fray. 'I know Peter wasn't happy when he came off,' says Kelly. 'He was such a fantastic pro and I am glad he did play after being in the team all season. He was a fantastic force and he was the anchorman of the team. But before I went on, Don Howe said to me, "Eddie, you could win this game for us if you start going at them through the middle of the park, attacking their centre-backs." It was a great boost.'

Howe made another tactical change in an attempt to make the most of Graham's impressive form. He explains, 'Charlie wasn't having the best of games that day so we kept him out of the way in midfield and pushed George Graham forward.'

Radford was clearly Graham's rival for the best Arsenal player on view, his powerful running making space on the left and allowing him to cut inside the challenge of Lloyd to shoot at Clemence. Soon afterwards, he dropped deep into his own half to receive the ball from Armstrong and set off on another run before claiming that his cross had struck Lloyd's arm. 'I had never felt so good,' he says. 'I could have played another game right afterwards. I don't know what it was, but I was at the peak of my game and the adrenaline was flowing. It wasn't until I watched the game on television that I saw how deep I went. I was back winning headers in our own box.'

Liverpool found an additional attacking threat with the introduction of Thompson as substitute for the ineffective Evans, although Shankly had been dithering over the switch since half-time. Thompson recalls, 'A couple of minutes after half-time Shanks suddenly calls over, "Get your boots on, you're going on." Bob Paisley asked who was coming off. Shanks answers, "Evans. Toshack." So Bob says, "You can't take them both off!" He didn't really know who to take off. He kept changing his mind and it went on like that for ages.'

Thompson's first touch was to push the ball away from Rice before crossing deep for Toshack to cause more problems. Then he linked with Heighway to set up a shot for Lindsay, whose execution left much to be desired. Paisley, seated on the bench with other future Liverpool managers Joe Fagan and Ronnie Moran, attended to Hughes after he took a blow in the face, but it was the onset of cramp that was quickly becoming the biggest threat to the players' fitness.

After 74 minutes, Radford's delivery from the right found Kennedy at the near post to stab a shot narrowly wide and minutes later Graham came even closer twice within 30 seconds. First, he rose above Lloyd to head Radford's near-post throw against the crossbar. Then, as Armstrong's corner floated deep into the penalty area, he won another header six yards out and saw Lindsay stick out a leg to divert the ball away from the foot of the post. It was Graham again, six minutes from time, who hit a first-time shot at Clemence from 20 yards. 'I was doing really well in their box and winning headers,' says Graham. 'I thought, "Fucking hell, I'm going to score today."'

Hall, Liverpool's busiest player, cut in from the left to hit a dipping shot over the bar and, with extra-time approaching, Kennedy turned to shoot left-footed beyond the dive of Clemence and the far post. The last action of the 90 minutes was Liverpool's second corner, from which Hall headed harmlessly at Wilson.

Thirty minutes of extra-time remained to break the deadlock or the teams would be heading to Hillsborough for a replay three days later. At Sheffield Wednesday's printing plant in Yorkshire, the presses began rolling on the match programme. Howe instructed Kelly to push up on Hughes and put him under pressure, while Mee offered words of encouragement to Arsenal players for whom the season would apparently never end. Seven of them discarded tie-ups in the middle of the field and rolled socks around their ankles in preparation for one last effort.

Within two minutes, however, the task ahead became even greater. Thompson pushed the ball to Heighway, but there seemed to be little danger as he advanced down the left wing with Rice in pursuit. By the time Heighway was level with the six-yard box just inside the left edge of the penalty area, Rice's position meant that pulling a cross back across goal was no longer an option. Instead Heighway suddenly drilled the ball low towards the near post. It eluded Wilson's jack-knife dive to his right, skimmed off the inside of the woodwork and settled into the far corner of the goal.

Four times in the final few minutes of normal time, Wilson had successfully dealt with crosses aimed at Toshack and he had moved a yard or two away from his near post in anticipation of another ball across the box. 'Tosh was the big threat,' Wilson explains. 'The orders to me were to go for him as much as I could because he would probably win most things in the air against Peter and Frank. There were a lot of crosses, half of them I actually caught and the others I took off his head and got the loose ball. My positioning for the goal was based on the whole afternoon spent going for crosses. When Heighway cut in he was in a position to cross, so I was glancing and thinking, "Where are you, Tosh?" It had worked for me so far, but what I didn't realise was that I was a good yard out so when he pinged it, it was, "Oh, shit." I remember going backwards and the ball just clipped the bottom of the post and flew in the far side. I turned round and Peter Simpson had his head down and Frank was like, "You ...!" I knew what he was thinking because at that moment it was looking like five Wembley finals and five defeats for him.'

But Arsenal's season had seen them climb bigger mountains than this one. 'I just picked the ball out of the net like I usually did,' Simpson recalls. 'It's strange. In all the finals I played in, I think I picked the ball out of the net every time. But even then it was just a question of, "Right, how long have we got?"'

It might not have been that straightforward had Wilson not redeemed himself two minutes later. Toshack won a header, Hall lashed a volley on the turn from just outside the six-yard box and the keeper's reflexes saw him stick out a left hand to block the effort. As Liverpool swept forward on a wave of noise from their fans, McNab's crude trip ensured Heighway did not repeat his heroics and Rice made a timely tackle to deny Hughes.

Eleven minutes of extra-time had elapsed when Kennedy rolled the ball forward. Radford, his back to goal, teed up the ball and hooked it over his head into the penalty area, where a line of red shirts prepared to repel invaders. Hughes could not prevent the ball dropping and it was Kelly who made first contact, swinging his right leg and sending the ball bundling towards goal. Graham flicked out his right boot as Clemence dived and the ball continued its playful path past the keeper's right hand into the net. It was a shambles of a goal, but it meant Arsenal were level and Graham, moving as fast as he had all afternoon, galloped from the scene with arms raised.

On *The Big Match* the following day Jimmy Hill would reveal footage from behind the goal that 'proved' Graham had not made contact. Kelly, who was subsequently awarded the goal, says, 'I never thought it had been me who scored, but Bob McNab, who was doing some work for ITV, told me the next day I had got the last touch. So that was more celebrating I had to do! But there was no haggling about it, we weren't that type of team.' Graham adds, 'I always thought it brushed my shin and everybody thought I had scored, but it didn't bother me.'

Arsenal's fans celebrated by striking up a chorus of the Liverpool anthem, 'You'll Never Walk Alone', and Radford fired a powerful shot at Clemence from well beyond the edge of the box. As the teams changed ends and Arsenal prepared to attack towards their own fans, Graham became the latest player to suffer an attack of cramp. Only goalkeeper Wilson and four of the Liverpool team persisted with socks pulled up to their knees. The Wembley pitch wore discarded tie-ups like medals of victory over the frailties of the human condition.

As play resumed, Toshack and Kennedy made futile attempts at goal. Then Thompson made it to the byline to submit a cross that just skimmed off the top of Toshack's head. The ball went straight back to the other end where Smith made a bold challenge on Kennedy. Moments later, Radford was left waving his arms in frustration as Armstrong skipped past Lindsay and stuck his cross behind the goal. Clemence took the resulting goal-kick and what followed would pass into football lore.

Unchallenged, Graham headed the keeper's clearance back towards the Liverpool end. Radford headed to George, received a return ball and, after jockeying towards Lawler, squared a pass back to George. The youngster pushed the ball one stride ahead, pulled back his right foot and unleashed an extravagant shot that whistled past Clemence's right arm from 20 yards. After 111 gruelling minutes, Arsenal were ahead at last. George lay down on his back, arms stretched above his head. It was as though he were placing an exclamation mark after his contribution. He lifted his head a little off the turf and waited for his teammates' arrival with a look that said, 'Well, what about that then?' It was a moment of pure Charlie. He had done little all afternoon, but now he had won the Double and made sure that everyone would remember it.

George, who had pushed forward again after Arsenal's equaliser, recalls, 'A lot of people were tired, but I could always hit the ball from anywhere. It was part of my game. I may have been the only one capable of scoring a goal like that.'

Graham agrees. 'Only Charlie could have scored that goal. He had a thunderbolt of a shot and it didn't matter who he was playing, he had one of those Peter Lorimer-type shots. A short backswing and *Bang*. I don't know if he lay down because of exhaustion or what, but we still have a laugh with him about that.'

After his teammates pulled him to his feet and finished their embraces, George turned to salute the Arsenal fans behind the goal into which he had deposited the ball. But there were still nine minutes to play. Wilson says, 'There is a picture in the Arsenal training ground of when Charlie scored. Everyone is around him and there I am just walking towards the Royal Box, just looking – no excitement, nothing. We were just a few minutes from winning the Double and every time they attacked and the ball went out of play I was asking Barry Davies, who was down behind the goal and who I knew from the BBC, how long there was left.'

Lawler gave the Gunners a scare when he volleyed over following a nod down by Toshack. Simpson was happy to hammer the ball as far and high as possible away from the Arsenal box, while Radford helped out near his own area before getting forward to fire another long shot at Clemence. With one minute to play, Simpson headed out for a corner. As Hall prepared to take an inswinger from the left, Wilson, red cap protecting him from the sun, bounced up and down on the line. McNab slapped the keeper's rump in encouragement. There was no doubt about Wilson's intentions. 'Bob McNab came to me and whacked me and said, "Go and get it. Wherever it is, go and get it." It was near post and I went through a lot of players and it stuck and there was this great roar from the Arsenal fans at the other end.'

As Wilson cleared, the final whistle was blown. The FA Cup was won, the Double achieved. The history of English football had a new chapter.

Graham gleefully swatted away the ball as it landed next to him. George pumped his fists. Even the referee, Burtenshaw, sank to his knees and punched the air, a strange act he later put down to relief at the game concluding without major controversy. All over the field, players in yellow shirts hugged each other. Wilson sympathised with Smith before seeking out his opposite number, Clemence, to assure him, correctly, that there would be plenty more opportunities to savour Wembley. Wilson recalls, 'Bertie had lost the plot, he was so excited. For him, it was extraordinary behaviour. It was hardly in his nature to say, "Well done." He was hugging and kissing everybody.'

Once more, 'Good Old Arsenal' echoed around Wembley as the players gathered at the foot of the steps. Wilson wrapped his arms around McLintock one more time before the captain went up the famous Wembley steps. 'I was trying to slow Frank down. He was out on his feet, so I was trying to tell him to take it in.' Several times McLintock's progress up the steps was halted by fans leaning across the barrier to embrace him, every one seeming to drain a little more energy from the weary warrior. McLintock finally made it, accepted the silver trophy with its yellow and blue ribbons from the Duke of Kent and bore it aloft in the direction of the Arsenal fans. Behind the skipper, George had momentarily lost his cockiness and swagger. Instead, he wept. A few minutes later, the boy who only five years earlier had been standing among the Gunners' fans on Highbury's North Bank was holding up the FA Cup in front of those same supporters.

While George held one handle of the trophy, McLintock grasped the other, but the elation the skipper had felt at White Hart Lane five days earlier was missing. 'It went over my head,' he says with obvious regret. 'I had made a Footballer of the Year speech at the Hilton on the Thursday night and at about half past two that night I was still awake, turning over thoughts and thinking of the final. Also, we had been up late celebrating on the Monday and now we'd had to play extra time in 90 degrees. I had been up against Toshack, so I'd had to jump magnificently every time, and then there was the effect of shouting at the boys over the season. When the final whistle went, I was gone. My battery must have been at its lowest point and that was it. I had to pick myself up to go up the steps for the Cup. Even afterwards, I never got the feeling I'd had with other occasions. I think I had given everything I had and there was nothing left to give. I was just an empty shell. I saw other players being so chuffed for me because I had finally won at Wembley and I was smiling away and I had a good drink later on, but nothing was there. I told my wife, "I can't feel anything." It went over my head. It was a horrible feeling. It got better over time when I sensed what we had done, but it was a shame. I would love to have felt the way I'd felt after we beat Tottenham.'

Graham was named as the Man of the Match. 'A lovely trophy with the Twin Towers on it,' he explains. 'Probably the nicest one I have got. The Cup final capped that season for me. I just loved being on the ball that day because Wembley slows everybody down. I even remember nutmegging Tommy Smith. It was a big occasion and I thought, "I am going to show them I can play." After the game, I realised I had reached the heights that not many other payers can reach. I had won Man of the Match and we had won the Double. Mind you, several other players could have won the award, especially John Radford, who was excellent that day.'

As the analysis of the previous 120 minutes of football got underway, Shankly revived the 'Lucky Arsenal' theme. 'The Cup was there for the winning,' he said. 'I thought a break would win it and Arsenal got a break for their equaliser. One goal in extra time is enough to win any game. You don't give away goals like that equaliser. Ray Clemence was coming for the ball thinking Tommy Smith was leaving it and Tommy deflected it past him. It hit Graham on the leg and bounced in.'

Emlyn Hughes would later attribute Arsenal's victory to their opponents' poor choice of shirts. He explained, 'The sun was beating down and it drained all my energy. For some reason we were wearing heavy, thick, long-sleeved shirts. I may be accused of making excuses for my own bad performance, but I'm convinced that our choice of shirts cost us the trophy – especially as we went into a gruelling extra time.'

Standing in their street clothes, two players watched the teams' laps of honour with differing degrees of attachment. On the Liverpool bench, Kevin Keegan was as disappointed as if he himself had been playing, but his time was to come. He would mark his Liverpool debut with a goal in the opening game of the following season and would be the king of Wembley on Cup final day three years later when Liverpool trounced Newcastle in what turned out be Bill Shankly's farewell.

For Jon Sammels, meanwhile, the sight of his friends celebrating the greatest triumph in the history of the club he loved was unbearably cruel. He could not bring himself to attend the victory banquet back at the Grosvenor House Hotel later that night, and a £100,000 transfer to Leicester awaited his signature. 'Arsenal wanted to get me a medal, but I said no,' he reveals. 'I was pleased for everybody that we had won, but you have got to be on the pitch and put a bit of sweat in for it. It was nice that they tried to get it for me, but a medal would not have felt right. I was down on the bench so I was part of it – but not part of it.'

Having left the field for the 64th and final time since the previous August, the only duties remaining for the Arsenal players in their historic season were to attend the club's official celebrations that evening and parade their trophies through the streets of Islington on a bus the following day. 'Going back to north London after beating Liverpool, seeing all the people there, filled you with a huge sense of pride,' Pat Rice remembers. But it was little wonder that McLintock could hardly get through the civic formalities without falling asleep. No other team had ever achieved so much in so many games. The previous Double had been won by a Tottenham team which, unencumbered by the League Cup or European competition, had played only 49 matches. The first Double had been won by Preston North End in 27 games and emulated by Aston Villa in 37 matches. Even the Leeds team that had earned huge sympathy after losing out on three trophies one year earlier had played two games fewer in their crowded, truncated season than this Arsenal team.

When the going had been at its toughest, when the gap to Leeds had seemed unbridgeable and when the Twin Towers seemed more distant than ever, it was the virtues of resolve, discipline and unbreakable team spirit that had got Arsenal through. This was a team largely without personal agendas, a team that remained closely bonded in spite of a pay structure that in less successful times could have been divisive and a squad dynamic that could have led to the development of cliques. The first team consisted of three distinct groups of players. There were the older ones who had come through the ranks: Simpson, Storey, Radford, Armstrong and Sammels. Then there were the youngsters who had followed the same path through the youth and reserve teams: George, Kelly, Kennedy and Rice. The third group consisted of those who had arrived from other clubs: McLintock, Graham, McNab and Wilson.

Graham says, 'In any team there are factions. You can have fantastic camaraderie but there will always be players you gel with more than others. A lot of people think you do everything together, but you don't. You don't all have to sit and laugh and joke together at dinner, but in a good team you gel when you start training and playing. You must have team spirit and camaraderie and that is down to a combination of many things. I have nothing but admiration for the way Bertie and Don built that team and had players, and people, who complemented each other.'

The players were secure enough with each other not to let internal criticism cause any damage. 'We didn't mind falling out with anyone if the team won,' says McLintock. 'Nowadays no one can criticise the modern player and nobody says anything at half-time.'

The team's absolute belief in each other and the methods employed by Howe and Mee meant that defeat was never considered. 'When you are really good at something you do it with a quiet authority,' McLintock continues. 'We felt as though we would keep our opponents out and I can hardly ever remember us drawing a match after we were one up late in the game. Mentally, we were so tough and in the last five minutes we would just get the ball and turn their defence. The resilience of that team up against the odds was amazing.'

Such qualities had matured during the previous four years, while the team had been growing up together, crawling from the wreckage of two League Cup final defeats and finding their feet with a European success. 'They were a gang of lads who wanted to work in order to win,' says Howe. 'They worked at things in training, they applied themselves. That attitude was born out of failure in the League Cups. That could have broken up the team, but they showed their character and their togetherness.'

The closeness of the team was enhanced by the fact that, in the course of a nine-month season, only 16 players had been used. Of those, Peter Marinello and Sammy Nelson had featured in as few as half a dozen games between them.

None of the Arsenal squad had begun the season among the nation's most-recognised footballing stars. Instead of film star faces they offered organisation and determination. And the fact that it was not a Brazilian blend of flair and flash that won the Double, Charlie George's Wembley winner notwithstanding, was not to everyone's liking. Yet that lack of appreciation from some quarters has served only to bring the Arsenal players closer together in defence of their achievement, both at the time and in subsequent years. Besides, how much is widespread public approval worth when weighed against the gold of winners' medals and the prize that their manager had teased them with when he addressed the team, hands trembling, late in the season?

From the schoolteacher in goal to the North Bank kid whose shot won the Cup, they are, just as Bertie Mee promised, in the history book for all time.

POSTSCRIPT

BY THE TIME THE 1971-72 SEASON KICKED OFF, ARSENAL'S DOUBLE-winning team had already begun to disband. Following Jon Sammels's unsurprising move to Leicester, came the more shocking news that Don Howe was returning to his former club, West Bromwich Albion, as manager. His departure was greeted with the same anger and disbelief among the players that had followed Dave Sexton's move to Chelsea four years earlier. They felt they had lost an indispensable ingredient and several of them still believe that Arsenal could have retained Howe's services had they hinted that the door was open for him to eventually succeed Bertie Mee.

Mee himself said, 'There is no need to repeat how highly I rate Don Howe as a coach and how sorry I am to see him leave Highbury.' The testimonials coming from Arsenal became somewhat less glowing, however, when Howe appointed Gunners trainer George Wright and youth team coach Brian Whitehouse to his new staff. The move affronted Arsenal chairman Denis Hill-Wood, who said, 'Loyalty is a dirty word these days, I suppose. It all just staggers me. There is nothing I can do about what West Brom have done in raiding our staff, except just ignore them.'

Steve Burtenshaw followed the path previously trodden by Howe in stepping up to first team coach. With Alan Ball bought as a £220,000 Christmas present for the fans, the Gunners reached another FA Cup final, once again beating Stoke in a replayed semi-final. The old enemies, Leeds United, were the opponents at Wembley, where Geoff Barnett played in goal in place of Bob Wilson, injured in the first semi-final tie. Arsenal lost 1–0 to a headed goal by Allan Clarke.

Two days later, Leeds lost 2–1 at Wolves in a game that cost them their chance to achieve the Double within 12 months of Arsenal's feat. It was the match from which Wolves centre-half Francis Munro's accusations of attempted bribery would stem some time later. On the climactic night of the season, Arsenal held Liverpool 0–0 at Highbury, denying Bill Shankly's team the Championship and allowing Brian Clough to win a first League title with his gifted Derby team. In another tight First Division race, it was Manchester City who at one stage seemed to have the upper hand. But Malcolm Allison's decision to sign Rodney Marsh for £200,000 from Queens Park Rangers late in the season is generally considered to be the moment that the team lost its rhythm and crucial points.

Tottenham had made the biggest summer signing of 1971 when they brought Ralph Coates down from Burnley for £180,000. They proceeded to win the second of the three trophies they would carry off in successive years when they beat Wolves in an all-English final of the UEFA Cup, as the Fairs Cup had been renamed. With Leeds having concluded the 1970–71 season by beating Juventus on away goals to win the Fairs Cup, Tottenham's success meant that the tournament was won by an English club for the fifth successive year, a streak Liverpool extended the following season. Shankly's maturing team, with Kevin Keegan emerging as its star, also won the League Championship in that 1972–73 season, setting the stage for their domination of the latter part of the decade under Shankly's successor, Bob Paisley.

Manchester United began the 1971–72 season under former Leicester manager Frank O'Farrell. George Best was in the mood and on top of his game as they dominated the first few months of the season, but they tailed off disappointingly in the second half of the campaign and by the next season Tommy Docherty was beginning his reign at Old Trafford. The unthinkable happened in 1974 – relegation to Division Two – although it gave Docherty the opportunity to rebuild a team that bounced back as one of the most exciting in the game.

Stoke's talented team under Tony Waddington finally earned the club its first trophy by lifting the 1972 League Cup. Former Arsenal veteran George Eastham scored the goal that secured a 2–1 win against Chelsea, who had beaten Real Madrid in a replay to win the previous year's European Cup-Winners' Cup. In another footnote to the 1970–71 season, another English team had lifted a trophy on foreign soil when relegated Blackpool triumphed against Bologna in the final of the Anglo-Italian Cup.

On the international front, Sir Alf Ramsey eventually became a victim of his failure to get England to the final stages of the 1972 European Championship and 1974 World Cup finals, but Don Revie was no more successful in his place. Having failed to qualify for the 1976 European Championship finals, Revie saw the writing on the wall after an important World Cup qualifying defeat in Italy. Before the return game was played at Wembley in the autumn of 1977, he had accepted a small fortune to become the coach of the United Arab Emirates team. Never the most popular of football figures, he was now painted as a traitor. Some years after returning to England he was diagnosed with motor neurone disease and one of England's most successful and controversial post-war managers died in 1989 at the age of 61.

By the time Revie was flying off to riches in the desert, Arsenal were unrecognisable from the team that had denied him in 1971. The Gunners had to content themselves with fifth place in the table and their FA Cup final defeat in 1972 before finishing as First Division runners-up to Liverpool and losing to Sunderland in the semi-final of the FA Cup the following year. That was to be the last semblance of success for Bertie Mee.

Three unsatisfactory seasons followed, including a battle against relegation for much of 1974–75, and in the summer of 1976 Mee made his exit from Highbury. Former skipper Terry Neill inherited the job and, with Don Howe restored as coach, reached three consecutive FA Cup finals and a European Cup-Winners' Cup final. The only victory in those games was in 1979 when Pat Rice lifted the Cup after a thrilling 3–2 win against Manchester United, by that time managed by former Gunners' coach Dave Sexton.

Mee's football career resumed when Graham Taylor offered him the post of assistant manager at Watford, where he eventually became general manager and a club director. Bertie Mee died during the preparation of this book in October 2001, aged 82. Rice also ended up at Watford, spending four years as a player at Vicarage Road, before returning to Highbury as a coach and rising through the ranks to become assistant manager to Arsene Wenger and winning another Double in the 1997–98 season.

Bob Wilson's retirement in 1974 enabled him to launch a full-time television career, although his influence was still being felt at Highbury almost 30 years later. As the club's goalkeeping coach, he has played a significant role in the career of England goalkeeper David Seaman.

Bob McNab left Highbury in 1975 and had spells with Wolves, Barnet and the North American Soccer League before settling in the sunshine of California, where he runs a sports recruitment agency. At Barnet, he teamed up briefly with Jimmy Greaves, who was enjoying a successful spell with the Southern League team after retiring from professional football on the final day of the 1970–71 season with a record of 357 League goals in 516 matches. McNab remains an avid football fan, despite his dislike of American network ESPN's 'soccer' commentators, and is a frequent visitor to England to conduct business, visit family and play golf.

Peter Simpson remained at Arsenal until 1978 and ended his career with the New England Teamen in the NASL. Having come close to settling in the United States, he remains typically downbeat about his contribution as a player in America. 'I wish we had gone three or four years earlier, I might have settled over there. I didn't play well, I had a few injuries and I couldn't give back as much as I should have done.' Simpson eventually entered the building trade.

Eddie Kelly was another who left the game after a post-Highbury career that took in Queens Park Rangers, Leicester (twice), Notts County, Bournemouth and Torquay. Having settled in Torquay, he had a brief spell coaching the young players at Halifax, before moving back to Devon in the summer of 2001.

Peter Storey's Arsenal career lasted until the latter part of Terry Neill's first season as manager. In March 1977, surplus to first team requirements, he signed for Fulham and played 17 games before the conclusion of the season marked the end of his career in professional football. For a man who met football's challenges head on, life in the real world proved to be a difficult experience. In 1980, he was given a two-year jail sentence for his part in a plot involving counterfeit coins and in 1982 he was sentenced to six months for selling cars bought on hire purchase. In 1990, he was sentenced to four weeks in jail for attempting to smuggle pornographic video tapes into the country.

Storey himself politely declines the opportunity to give his version of events. 'I don't want to say anything because people don't believe you anyway. I have tried to say things before but people keep knocking you down and I can't be bothered any more.' It is left to teammates to speak up for their colleague and Sammy Nelson's sentiments are typical. 'Peter wasn't a crook. He was unfortunate to get involved with the wrong people and he bore the brunt of it.'

Storey has put such matters behind him. He is married, living in Richmond, Surrey, and working as a chauffeur. Still an Arsenal fan, he has three sons who are Highbury season ticket holders, attends a few games every season and remains in contact with some of his former colleagues.

Take any group of 15 young men from 1971 and project forward 30 years or so and there will be some unhappy tales to tell. As well as the personal battles of Storey and the tragedy of George Armstrong's death in October 2000, there is the story of Ray Kennedy's very public fight against illness. Transferred to Liverpool in the summer of 1974, Bill Shankly's last signing, Kennedy made a slow start to his Anfield career until a move back into midfield brought him 17 England caps, three European Cups, five more League Championships and winners' medals in the League Cup and UEFA Cup. Towards the end of his League career, which concluded at Swansea, Kennedy noticed the first symptoms of what was eventually diagnosed as Parkinson's disease. One of the most successful players ever to kick a football, Kennedy now lives back in his native North-east, dealing with an illness – and the side-effects of medication – that makes the completion of even the most mundane everyday task an exhausting achievement. When he sees film of his playing days, he admits, 'I can't believe that is me. I look at myself now and wonder how I did it and what this terrible disease has done to me. I can't make any plans like going to watch football live. I just hope I'll be having a good day and able to catch it on television.'

Kennedy's best friend at Highbury, John Radford, finished his Arsenal career in 1976 with 149 goals to his name. Sold for £80,000, he played 28 games for West Ham without scoring once before finishing his League career at Blackburn Rovers, for whom he scored in his first game. Returning south he spent several years as manager of non-League Bishop's Stortford, where he still lives.

Peter Marinello's ill-fated residence at Highbury ended in 1973, after only 43 games and five goals, with a transfer to Portsmouth. The potential remained largely unfulfilled, although he continued to play until 1983 with spells at Motherwell, Fulham and Hearts and the NASL's Phoenix Inferno. John Roberts left Arsenal during the 1972–73 season, but went on to win 22 Wales caps during a career that took in Birmingham, Wrexham and Hull City. Already a Northern Ireland international by the year of the Double, Sammy Nelson established himself as the successor to McNab in Arsenal's left-back position and became one of the North Bank's favourites during the Terry Neill years. He continued playing for Arsenal until 1981, signing for Brighton after being replaced in the first team by England left-back Kenny Sansom. Now working in the insurance business, his skills as social secretary play a large part in keeping the 1970–71 team in contact with each other.

Don Howe finally became manager of Arsenal when Terry Neill was sacked in 1983 and it was his resignation three years later that heralded the return of George Graham to Highbury as Arsenal boss. Howe served as an England coach under Ron Greenwood, Bobby Robson and Terry Venables and won the FA Cup in 1988 as coach of Wimbledon, where he helped former Arsenal striker Bobby Gould plot the downfall of a great Liverpool team.

With Graham in the manager's seat, Arsenal enjoyed nine years of almost unbroken success until his much-publicised financial dealings with Norwegian agent Rune Hauge precipitated a one-year FIFA suspension and his hasty departure from the club he still loves. On his return to football, Graham proved he had forgotten none of the managerial skills he learned from, among others, Bertie Mee by helping to develop a promising young Leeds side and then winning the League Cup for, of all teams, Tottenham Hotspur.

Frank McLintock was sold to Queens Park Rangers for £25,000 in April 1973, his place in the Arsenal team taken by Jeff Blockley, who failed to live up to his £200,000 transfer from Coventry. In 1976, reunited with Dave Sexton, McLintock almost won another League Championship as Rangers battled Liverpool right to the last day of the season. A managerial career at Leicester and Brentford never mirrored the success of his playing days, but McLintock found a comfortable home in the world of the media.

If the transfers of Graham, Kennedy and McLintock disappointed the North Bank as they saw Arsenal's post-Double fortunes plummet, then the sale of Charlie George to Derby for a mere £90,000 in the summer of 1975 was like flogging the family silverware. It could have been worse, however, as he very nearly ended up at Tottenham. Proof of the place George retained in Highbury's hearts came when he played his first game back at Arsenal in Derby colours and a Gunners fan raced on to the pitch to present him with a bouquet as his name echoed round the stadium. After going on to play for Southampton, Nottingham Forest, Hong Kong club Bulova, Bournemouth and Derby once more, George called it a day on a career that achieved much yet is still thought by many to have come up short of its potential. Red and white continues to flow through the veins of the man whose Wembley goal remains one of the Gunners' great moments. He loves the club as much as the fans continue to worship him, and he works in the Arsenal club museum – quite appropriate for a man who helped shape Arsenal's history on a sunny afternoon in the spring of 1971.

The Willow Foundation

THE WILLOW FOUNDATION (REGISTERED CHARITY NO. 1079977) WAS launched in August 1999 by Bob and Megs Wilson as a memorial to their daughter, Anna, who died from a rare form of cancer in December 1998, shortly before her 32nd birthday. The Foundation was born out of the belief that the quality of life of young adults living with life-threatening or serious illness can be improved by providing 'special days' away from the routine of illness and treatment.

'Our desire to help young people with life-threatening illnesses grew from our own experiences with Anna,' says Wilson. 'She wanted quality of life, quality of time and, most importantly, she wanted to be treated as normal. The more we lived with Anna's cancer the more we realised that special days can often do more than conventional medicine.'

A percentage of royalties from the sale of this book are being donated to the Willow Foundation. Anyone interested in finding out more about the work of the Foundation or making a donation should contact: The Willow Foundation, Sylvia Adams House, 24 The Common, Hatfield, Hertfordshire, AL10 0NB. The Foundation's Internet site can be found at www.willowfoundation.org.uk